Basic Elements of Machine Design

Basic Elements of Machine Design

Dr. Rajkumar. E
Dr. Bikash Routh
Dr. G. Sundaramali
Dr. Narendiranath Babu. T

NAMYA PRESS.com

Published by

Namya Press

India: 213, Vardaan House, 7/28 Ansari Road, Daryaganj, Delhi-110002
USA: 10685-B Hazelhurst Dr. # 31013 Houston, Texas USA - 77043
Email: namyapress@gmail.com
Website: https://namyapress.com

Edition	:	First Published in 2024 (Namya Press)
Title	:	Basic Elements of Machine Design
Authors	:	Dr. Rajkumar. E, Dr. Bikash Routh, Dr. G. Sundaramali, Dr. Narendiranath Babu. T
ISBN	:	978-93-5545-754-7
Copyright	:	© Dr. Rajkumar. E, Dr. Bikash Routh, Dr. G. Sundaramali, Dr. Narendiranath Babu. T. 2024 All Rights Reserved

Acknowledgement

First and foremost, we would like to thank our families and loved ones for their unwavering support and understanding throughout this journey. Our heartfelt gratitude goes to the management of VIT for their unwavering encouragement and support throughout the process of writing this book

We would like to express our appreciation to our colleagues and peers who have provided valuable feedback, engaged in thought-provoking discussions, and offered their support throughout the writing process. Insights and perspectives have been instrumental in shaping the content and ensuring its relevance to the readers.

The well-organized chapters, clear explanations, and practical examples provided in the textbook greatly enhanced our learning experience. The inclusion of various design tools and techniques also helped students to develop a better understanding of how to apply the concepts in real-world scenarios. We hope that this book serves as a valuable resource and inspires further exploration and innovation in the field.

Once again, we would like to extend our gratitude for your efforts in creating a textbook that is not only informative but also easy to comprehend. Thank you for contributing towards our academic success.

Dr. Rajkumar. E
Dr. Bikash Routh
Dr. G. Sundaramali
Dr. Narendiranath Babu. T

Preface

Designing a new machine or system is not just about solving the problems of today, but about anticipating the needs of tomorrow. This requires a deep understanding of the industry in which the machine will be used, as well as an awareness of current and future trends. It also requires a willingness to adapt and change as new information becomes available, ensuring that the final product is as cutting-edge as possible.

As a professor or student in the field of mechanical engineering, we wanted to provide a comprehensive and practical resource that covers all the essential topics in machine design. It is designed for individuals who are interested in understanding the fundamentals of designing various machine components.

This book will cover topics such as stress analysis, material selection, and design calculations for important machine elements such as bearings, gears, shafts, and more. It will also provide hands-on experience through practical assignments and case studies.

In this book, we have included practical examples and case studies along with clear explanations and illustrations to help readers understand the concepts easily. The preface of the book gives an overview of the content and provides some insights into the importance of machine design in various industries.

We believe this book will be beneficial for professionals in the engineering field, as well as students who are looking to enhance their knowledge and skills in this area. Thank you for your support and we hope you find this textbook beneficial in your academic or professional endeavours.

Dr. Rajkumar. E
Dr. Bikash Routh
Dr. G. Sundaramali
Dr. Narendiranath Babu. T

Preface

Contents

1

Introduction to Engineering Design

Engineering design is a goal-oriented process that involves a great deal of creativity and forward-thinking. It is not just about creating something that works, but about creating something that is efficient, reliable, and innovative. When we think of machine design, we often think of engineers and technologists, but the truth is that many other professionals are involved in the design process as well. Scientists, architects, artists, and even poets all play a role in the creation of new machines and systems. Each brings their own unique perspective and expertise to the table, contributing to the overall success of the design process.

It is noticeable that designers work towards an improvement and a perfection of their products beyond disciplinary boundaries. Admittedly, the design itself will never be perfect, only the imperfection will be minimized. Since design conforms to constraints, requires choices, and involves compromise, it will never be perfect. Design nowadays is in most areas used to increase the user satisfaction, the brand identity, as well as the competitiveness in the sense of being better, quicker, and cheaper, etc., than others

Needs → Design process → Solutions

1. Write down the problem statement
2. Generate possible solutions
3. Evaluate each solution against the criteria and select the best one.
4. Document the solution

Fig. 1.1. Engineering design process

One of the key components of machine design is the creative aspect. While engineering is often thought of as a purely technical field, the truth is that creativity plays a major role in the design process. Engineers and designers must think outside the box, coming up with innovative solutions to complex problems. This requires a great deal of imagination and ingenuity, as well as a willingness to take risks and try new things. Another important aspect of machine design is the need to think ahead.

Engineering design serves as fundamental discipline to deliver appropriate design models and descriptions in order to meet a high number of product requirements,

- To enable robust manufacturing with high quality,
- To deliver sound profits on competitive markets,
- Fulfil customer expectations during use, and to enable a sustainable future.

Design research is concerned with the study, research, and investigation of man-made artifacts and systems. Within the manufacturing industry, design has been formally acknowledged as a separate discipline for the last 150 years. This is particularly true for the field of engineering, where scientific developments, especially those that occurred in the early 1940s, made significant contributions toward solving design problems. Multidisciplinary teams consisting of engineers, industrial designers, psychologists, and statisticians were set up. Initially, the focus of design research was on improving classical design by using systematic design methods. The Design Research Society was founded in London in 1966. In 1970, the Environmental Design Research Association was established.

1.1 The Fundamentals of Product Development

Developing good products involves examining and developing a holistic understanding of the entire product cycle from inception to disposal, also known as "cradle to grave". In reality, there is a wide variety of proven and effective design methods and CAx tools available. An engineer can choose the method or tool most appropriate to the task and stage of the product development process. The basic areas of product development are:

- Machine Elements and Systems
- Design Methods
- Computer-Supported Tools

Efficient interaction between these areas is dependent upon well-educated engineers who manage the fields along the whole process of product development and realization. Machine elements offer a huge number of solutions so it is necessary to distinguish between designing with machine elements and the designing of machine elements.

1.2 Design Methodology

The design methodology refers to the study of principles and procedures of design in a broad and general sense. It is concerned with how design is carried out. In doing so it analyses how designers work and how they think. The aim is to make rational decisions that adapt to the prevailing values. This is achieved by looking at rational methods of incorporating scientific techniques and knowledge into the design process.

What is Design?

Design is indeed an iterative and creative process that involves a series of steps and considerations. It requires clear definitions, controlled aims, and a systematic approach to achieve the desired outcome. The role of the designer, regardless of the discipline, typically involves three key principles:

- **Identifying the Need:** The designer's first task is to understand and define the problem or need that the design aims to address. This involves conducting research, gathering information, and analysing user requirements, market trends, and other relevant factors. By identifying the need, the designer can establish a clear direction for the design process.
- **Describing the Vision:** Once the need is identified, the designer formulates a vision or concept for the design. This involves envisioning the desired outcome, setting goals, and defining the design objectives. The designer must communicate and articulate this vision effectively to stakeholders, team members, and clients to ensure a shared understanding and alignment.
- **Producing the Result:** The final principle of design is the actual production of the design solution. This involves translating the vision into tangible outputs, such as sketches, prototypes, technical drawings, or digital models. The designer applies their creative thinking, technical expertise, and problem-solving skills to develop and refine the design, ensuring that it meets the defined objectives and requirements.

Throughout the design process, designers engage in an iterative cycle of ideation, evaluation, and refinement. They generate multiple ideas, concepts, and solutions, evaluate their feasibility and effectiveness, and iterate on the design based on feedback and insights. This iterative approach allows designers to continuously improve and optimize the design until the desired result is achieved.

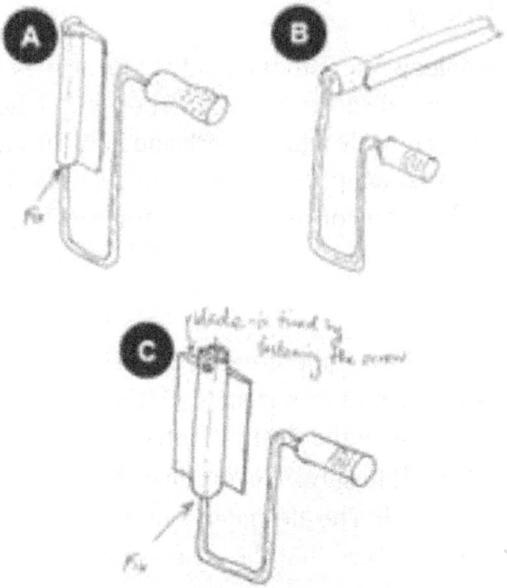

Fig. 1.2. Free hand sketch

To ensure a controlled and systematic design process, designers often follow established methodologies and frameworks, such as the Design Thinking process or the Engineering Design Process. These frameworks provide a structured approach to problem-solving, emphasizing user-centricity, collaboration, and iteration.

1.3 What is Machine Design?

Machine design is indeed a complex and time-consuming process that involves creating new machines or improving existing ones. It encompasses various stages, considerations, and factors that influence the final design. Some of the key aspects involved in machine design include:

- **Problem Identification:** The first step in machine design is identifying the problem or need that the machine is intended to address. This involves understanding the requirements, constraints, and objectives of the machine.

- **Conceptualization and Preliminary Design:** Once the problem is identified, designers generate multiple concepts and evaluate their feasibility. Preliminary design involves selecting the most promising concept and developing a basic design layout.
- **Detailed Design:** In this stage, designers delve into the specifics of the machine design. They consider factors such as type of loading (static, dynamic, impact), material selection, kinematics (motion and movement), and other relevant parameters. Detailed calculations, analysis, and simulations are performed to ensure the machine's functionality, strength, and reliability.
- **Component Selection and Integration:** Designers select appropriate components, such as gears, bearings, motors, and actuators, based on the machine's requirements. They integrate these components into the design, ensuring compatibility and optimal performance.
- **Manufacturing Considerations:** Machine design must take into account manufacturing processes and techniques. Designers need to consider factors like ease of manufacturing, cost-effectiveness, and scalability during the design process.
- **Testing and Validation:** Once the design is complete, prototypes are built and tested to verify its performance, functionality, and safety. Testing may involve load testing, stress analysis, and performance evaluation to ensure that the machine meets the desired specifications.
- **Iteration and Improvement:** Based on the test results and feedback, designers may need to iterate and refine the design to address any issues or optimize performance. This iterative process continues until the desired machine design is achieved.

Throughout the machine design process, designers must consider various factors, including the intended application, operating conditions, safety requirements, cost constraints, and environmental considerations. Collaboration with experts from different disciplines, such as mechanical engineering, materials science, and manufacturing, is often necessary to ensure a comprehensive and successful machine design.

Machine design dealt with the following requirements:

- **Deciding overall dimensions of the machine:** Determining the overall dimensions of the machine involves considering factors such as available space, functionality, ease of operation, and transportation requirements.

Designers need to ensure that the machine fits within the designated space and meets the desired performance criteria.

- **Deciding dimensions of each part and shape:** Once the overall dimensions are established, designers determine the dimensions and shape of each individual part of the machine. This involves considering factors such as structural integrity, functionality, manufacturability, and assembly requirements. Designers need to ensure that each part is appropriately sized and shaped to fulfil its intended purpose within the overall machine design.
- **Selecting appropriate mechanism:** The selection of the appropriate mechanism is crucial in machine design. Designers need to choose the mechanism that best suits the desired functionality and performance requirements of the machine. This can involve selecting mechanisms such as gears, linkages, cams, or other mechanical components that enable the desired motion, force transmission, or control.
- **Selecting material:** The selection of the appropriate material is essential to ensure the strength, durability, and performance of the machine. Designers consider factors such as mechanical properties, corrosion resistance, weight, cost, and availability when choosing the material for each part. The material selection should align with the specific requirements and operating conditions of the machine.

Selecting the correct manufacturing process: Designers need to select the most suitable manufacturing process for each part of the machine. This can include processes such as casting, machining, forging, welding, or additive manufacturing techniques. The choice of manufacturing process depends on factors such as complexity, cost, production volume, material properties, and desired tolerances.

- **Ergonomics and Aesthetics:** Considering ergonomics and aesthetics is important to ensure that the machine is user-friendly, comfortable, and visually appealing. Designers need to consider factors such as user interface design, control placement, accessibility, and overall aesthetics to enhance the user experience and make the machine visually appealing.

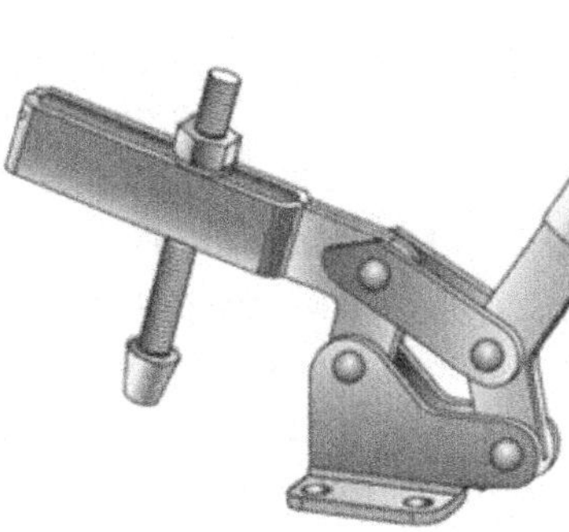

Fig. 1.3. Mechanism

1.4 Classifications of Machine Design

The machine design may be classified as follows:

1. Adaptive design

Some of the design works involves the adaptation or modification of existing designs, it is not accurate to say that this type of design requires no special knowledge or skill. Even when making minor alterations or modifications, designers need to possess certain expertise and capabilities to ensure the success of the design adaptation process. Here are a few reasons why:

- **Understanding of Design Principles:** Designers need to have a solid understanding of design principles, such as aesthetics, ergonomics, functionality, and user experience. This knowledge helps them make informed decisions when adapting existing designs to ensure that the modified design still meets the desired objectives and requirements.
- **Technical Competence:** Designers must possess technical competence in the relevant field to effectively modify existing designs. They need to understand the underlying engineering principles, manufacturing processes, and materials involved in the original design to make appropriate alterations without compromising the integrity or performance of the product.
- **Problem-solving Skills**: Even when making minor alterations, designers may encounter challenges or constraints that require problem-solving skills. They need to identify potential issues, find creative solutions, and ensure that the modified design functions as intended.

- **Knowledge of Market and User Needs:** Designers should have a good understanding of market trends, user preferences, and needs. This knowledge helps them adapt existing designs to better align with the target market and meet the evolving demands of users.
- **Communication and Collaboration:** Designers often work in multidisciplinary teams, collaborating with engineers, manufacturers, and other stakeholders. Effective communication and collaboration skills are essential to ensure that the modifications are implemented correctly and that all parties involved are aligned with the design changes.

While adapting existing designs may not require the same level of complexity as creating entirely new designs, it still demands a certain level of knowledge, skill, and expertise. Designers with ordinary technical training can certainly undertake such tasks, but their competence and understanding of design principles play a crucial role in achieving successful design adaptations.

2. Development design

Development design, also known as design development or advanced design, involves taking existing designs and transforming them into new ideas by incorporating new materials, manufacturing methods, or technologies. This type of design requires a significant level of scientific training, technical expertise, and design ability to successfully modify and innovate upon existing designs.

Designers working on development design projects need to possess the following skills and knowledge:

- **Scientific Training:** Development design often involves incorporating new materials, technologies, or scientific principles into the design process. Designers must have a solid scientific foundation and understanding of relevant scientific disciplines to effectively integrate these elements into the design.
- **Design Ability:** Designers need to have a strong design ability to envision and create new ideas based on existing designs. They must be able to think creatively, explore different possibilities, and generate innovative concepts that go beyond the original design.
- **Technical Expertise:** Development design often requires a deep understanding of technical aspects, such as materials science, manufacturing processes, engineering principles, and technological

advancements. Designers must be knowledgeable about these areas to select and implement new materials or methods that enhance the design.

- **Problem-solving Skills:** Development design involves overcoming challenges and finding solutions to complex problems. Designers must possess strong problem-solving skills to identify constraints, analyse feasibility, and develop strategies to modify the existing design effectively.
- **Research and Analysis:** Designers need to conduct extensive research to identify new materials, technologies, or manufacturing methods that can be integrated into the design. They must analyse the potential benefits, limitations, and implications of these new elements to ensure their successful incorporation.
- **Adaptability and Flexibility:** Development design often requires designers to adapt and adjust their approach as they encounter new information or challenges. They must be flexible in their thinking and willing to iterate and refine their designs based on feedback and new insights.

Development design is a specialized area that demands a high level of scientific training, technical expertise, and design ability. Designers in this field have the opportunity to transform existing designs into innovative and ground breaking products that may differ significantly from the original concept.

3. New design

New design, often referred to as innovative or ground breaking design, involves the creation of novel and original solutions that push the boundaries of existing design practices. It requires extensive research, technical expertise, and creative thinking to develop unique and unconventional design concepts. Designers working on new design projects must possess certain personal qualities and skills to effectively tackle the challenges involved. These qualities may include:

- **Curiosity and Open-mindedness:** Designers need to have a natural curiosity and a willingness to explore new ideas, technologies, and materials. They should be open-minded and receptive to unconventional approaches and perspectives.
- **Research Skills:** Extensive research is crucial in new design projects. Designers must be adept at conducting thorough research to gain insights

into user needs, market trends, emerging technologies, and other relevant factors that can inform their design decisions.

- **Technical Ability:** New design often involves pushing the boundaries of what is technically feasible. Designers must have a strong technical foundation and a deep understanding of materials, manufacturing processes, engineering principles, and other technical aspects relevant to their field.
- **Creative Thinking:** Innovative design requires designers to think outside the box and come up with fresh and imaginative ideas. They should be able to generate multiple concepts, explore unconventional approaches, and challenge established norms to create truly innovative solutions.
- **Problem-solving Skills:** New design projects often involve complex and ambiguous problems. Designers must possess strong problem-solving skills to analyze challenges, identify opportunities, and develop effective solutions that address user needs and overcome constraints.
- **Collaboration and Communication:** Collaboration with multidisciplinary teams is often essential in new design projects. Designers should be able to effectively communicate their ideas, collaborate with experts from different fields, and integrate diverse perspectives into their design process.

New design is a demanding and exciting field that requires a combination of technical expertise, research capabilities, and creative thinking. Designers who possess the necessary personal qualities and skills can embark on the challenging journey of creating innovative and ground breaking designs that shape the future of their respective industries.

The designs, depending upon the methods used, may be classified as follows:

(*a*) *Rational design*

Rational design, also known as analytical design, is an approach to design that relies on mathematical principles and formulas derived from the laws of mechanics and other scientific disciplines. It involves using theoretical models, calculations, and analysis to guide the design process and make informed decisions.

In rational design, designers apply scientific principles and mathematical equations to understand the behavior, performance, and structural integrity of a system or component. By utilizing mathematical formulas, such as those derived from the principles of mechanics, designers can predict and optimize various aspects of the design, including strength, stability, load-bearing capacity, and dynamic response.

Rational design typically involves the following steps:

- **Problem Definition:** Clearly defining the design problem and identifying the objectives, constraints, and requirements.
- **Mathematical Modeling:** Developing mathematical models that represent the physical behaviour and characteristics of the system or component under consideration. This may involve formulating equations based on principles of mechanics, physics, or other relevant scientific disciplines.
- **Analysis and Calculation:** Applying mathematical formulas and analytical techniques to analyse the model and calculate the desired design parameters, such as stress, strain, deflection, or performance metrics.
- **Optimization:** Using the calculated results to optimize the design by adjusting variables, dimensions, or materials to meet specific criteria or objectives.
- **Validation and Iteration:** Validating the design through testing, simulation, or comparison with real-world data. Iterative refinements may be made based on the validation results.

Rational design provides a systematic and rigorous approach to design, ensuring that the design meets desired performance criteria and adheres to scientific principles. It is commonly used in engineering disciplines, such as structural engineering, mechanical engineering, aerospace engineering, and many others, where the behaviour of materials and structures can be accurately described using mathematical formulas and principles.

This type of design depends upon mathematical formulae of principle of mechanics.

(*b*) *Empirical design*

Empirical design refers to a design approach that relies on empirical formulae, rules of thumb, and past experience rather than theoretical or analytical methods. It is a practical and often simplified approach to design that is based on observed data and established relationships.

In empirical design, designers use formulae or rules that have been derived from extensive testing, experimentation, or historical data. These formulae are typically developed through observation and analysis of real-world examples and are often specific to certain applications or industries.

The use of empirical design can be beneficial in situations where theoretical models or analytical methods are not readily available or practical. It allows designers to quickly estimate or predict the behaviour or performance of a system or component based on established relationships and past experience.

However, it is important to note that empirical design has limitations. It may not account for all variables or factors that can influence the design outcome, and its accuracy may vary depending on the specific context or conditions. Empirical design should be used with caution and validated against real-world data or testing whenever possible.

Empirical design is commonly employed in various fields, including civil engineering, structural design, mechanical engineering, and product development. It provides a practical and efficient approach to design, particularly when time, resources, or detailed analysis are limited.

(*c*) ***Industrial design.***

Industrial design is a field of design that focuses on the aesthetic and functional aspects of products, particularly those intended for mass production in industries. It involves the creation and development of designs for various products, including machine components, consumer goods, appliances, furniture, and more.

Fig. 1.4. Concept foldable scooter

In the context of manufacturing machine components, industrial design plays a crucial role in ensuring that the components are not only functional and efficient but also visually appealing and user-friendly. Industrial designers work closely with engineers, manufacturers, and other stakeholders to create designs that meet both technical requirements and market demands.

The industrial design process typically involves the following steps:

- **Research and Analysis:** Industrial designers conduct research to understand user needs, market trends, and technological advancements. They analyse existing products and identify opportunities for improvement.
- **Concept Development:** Based on the research findings, industrial designers generate multiple design concepts. These concepts explore different forms, features, and materials that align with the desired functionality and manufacturing feasibility.
- **Prototyping and Testing:** Selected design concepts are translated into physical or digital prototypes. These prototypes are tested and evaluated to assess their performance, usability, and aesthetics. Iterative refinements are made based on the test results.

Fig. 1.5. Digital Prototype (Concept bike)

- **Design Refinement:** The chosen design concept is further refined, considering factors such as manufacturability, cost-effectiveness, and sustainability. Industrial designers collaborate with engineers and manufacturers to ensure that the design can be efficiently produced at scale.
- **Production Documentation:** Detailed specifications, drawings, and documentation are created to guide the manufacturing process. These

documents provide instructions for fabricating, assembling, and finishing the machine components.

Industrial design aims to create products that not only meet functional requirements but also resonate with users, differentiate from competitors, and align with brand values. By considering production aspects from the early stages of design, industrial designers can optimize the manufacturing process, reduce costs, and enhance the overall quality of the machine components.

(*d*) *Optimum design*

Optimum design refers to the process of finding the best possible design solution for a given objective function while considering the specified constraints. The objective function represents the desired outcome or goal of the design, which could be maximizing performance, minimizing cost, reducing weight, or any other measurable criteria.

In optimum design, the goal is to find the design parameters or variables that optimize the objective function while satisfying the constraints. These constraints can include limitations on resources, manufacturing capabilities, safety regulations, or any other factors that must be considered during the design process.

To achieve an optimum design, various techniques and methodologies can be employed, such as mathematical optimization algorithms, simulation-based optimization, or heuristic approaches. These methods help explore the design space, evaluate different design alternatives, and identify the optimal solution based on the defined objective function and constraints.

In many cases, achieving an optimum design involves trade-offs between conflicting objectives. For example, improving performance may increase cost or weight. The designer must carefully balance these trade-offs to find the best compromise that meets the desired objectives within the given constraints.

Overall, optimum design aims to find the most efficient and effective solution that minimizes undesirable effects and maximizes the desired outcome, considering all relevant constraints and limitations.

(*e*) *System design*

System design refers to the process of designing a complex mechanical system, such as a motor car, to meet specific requirements and objectives. It involves the integration of various components, subsystems, and technologies to create a functional and efficient system.

In the context of motor car design, system design encompasses several aspects, including:

- **Functional Requirements:** Defining the intended purpose and functionality of the car, such as transportation, performance, safety, and comfort.
- **Component Integration:** Identifying and selecting the necessary components, such as the engine, transmission, suspension, braking system, electrical system, and interior features, and integrating them into a cohesive system.
- **Performance Optimization:** Balancing various design parameters, such as power, fuel efficiency, handling, and aerodynamics, to achieve optimal performance and meet regulatory standards.
- **Safety and Reliability:** Ensuring that the design incorporates appropriate safety features, crashworthiness, and reliability measures to protect occupants and meet industry standards.
- **Ergonomics and User Experience:** Considering human factors, ergonomics, and user experience to design a comfortable and intuitive driving environment.
- **Manufacturing and Cost Considerations:** Taking into account manufacturing processes, materials, and cost constraints to design a system that can be efficiently produced and meets budgetary requirements.

System design in motor car design involves a multidisciplinary approach, combining mechanical engineering, electrical engineering, materials science, and other relevant fields to create a well-integrated and functional product. Computer-aided design (CAD) and simulation tools are often used to aid in the design and analysis of the system.

(f) Element design

Element design refers to the process of designing individual components or elements of a mechanical system, such as pistons, crankshafts, connecting rods, and other similar parts. This involves considering various factors such as material selection, structural integrity, functionality, manufacturing processes, and performance requirements. The goal is to create a component that meets the desired specifications and can effectively perform its intended function within the larger mechanical system.

(g) *Computer aided design*

Computer-aided design (CAD) is a design process that utilizes computer systems to aid in various aspects of design creation, modification, analysis, and optimization. CAD software allows designers to create and manipulate digital models of objects or systems, providing a more efficient and accurate design process compared to traditional manual methods. CAD systems offer a wide range of tools and functionalities, such as 2D drafting, 3D modeling, simulation, rendering, and documentation, enabling designers to visualize and evaluate their designs before they are physically realized. CAD is widely used in various industries, including architecture, engineering, manufacturing, and product design.

Objectives of the Machine Design

- **Strength:** Ensuring the strength of the machine is crucial to withstand the applied loads and forces during operation. Designers need to select appropriate materials, determine suitable cross-sectional dimensions, and consider factors such as stress analysis and structural integrity to ensure the machine can handle the required loads without failure.
- **Rigidity:** Rigidity refers to the ability of the machine to resist deformation under load. Designers aim to minimize deflection and ensure that the machine remains stable and maintains its intended shape during operation. This involves selecting appropriate materials, optimizing structural design, and considering factors such as stiffness and vibration analysis.
- **Wear Resistance:** Machines often experience wear due to friction, abrasion, or other factors. Designers need to consider wear-resistant materials, surface treatments, lubrication systems, and appropriate design features to minimize wear and prolong the machine's lifespan.
- **Minimum dimensions and weight:** Designers strive to minimize the dimensions and weight of the machine while maintaining its functionality and performance. This can involve optimizing the design, using lightweight materials, and employing efficient structural configurations to reduce the overall size and weight of the machine.
- **Manufacturing:** Designers need to consider the manufacturability of the machine design. This includes selecting manufacturing processes that are suitable for the chosen materials, ensuring ease of assembly, and

minimizing production costs. Designers also consider factors such as tolerances, surface finishes, and part complexity to facilitate efficient and cost-effective manufacturing.

- **Safety:** Safety is a critical objective in machine design. Designers need to incorporate safety features, such as guards, emergency stop mechanisms, interlocks, and warning systems, to protect operators and prevent accidents. Compliance with relevant safety standards and regulations is essential to ensure the machine's safe operation.
- **Reliability:** Designers aim to create machines that are reliable and perform consistently over time. This involves considering factors such as component selection, robust design, redundancy, and preventive maintenance to minimize downtime and ensure the machine's reliability in various operating conditions.
- **Cost:** Cost is an important objective in machine design. Designers need to balance the desired functionality, performance, and quality of the machine with the available budget. This involves optimizing the design, selecting cost-effective materials and manufacturing processes, and considering the overall lifecycle costs of the machine.

1.5 Steps Involved in the Machine Design Procedure

Identifying the need for the equipment or machine:

We must first locate the source of the problem inside the system. Whether the problem is present or not. Try to find out the problem inside system or outside of the system (problems facing by a person). We should find out the need for the machine or a system before designing any part or machine. If there is no need of the machine or part they there is no point in the designing or manufacturing it.

Selecting the possible mechanism:

Choose and examine the optimum mechanisms and movements for the particular machine. There should be optimized mechanism for movement of the machine/part. Be cautious in selecting the right or suitable mechanism, because this will decide the course of the direction of the machine/part.

Analysis of forces:

Then determine the forces affecting each machine part, whether it is moving or stationary. This will help you in selection of right material and dimensions.

The following two types of loading is used for the machine components.

- Static loading
- Variable loading

Static loading is a stationary force, whose magnitude point of application and direction remains unchanged. This load produces axial compression or tension, shear load, bending or torsion load.

In variable loading, the stresses vary with time and fluctuates between different levels. The failure under repeated or fluctuated stresses is known as fatigue failure.

Selection of material:

After deciding the mechanism and analysing the forces acting on the machine element, we have to select the suitable material to manufacture the element. According to the application, forces acting on it, availability in the market, and cost we have to select by material by considering this factors.

Design of machine components

Designing a machine is no simple task. It requires a deep understanding of the forces that will act upon it and the materials that will be used. By carefully assessing these factors, engineers can determine the right proportions for each component, ensuring that they can withstand the stresses they will encounter during operation.

The first step in the design process is to assess the forces that will be exerted on the machine. These forces can come from a variety of sources, such as the weight of the load it will carry, the pressure it will endure, or the vibrations it will experience. By analysing these forces, engineers can determine the maximum stresses that each component will face.

Once the forces have been assessed, the next crucial step is to choose the appropriate materials for each component. Different materials have different properties, such as strength, flexibility, and durability. By selecting materials that can withstand the anticipated stresses, engineers can ensure the longevity and reliability of the machine.

However, it is not enough to simply choose strong materials. Every element of the machine must receive the proper level of safety. This means that the stresses experienced by each component must be less than the maximum stresses that the material can withstand. By incorporating a safety factor into the design, engineers can account for unforeseen circumstances or variations in operating conditions, ensuring that the machine remains robust and secure.

To achieve this level of safety, engineers employ various design techniques. One common approach is to use redundancy, where multiple components are used to perform the same function. This ensures that even if one component fails, the machine can still operate safely. Additionally, engineers may incorporate features such as overload protection or fail-safe mechanisms to further enhance the safety of the machine.

In the world of machine design, precision is paramount. Every component must be carefully crafted to meet the required specifications. This involves determining the right proportions for each element, ensuring that they can withstand the anticipated forces without compromising safety. By employing advanced modeling and simulation techniques, engineers can test and refine their designs before they are brought to life.

Computer-aided design (CAD) software plays a crucial role in this process. It allows engineers to create detailed 3D models of the machine and simulate its behaviour under different conditions. By virtually testing the design, engineers can identify potential weaknesses or areas of improvement, enabling them to refine the proportions and enhance the safety of the machine.

Furthermore, advancements in materials science have opened up new possibilities in machine design. Engineers now have access to a wide range of innovative materials, each with its own unique properties. For example, carbon fibre composites offer exceptional strength-to-weight ratios, making them ideal for applications where weight reduction is critical. By leveraging these materials, engineers can design machines that are not only strong and safe but also lightweight and efficient.

Modification:

Following the overall design of the machine's component parts, we must change the machine to better utilize available resources and to do it at a lower cost. Because sometimes when designing a machine, we examine every factor, but in practice, we also need to take the machine's entire cost into account as well as the resources that are readily available on the market.

Detailed Drawing:

When creating part drawings, we focus on the individual components of the machine. This involves carefully measuring and documenting the dimensions of each part, as well as noting any specific features or characteristics that are important for the assembly process. These drawings serve as a detailed guide for manufacturing and assembly, ensuring that each part is produced to the correct specifications.

Subassembly drawings are then created to represent groups of parts that come together to form a larger component of the machine. This could be a complex mechanism, a housing for machine components, or any other subassembly that is integral to the overall function of the machine. These drawings show how the individual parts fit together and interact, providing essential information for the assembly process.

Finally, assembly drawings bring together all the individual parts and subassemblies to represent the complete machine. These drawings are essential for understanding how the machine is put together, including the order of assembly, the relationships between components, and any specific instructions or considerations that need to be taken into account during the assembly process.

Throughout this process, attention to detail is paramount. Every measurement, every dimension, and every annotation must be accurate and precise to ensure that the final machine functions as intended. This requires a combination of technical skill, knowledge of engineering principles, and a meticulous approach to documentation.

Production:

Components are made in factories in accordance with the drawing, then assembled in accordance with the designs. This process begins with the initial concept and design phase, where the overall function and purpose of the machine are carefully considered. Once the design is finalized, the next step is to create detailed drawings and specifications for each individual component. These drawings serve as a guide for the manufacturing process, ensuring that each part is made to exact specifications.

The intricate process of machine design involves careful planning, precise measurements, and a deep understanding of how each component works together to achieve a specific function.

Once the components are manufactured, they are carefully inspected to ensure that they meet the required standards. This is a crucial step in the process, as any deviation from the design specifications can result in a machine that does not function properly. Once the components have been approved, they are then assembled according to the designs.

The assembly process requires a high level of precision and attention to detail. Each component must be carefully aligned and connected to ensure that the machine functions as intended. This often involves the use of specialized tools and equipment to ensure that everything comes together seamlessly.

Throughout the entire process, it is important to constantly monitor and test the machine to ensure that it meets the required standards. This may involve running simulations, conducting stress tests, and making any necessary adjustments to ensure that the machine operates safely and efficiently.

Quality Checking:

While ensuring high calibre and safety are indeed crucial design principles for creating machines or machine components, there are additional fundamental design principles that are commonly applied in the process. These principles help guide the design and development of machines to ensure their functionality, efficiency, and reliability. Here are some of the fundamental design principles used in creating machines:

- **Functionality:** The primary purpose of a machine is to perform a specific function or task. Designers must ensure that the machine is designed to fulfil its intended purpose effectively and efficiently. This involves understanding the requirements, constraints, and desired outcomes of the machine and incorporating the necessary features, mechanisms, and controls to achieve its functionality.
- **Efficiency:** Machines should be designed to operate with optimal efficiency, minimizing energy consumption, material waste, and time required to perform the desired task. Designers consider factors such as power requirements, mechanical efficiency, and overall system performance to maximize the efficiency of the machine.
- **Reliability and Safety:** Machines must be designed to operate reliably and safely. Designers incorporate safety features, such as guards, emergency stop mechanisms, and fail-safe systems, to protect users and prevent accidents. Reliability is achieved through robust design, appropriate material selection, and consideration of potential failure modes and preventive measures.
- **Ergonomics:** Designers consider the ergonomics of the machine to ensure that it is user-friendly and comfortable to operate. This involves designing controls, interfaces, and access points that are intuitive, easy to use, and minimize physical strain on the operator.
- **Maintainability:** Machines should be designed with ease of maintenance and repair in mind. Designers consider accessibility to components,

modularity, and standardization to facilitate maintenance, reduce downtime, and extend the machine's lifespan.

- **Cost-effectiveness:** Designers strive to create machines that are cost-effective in terms of manufacturing, operation, and maintenance. This involves optimizing material usage, minimizing complexity, and considering the overall lifecycle costs of the machine.
- **Environmental Considerations:** Designers increasingly take into account the environmental impact of machines. This includes designing for energy efficiency, using sustainable materials, and considering end-of-life disposal or recycling options.

These fundamental design principles, along with quality control measures, ensure that machines are designed to meet the required standards, perform their intended functions reliably, and prioritize the safety of users. By adhering to these principles, designers can create machines that are efficient, reliable, user-friendly, and environmentally responsible.

1.6 Design Parameters

In Engineering, something can be proven either by observation or by measurement. We have to investigate a model that describes design in terms of a logical representation. The design process can be effectively understood and improved by identifying its three basic elements: inputs, outputs, and the methods used in between. This clarity helps in streamlining the operation and increasing the probability of success while reducing risks.

- **Inputs:** The inputs in the design process refer to the information, resources, and requirements that are provided at the beginning of the design project. These inputs can include client briefs, user needs, market research, technical specifications, budget constraints, and any other relevant information. Clearly defining and understanding the inputs is crucial as they form the foundation for the design process.
- **Outputs:** The outputs of the design process are the tangible or intangible results that are generated at the end of the process. These can include design concepts, prototypes, technical drawings, specifications, user interfaces, or any other deliverables that fulfil the objectives of the design project. Defining the desired outputs helps in setting clear goals and expectations for the design process.

- **Methods:** The methods used in the design process refer to the techniques, tools, and approaches employed to transform the inputs into the desired outputs. This can include research methods, ideation techniques, prototyping processes, testing methodologies, and various design tools and software. Having a well-defined and structured method helps in ensuring consistency, efficiency, and effectiveness throughout the design process.

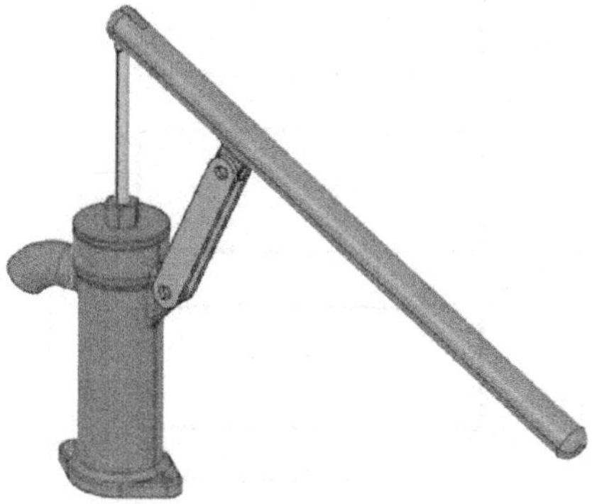

Fig. 1.6. Hand pump

By clearly identifying these three elements and defining the roles and responsibilities of the design team in advance, the design process becomes more transparent and manageable. It allows for better communication, collaboration, and coordination among team members, reducing uncertainties and fears. Additionally, by recognizing and addressing any broken processes or bottlenecks, the design process can be improved, repeated, and modified to achieve better results. Regular evaluation and feedback loops within the design process also contribute to continuous improvement. By analysing the inputs, outputs, and methods used, designers can identify areas for enhancement, refine their approach, and optimize the overall design process.

Therefore, design can be quantitatively measurable and could be evaluated and optimized.

1.7 Design Process

Design process consists of six different phases as shown in figure 1.7.

- **Recognition of need**: Before beginning the design of a component, sort out the problem exists, for which a product can be designed.

- **Define the problem**: Specify the general outline of the problem to be solved. This includes the cost, operating performance and characteristics functions.
- **Synthesis**: Suggest possible alternate design solution or if some shortcomings are there; improve this using computer aided design software.

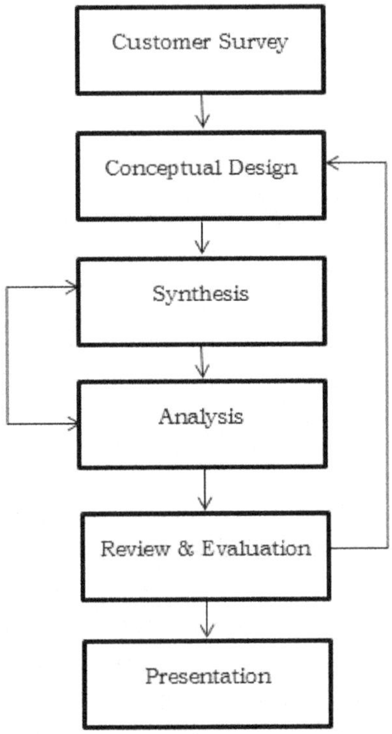

Fig. 1.7.CAD design process

- **Analysis and optimization**: The product is analysed with the help of computer aided Engineering software and interprets the results obtained from them. This process will go on till the designed is optimized.
- **Evaluation of design**: Measure and test the product to be safe to use in real time environment. Tests are to be conducted on prototype model.
- **Presentation**: Make the final presentation with Bill of material and drawing of the design by mentioning its material, size and assembly list. It means a database of the design is created for manufacturing.

1.8 The Applications of Computers for Design

The modern computer aided design system can be grouped into four functional areas as shown in figure 1.8.

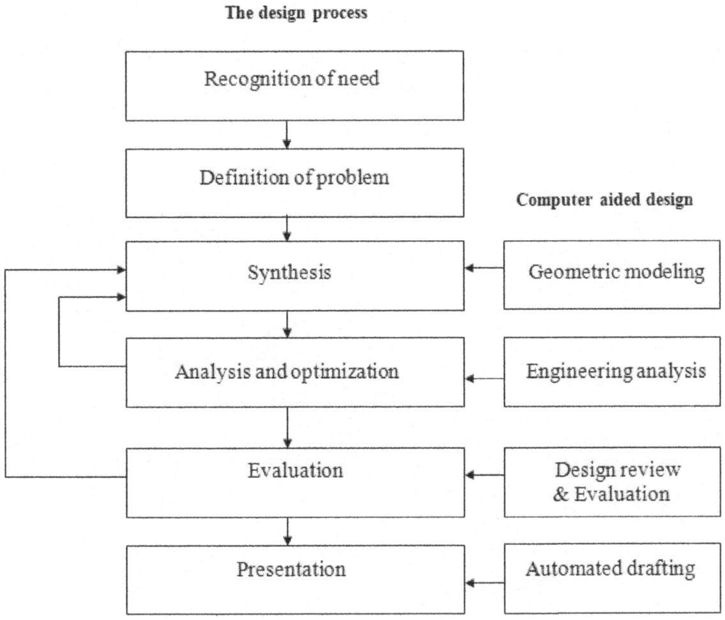

Fig. 1.8. Computer aided design **process**

Geometric modelling:

In CAD, geometric modelling is concerned with the computer compatible mathematical description of the geometry of an object. The mathematical description allows the image of the object to be displayed and manipulated on a graphics terminal through signals from CPU of the CAD system.

The software that provides geometric modelling capabilities must be designed for efficient use both by the computer and the human designer.

Analysis:

The analysis may involve stress – strain calculations, heat transfer computations or the use of differential equation to describe the dynamic behaviour of the system being designed. The computer can be used to aid in this analysis work.

Design review and evaluation:

Checking the accuracy of the design can be accomplished conveniently on the graphic terminal. Design review can be carried out by different procedures. E.g. Layering and interference checking. Some of the CAD systems provide kinematics as it evaluation feature. The available kinematics package provides the capability to animate the motion of simple designed mechanism such as hinged components and linkages. This capability enhances the designer's visualization of the operation of the mechanism and helps to ensure against interface with other components.

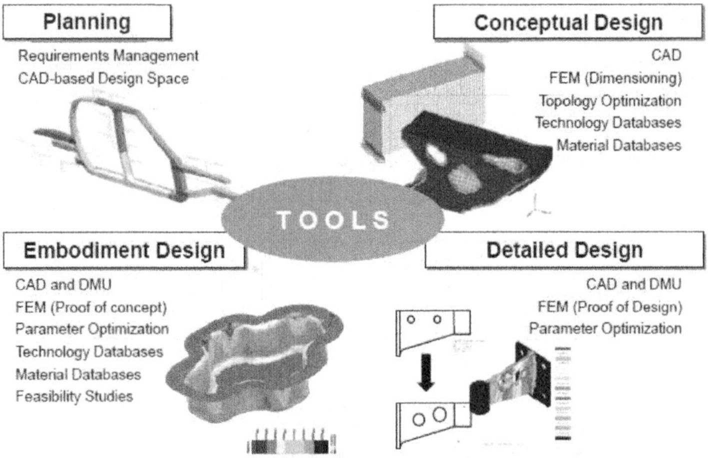

Fig. 1.9. Tools used in various designs

Automated drafting:

Automated drafting involves the creation of hard copy engineering drawings directly from the CAD database is that it can be used to develop a parts classification and coding system. Product optimization is the practice of making changes or adjustments to a product to make it more desirable. Optimization is finding an alternative with the most cost effective or highest achievable performance under the given constraints by maximizing desired factors and minimizing undesired ones. In comparison, maximization means trying to attain the highest or maximum result or outcome without regard to cost or expense. Optimization is mainly concerned with quality of the product and when it comes to quality Taguchi principles and experiments play an important role in product design.

1.9 Benefits of CAD

- Improved Engineering productivity.
- Shorter lead time.
- Reduced engineering personal requirements.
- Customer modifications are easier to make.
- Minimized transcription errors.
- Improved accuracy of design.
- In analysis, easier recognition of component interactions.
- Assistance in preparation of documentation.
- Designs have more standardization.
- Improved productivity in tool design.
- Assistance in inspection of complicated parts.
- Saves materials and machining time by optimizing algorithms.

CAx Technologies

The product design and development are developed and supported by computer software. It is termed as CAx technologies i.e. Computer Aided something. These tools are supporting the engineering activities.
The most often used abbreviations are:

- **CAD** – Computer Aided Design
- **CAM** – Computer Aided Manufacturing
- **CAE** – Computer Aided Engineering
- **CAPP** – Computer Aided Process Planning
- **CAQA** – Computer Aided Quality Assurance
- **CAPPS** – Computer Aided Production Planning and Scheduling
- **CAST** – Computer Aided Storage and Transport

What is Product Design?

Design not only functions through the honed application of guidelines or rules, but is also based on the perception of the environment/surroundings and therefore the social developments or trends that result from an accountable perspective. Rather than thinking in terms of conventional patterns, designers should recognize and analyse deficits and deficiencies through observation and self-experiments, and be able to generate appropriate superior solutions. This expertise provides the basis for every creative process. Digital and manual presentation techniques are both necessary tools in the design process for the visualization of new concepts. Styling is a part of a comprehensive process.

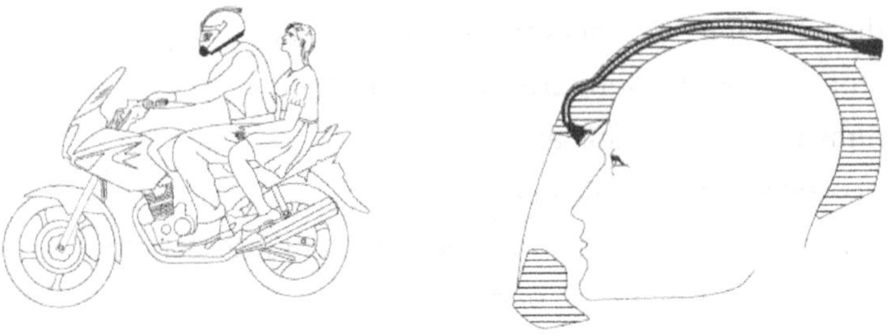

Fig. 1.10. Product design

Product design and engineering involves working out all the technical details of the product. The success of innovative engineering process depend on short and iterative development cycles which offers the possibility of high quality products, cost efficient on the market and thus to stand up to today's tough competitive pressure. The design engineers seek the answers to the following questions:

- How should the product look like?
- How will it work?
- If it has to be powered, what power source should it use?
- What is the best shape and size?
- How will the parts be made and assembled?

Designing is the idea generating phase with sketches and mock-ups as outputs. This is achieved by applying scientific and mathematical knowledge in engineering the product.

Designer's major tasks are:

- Collecting ideas
- Sketching ideas resulting in thumbnail and rough sketches.
- Rendering sketches
- Making mock-ups
- Making detailed assembly and schematic drawings.
- Building and testing prototype.

1.10 Digital Prototyping

The employment of virtual prototypes in the early phases of product development optimizes the whole development process. The digital demonstration allows an early modification and optimization of the prototype. By combining CAD technologies, Rapid prototyping, and Reverse Engineering, prototypes can be produced faster and cheaper as before. Furthermore, it leads to a cost-saving increase in the variety of prototypes. By means of virtual prototypes, product features can be easily verified and thus development times can be reduced enormously. Digital Prototyping has the following three areas: CAD, simulation and Virtual Reality. Simulation and CAD-data produce quantifiable results, whereas the connection with VR-technologies enables a qualitative evaluation of the results.

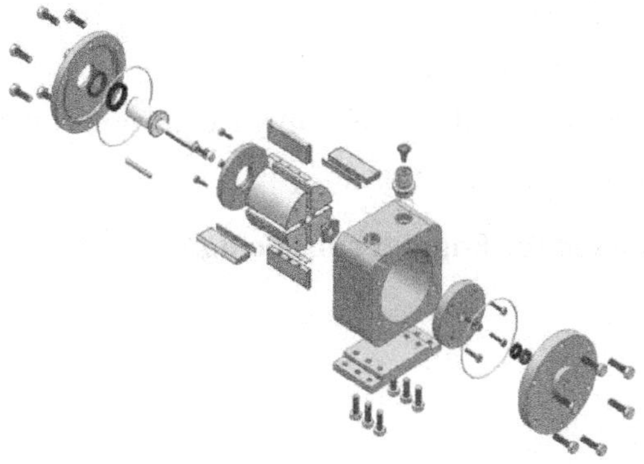

Fig. 1.11. Digital prototype (Disassembly of a product)

Factors Involved in Rapid Product Development

- Understanding the Industry's pre-requisites and requirements to realize the rapid prototyping and manufacturing evolution.
- Select role and power of Rapid Prototyping or Virtual Prototyping for each product requirements.
- Improving new developments in RP – Rapid Prototyping and RM – Rapid Manufacturing.
- Managing CAD/CAM systems to enhance accuracy and efficiency.
- More extensive utilization of IT- Information Technology and KM- Knowledge Management to support product development.

- Introduce simulation technologies into the Rapid Product development Technologies.
- Abandoning slow, time consuming traditional product design processes by employing latest rapid prototyping and simulation solutions. Redefining the ideal skill set for product design manager.
- Defining, measuring and continually improving design investments.
- Understanding and applying the latest product innovation strategies through Rapid Product Development technologies.

Factors Influencing the Selection of Materials for Machine Components

The following factors influence the selection of materials for machine components

- Availability of materials
- Cost associated with the materials
- Method of processing and manufacturing considerations
- Mechanical properties of material

Common Materials used for Engineering Design

- Cast iron
- White cast iron
- Malleable cast iron
- Grey cast iron
- Spheroidal cast iron
- Alloy cast iron
- Wrought iron
- Low carbon steel
- Medium carbon steel
- High carbon steel
- Alloy steel
- Aluminium
- Copper
- Titanium
- Plastic
- Rubber

1.11 Indian Standards for Engineering Materials

In grey cast iron FG 150, the number indicates the ultimate tensile strength in $N/_{mm^2}$

Composition of alloy steel 55Cr3 is

- 0.5 – 0.6% of carbon
- 0.10-0.35% of silicon
- 0.6-0.8% of manganese and
- 0.6-0.8% of chromium.

1.12 Classification of Materials for Engineering Use

Engineering materials are broadly classified as follows

- Metals and their alloys
- Non-metals

1) Metals

These are further classified into two types

1. Ferrous Metals: In these metals, the main constituent is iron. The various ferrous metals used in engineering are wrought iron, cast iron and alloy steel, etc.,

2. Non Ferrous Metals: Non-ferrous metals are those metals, which do not contain iron as their main constituent.

Examples: Copper, zinc, brass, bronze, tin, aluminium, gun metal.

3. Non-metals: These are shiny and solid substances that can be formed to any geometrical shape. Non-metals cannot conduct electricity or heat.

Examples: Glass, plastic, wood, rubber, etc.

Significance of Preferred Numbers in Machine Design

Preferred numbers, also known as standard numbers or preferred values, are indeed a series of numbers that are commonly used to determine the parameters of various products. These numbers are selected based on specific criteria to ensure functionality, usability, compatibility, and cost-effectiveness.

- **Function of component:** The function of a component or product plays a significant role in determining the preferred numbers used for its parameters. For example, in power transmission systems, preferred numbers may be employed to determine the capacity of the system, such as the power rating or torque. The chosen numbers should align with the functional requirements and performance characteristics of the component or system.

- **Uses of product:** The intended uses of a product also influence the selection of preferred numbers. Different applications may have specific requirements or standards that dictate the parameters of the product. For instance, in the case of electrical resistors, preferred numbers are often used to determine the resistance values available to ensure compatibility with standard circuits and systems.
- **Compatibility:** Compatibility with existing systems, components, or standards is another important consideration in selecting preferred numbers. By using numbers that align with established standards or commonly used values, compatibility and interchangeability between different products or components can be ensured. This facilitates ease of integration, replacement, or maintenance.
- **Cost of product:** The cost of the product is a significant factor in determining the preferred numbers used for its parameters. By selecting numbers that align with standard manufacturing processes, material sizes, or packaging options, economies of scale can be achieved, leading to cost savings in production. Additionally, using preferred numbers can help streamline inventory management and reduce complexity in sourcing or manufacturing.

Machine elements like gears, shafts, clutches and brakes, pulleys, belts, chain, sprocket are used to transmit power from one place to another.

Design Procedure Based on Strength and Rigidity

Design Procedure Based on Strength

The objective of this design is that the machine element should not fail due to the force acting on it. It should resists these forces and have sufficient strength to prevent failure. The element may fail due to either fracture or general yielding. The criteria of design is that the strength of material must be greater than the induced stresses in the component or machine. Ductile and brittle materials usually fails by yielding and fracture respectively.

Design Procedure based on Rigidity

The objective of this design is that, the machine components should not deflect or bend due to the force acting on it. The components should be rigid enough to withstand the loads. It is generally used in the design of machine tools and instruments. The criteria of design is the maximum permissible deflection and permissible angle of twist.

Mechanical Properties of Engineering Materials

- The performance requirements of a machine are crucial in determining the properties of the materials to be used. We will explore how performance requirements are compared with the properties of materials to select the best suitable material for machine design.
- When designing a machine, it is essential to consider the physical, chemical, mechanical, and manufacturing properties of materials. These properties play a significant role in determining the suitability of a material for a specific application. For example, the stress level estimated for any machine member is compared with the strength of the available materials. This comparison helps in selecting a material that can withstand the required stress levels without failing.
- Physical properties such as melting point, coefficient of thermal expansion, thermal conductivity, specific heat, specific gravity, electrical conductivity, and magnetic properties are essential considerations in machine design. For instance, in high-temperature applications, materials with high melting points and good thermal conductivity are preferred to ensure the stability and efficiency of the machine.
- Chemical properties, including corrosion resistance and reactivity with acids, bases, and water, are crucial in environments where the machine is exposed to harsh chemicals or corrosive substances. Selecting materials with excellent corrosion resistance can prolong the lifespan of the machine and reduce maintenance costs.
- Mechanical properties such as hardness, toughness, ductility, and malleability are vital in determining the structural integrity and performance of machine components. For example, in applications where impact resistance is essential, materials with high toughness are preferred to prevent brittle failure.

- Manufacturing properties such as castability, weldability, formability, and machinability are also significant factors in material selection. These properties influence the ease of manufacturing and assembly of machine components, ultimately affecting the overall production cost and efficiency.

Mechanical Properties of Metals: The mechanical properties of the metals are those which are associated with the ability of the material to resist mechanical forces and load. These mechanical properties of the metal include; Strength, stiffness, elasticity, plasticity, ductility, brittleness, malleability, toughness, resilience, creep and hardness.

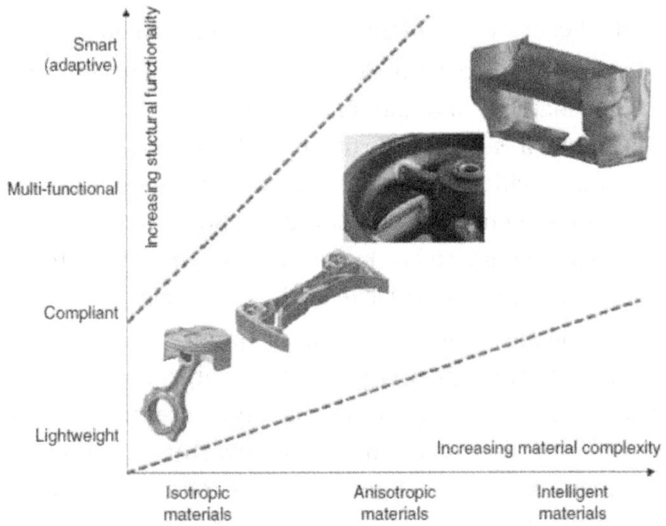

Fig. 1.12. Material properties and structural functionality

- **Strength:** It is the ability of a material to resist the externally applied forces without breaking or yielding. The internal resistance offered by a part to an externally applied force is called stress.
- **Stiffness:** It is the ability of a material to resist deformation under stress. The modulus of elasticity is the measure of stiffness.
- **Elasticity:** It is the property of a material to regain its original shape after deformation when the external forces are removed.
- **Plasticity:** It is property of a material which retains the deformation produced under load permanently.

- **Ductility:** It is the property of a material enabling it to be drawn into wire with the application of a tensile force. A ductile material must be both strong and plastic. The ductility is usually measured by the terms, percentage elongation and percentage reduction in area. The ductile material commonly used in engineering practice are mild steel, copper, aluminum, nickel, zinc, tin and lead.
- **Brittleness:** It is the property of a material opposite to ductility. It is the property of breaking of a material with little permanent distortion. Cast iron is a brittle material.
- **Malleability:** It is a special case of ductility which permits materials to be rolled or hammered into thin sheets. The malleable materials commonly used in engineering practice are lead, soft steel, wrought iron, copper and aluminum.
- **Toughness:** It is the property of a material to resist fracture due to high impact loads like hammer blows. The toughness of the material decreases when it is heated.
- **Resilience:** It is the property of a material to absorb energy and to resist shock and impact loads. This property is essential for spring materials.
- **Creep:** When a part is subjected to a constant stress at high temperature for a long period of time, it will undergo a slow and permanent deformation called creep. This property is considered in designing internal combustion engines, boilers and turbines.
- **Fatigue:** When a material is subjected to repeated stresses, it fails at stresses below the yield point stresses. Such type of failure of a material is known as fatigue. This property is considered in designing shafts, connecting rods, springs, gears, etc.
- **Hardness:** It is the property of the metals; it adopts many different properties such as resistance to wear, scratching, deformation and machinability etc.

1.13 Types of Stresses

There are several types of stresses that can act on a material or structural element. Here are some common types of stresses:

- **Tensile Stress:** Tensile stress occurs when a material is subjected to pulling or stretching forces that try to elongate it. It is characterized by the stress acting perpendicular to the cross-sectional area of the material, causing it to elongate.

- **Compressive Stress:** Compressive stress is the opposite of tensile stress. It occurs when a material is subjected to compressive forces that try to shorten or compress it. Compressive stress acts perpendicular to the cross-sectional area of the material, causing it to shorten.
- **Shear Stress:** Shear stress arises when two forces act parallel to each other but in opposite directions, causing one layer of a material to slide or deform relative to another layer. Shear stress acts parallel to the cross-sectional area of the material.
- **Bending Stress:** Bending stress occurs in structural elements subjected to bending moments. It results from the combination of tensile and compressive stresses on opposite sides of the element. The top surface experiences tensile stress, while the bottom surface experiences compressive stress.
- **Torsional Stress:** Torsional stress occurs in structural elements subjected to torsional (twisting) moments. It causes shear stress within the material, resulting in deformation or failure.
- **Bearing Stress:** Bearing stress occurs when two surfaces come into contact and transmit forces. It is the stress developed at the contact area between the two surfaces.
- Fatigue Stress: Fatigue stress refers to the stress that occurs when a material is subjected to repeated or cyclic loading. It can lead to progressive damage and failure over time, even if the applied stress is below the material's ultimate strength.

Working Stress

Working Stress: When designing machine parts, it is desirable to keep the stress lower than the maximum or ultimate stress at which failure of the material takes place. This stress is known as the working stress.

When some external system of forces or loads acts on a body, the internal forces (equal and opposite) are set up at various sections of the body, which resist the external forces. This internal force per unit area at any section of the body is known as ***unit stress*** or simply a ***stress.*** It is denoted by a Greek letter sigma (σ). Mathematically,

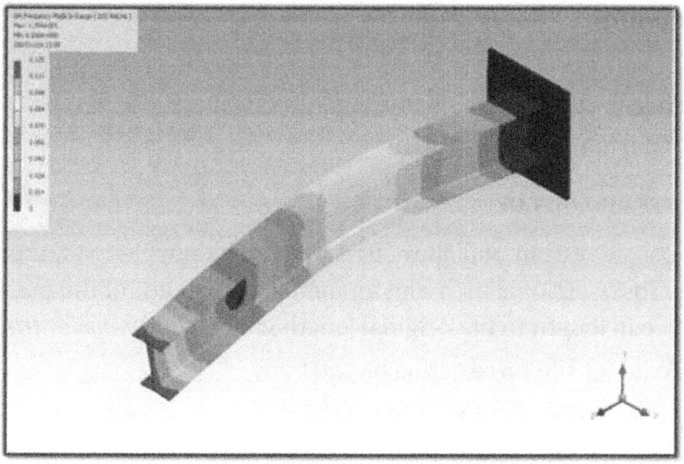

Fig. 1.13. Stress analysis

Stress, $\sigma = P/A$

Where

P = Force or load acting on a body, and

A = Cross-sectional area of the body.

Unit Strain

When a system of forces or loads act on a body, it undergoes some deformation. This deformation per unit length is known as ***unit strain*** or simply a ***strain.*** It is denoted by a Greek letter epsilon (ε). Mathematically,

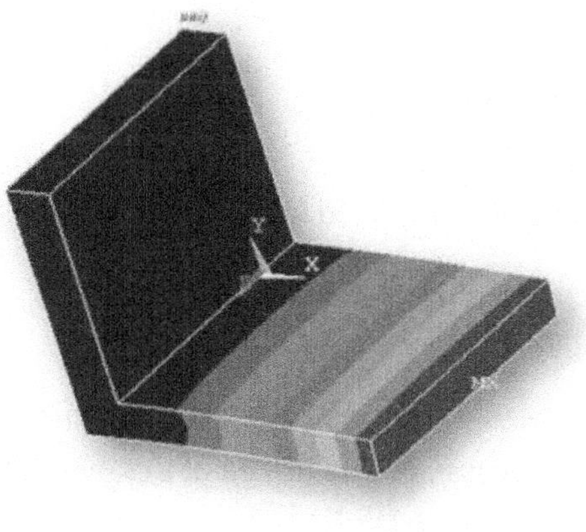

Fig. 1.14. Strain analysis

Strain, $\varepsilon = \delta l / l$ or $\delta l = \varepsilon . l$

Where

δl = Change in length of the body, and

l= Original length of the body.

Tensile Stress and Strain

A little consideration will show that due to the tensile load, there will be a decrease in cross-sectional area and an increase in length of the body. The ratio of the increase in length to the original length is known as *tensile strain.*

Let P = Axial tensile force acting on the body,

A = Cross-sectional area of the body,

l = Original length, and

δl = Increase in length.

Then

Tensile stress, $\sigma t = P/A$

and tensile strain, $\varepsilon t = \delta l / l$

Young's Modulus or Modulus of Elasticity

Hooke's law* states that when a material is loaded within elastic limit, the stress is directly proportional to strain, *i.e.*

where E is a constant of proportionality known as ***Young's modulus*** or ***modulus of elasticity.*** In S.I. units, it is usually expressed in GPa *i.e.* GN/m^2 or kN/mm^2. It may be noted that Hooke's law holds good for tension as well as compression.

Direct Equation (Axial Stress):

The direct equation, also known as the axial stress equation, calculates the stress in a structural member subjected to an axial load (tension or compression). It is given by:

$$\sigma = \frac{P}{A}$$

Where: σ is the axial stress (force per unit area), P is the axial load applied to the member, and A is the cross-sectional area of the member.

Bending Equation (Flexural Stress):

The bending equation, also known as the flexural stress equation, calculates the stress in a structural member subjected to bending moments. It is given by:

$$\sigma = \frac{M\,c}{I}$$

Where: σ is the flexural stress, M is the bending moment applied to the member, c is the distance from the neutral axis to the point of interest (also known as the distance to the extreme fiber), and I is the moment of inertia of the cross-sectional area of the member.

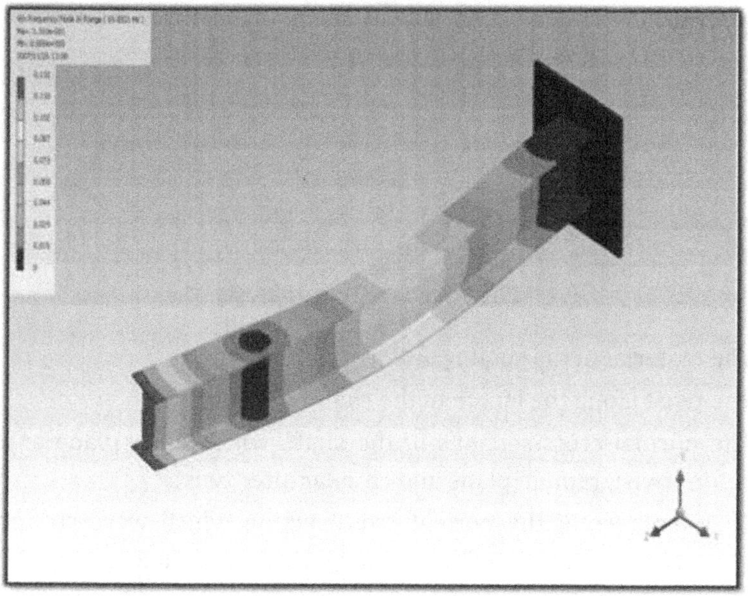

Fig.1.15. Bending analysis

Torsional Equation (Shear Stress):

When a body is subjected to two equal and opposite forces acting tangentially across the resisting section, as a result of which the body tends to shear off the section, then the stress induced is called ***shear stress.*** The torsional equation calculates the shear stress in a structural member subjected to torsional (twisting) moments. It is given by:

$$\tau = \frac{Tr}{j}$$

The above equation **is** known as ***torsion equation.*** It is based on the following assumptions:

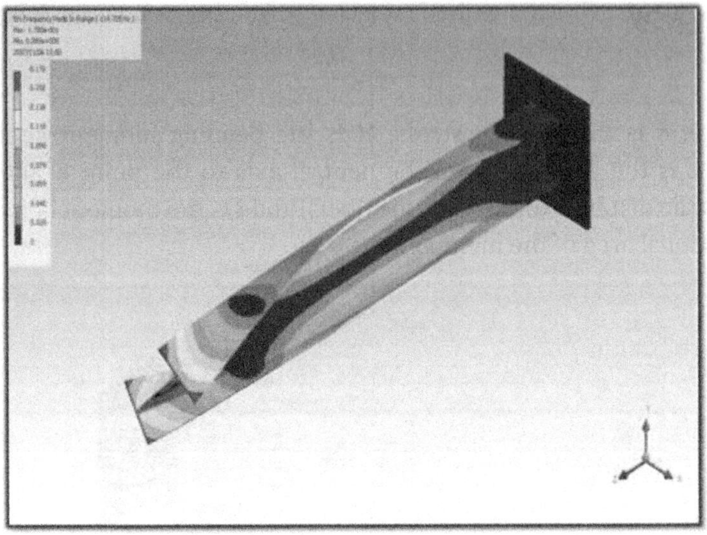

Fig. 1.16. Twisting analysis

- The material of the shaft is uniform throughout.
- The twist along the length of the shaft is uniform.
- The normal cross-sections of the shaft, which were plane and circular before twist, remain plane and circular after twist.
- All diameters of the normal cross-section which were straight before twist, remain straight with their magnitude unchanged, after twist.
- The maximum shear stress induced in the shaft due to the twisting moment does not exceed its elastic limit value.

Where: τ is the shear stress, T is the torsional moment applied to the member, r is the radial distance from the center of the member to the point of interest, and J is the polar moment of inertia of the cross-sectional area of the member.

Linear and Lateral Strain

Linear strain and lateral strain are two types of strain that describe the deformation of a material under the influence of external forces or loads. Linear strain, also known as axial strain or longitudinal strain, refers to the change in length of a material along its longitudinal axis. It is calculated as the ratio of the change in length (ΔL) to the original length (L) of the material:

Linear Strain = ΔL / L

Linear strain can be either positive (tensile strain) or negative (compressive strain), depending on whether the material is being stretched or compressed. Tensile strain occurs when the material elongates, resulting in a positive linear strain value. Compressive strain occurs when the material contracts, resulting in a negative linear strain value.

Lateral strain, also known as transverse strain or shear strain, refers to the change in dimensions of a material perpendicular to the applied force. It is calculated as the ratio of the change in width or thickness (ΔW) to the original width or thickness (W) of the material:

Lateral Strain = ΔW / W

Lateral strain is typically associated with shear forces or loads that cause the material to deform in a perpendicular direction to the applied force. It represents the change in shape of the material rather than its length.

It is important to note that linear strain and lateral strain are related to each other through the Poisson's ratio (ν) of the material.

Poisson's ratio is a material property that describes the ratio of lateral strain to linear strain. It is typically denoted by the Greek letter "nu" (ν) and is a dimensionless value.

Mathematically,

$$\frac{\textit{Lateral strain}}{\textit{Linear strain}} = \text{constant}$$

In most materials, when a material is subjected to tensile strain (positive linear strain), it tends to contract laterally (negative lateral strain). Conversely, when a material is subjected to compressive strain (negative linear strain), it tends to expand laterally (positive lateral strain). Poisson's ratio quantifies this relationship between linear strain and lateral strain.

Consider a circular bar of diameter *d* and length *l*, subjected to a tensile force *P* as shown in figure 1.17

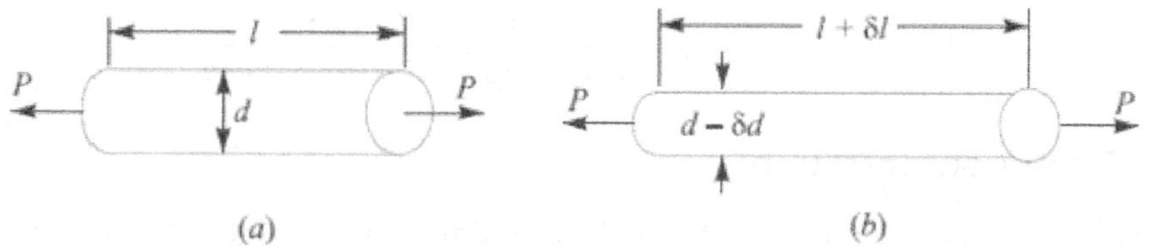

Fig. 1.17. Linear and lateral strain

A little consideration will show that due to tensile force, the length of the bar increases by an amount δl and the diameter decreases by an amount δd, as shown in Fig. (b). similarly, if the bar is subjected to a compressive force, the length of bar will decrease which will be followed by increase in diameter.

Factor of Safety

The calculation of the factor of safety involves comparing the ultimate strength or capacity of the structure (the maximum load or stress it can withstand) to the working or design load/stress (the actual load or stress applied during normal operation). The formula for calculating the factor of safety is as follows:

$$Factor\ of\ safety = \frac{Ultimate\ strength}{Working\ load\ or\ Stress}$$

The ultimate strength is determined through testing, analysis, or reference to material properties, and it represents the maximum load or stress that the structure can handle before failure. The working load or stress is the actual load or stress that the structure is subjected to during normal operation.

A factor of safety greater than 1 indicates that the structure is designed to handle loads or stresses higher than the expected operating conditions, providing a safety margin. For example, if a structure has a factor of safety of 2, it means that it can handle twice the working load or stress without failure.

- In case of ductile materials; e.g. mild steel, where the yield point is clearly defined, the factor of safety is based upon the yield point stress.

In such cases;

$$Factor\ of\ safety = \frac{Yield\ point\ stress}{Working\ or\ Stress}$$

- In case of brittle materials e.g. cast iron, the yield point is not well defined as for ductile materials. Therefore, the factor of safety for brittle materials is based on ultimate stress.

In such cases:

$$Factor\ of\ safety = \frac{Ultimate\ stress}{Working\ or\ design\ Stress}$$

1.14 Stress Concentration

Stress concentration refers to the localized increase in stress levels within a material or structure, typically occurring around geometric features such as holes, notches, sharp corners, or changes in cross-sectional area. These areas of stress concentration can significantly weaken the material and increase the likelihood of failure or fracture. T h is irregularity in the stress distribution caused by abrupt changes of form is called ***stress concentration.***

Ductile Fracture

Normal fracture process stages:

- Necking
- Formation of small cavities (microvoids) in the interior of the cross section,
- Deformation continues, these microvoids enlarge, come together, and to form an elliptical crack,

Which has its long axis perpendicular to the stress direction.

- The crack continues to grow in a direction parallel to its major axis by this microvoid coalescence process.
- Finally, fracture occurs by the rapid propagation of a crack around the outer perimeter of the neck, by shear deformation at an angle of about 45° with the tensile axis. This is the angle at which the shear stress is a maximum as shown in figure 1.14.

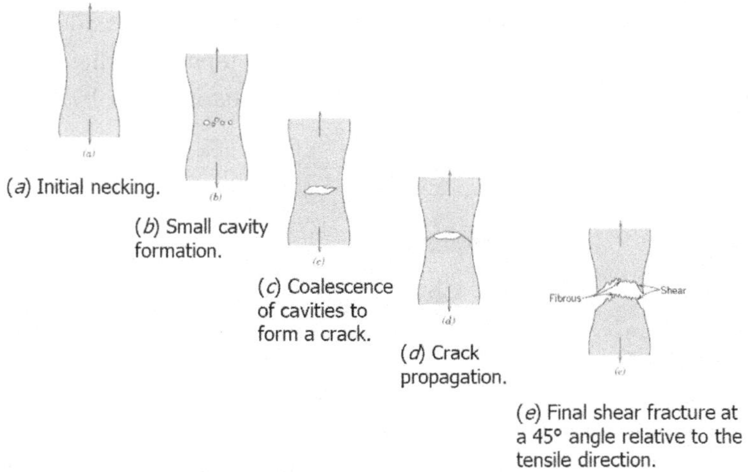

Fig. 1.18. Stages of fracture

- The magnitude of the localized stress diminishes with distance away from the crack tip.

- At positions far removed, the stress is just the nominal stress.
- Due to their ability to amplify an applied stress in their locale, these flaws are sometimes called **stress raisers.**

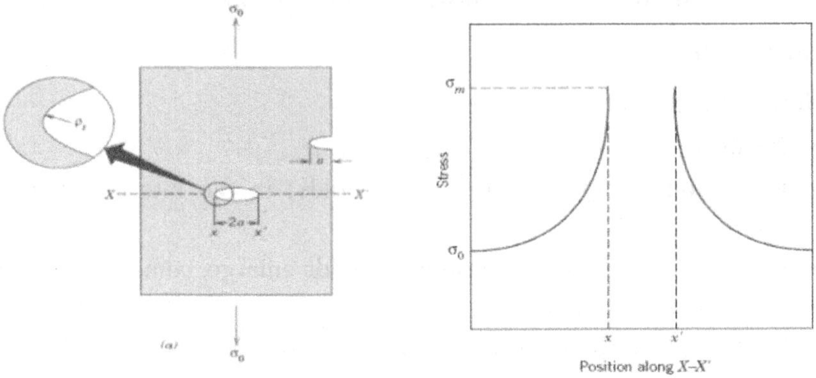

Fig. 1.19. Stress raisers

Concept of Stress Concentration

In a machine element, if there is a discontinuity such as sudden change in cross section, a fillet Hole, groove or notch; highly localized stresses are induced at such places. Such discontinuities are called stress raisers and the localized stress effect they produce is termed as stress concentration. Consider an elliptical hole in an infinitely large plate loaded in uniform tension. Using the theory of elasticity the theoretical stress concentration factor is given by the equation below.

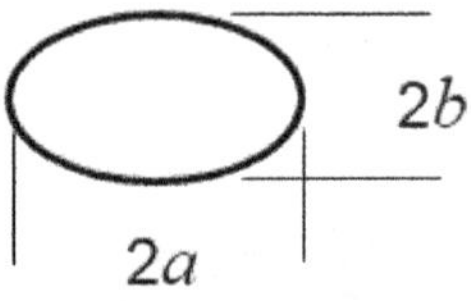

$$K_t = 1 + \frac{2b}{a}$$

Stress concentration factor is found using experimental methods.

- **Photo elasticity:** a plane polarized light is passed thru a phot elastic material (all transparent plastics) resulting in a colorful fringe pattern indicating the intensity of the stress.

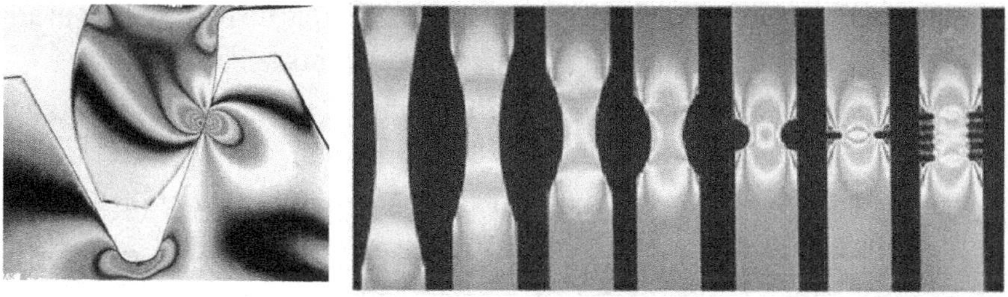

Fig. 1.20. Photo elasticity

- **Brittle Coating:** a specially prepared lacquers are usually applied by spraying on the actual part. After air drying, the part is subjected to stress. A pattern of small cracks appear on the surface. Data could be used to locate strain gages for precise measurement of the stress. The method is sensitive to temperature and humidity.
- **Electrical strain gauges:** The method is the most popular and widely accepted for strain measurements and stress analysis. The strain gauge consists of a grid of strain-sensitive metal foil bonded to a plastic backing material. When the gauge is subjected to a mechanical deformation, its electrical resistance changes proportionally. The change in voltage is converted to strain and the stress is calculated from the strain.

Fig. 1.21. Electrical strain gauges

Finite Element Method

- The CAD model is subdivided into many small pieces of simple shapes called *elements*.
- FEA program writes the equations governing the behavior of each element taking into consideration its connectivity to other elements.

- These equations relate the unknowns, for example displacements in stress analysis, to known material properties, restraints and loads.
- The program assembles the equations into a large set of simultaneous algebraic equations (thousands or even millions).
- These equations are then solved by the program to obtain the stress distribution for the entire model.

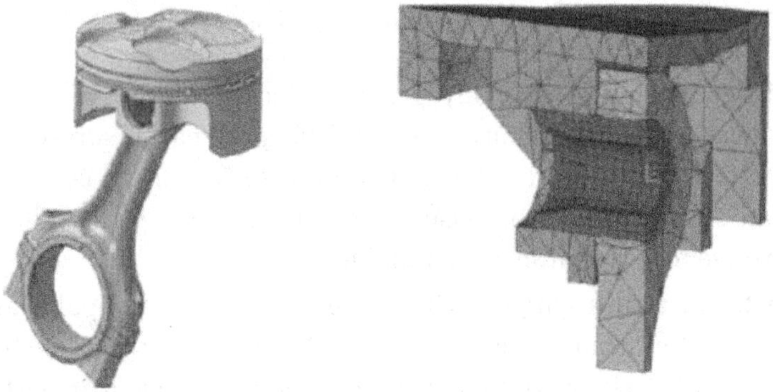

Fig. 1.22. FEA method

It occurs for all kinds of stresses in the presence of fillets, notches, holes, keyways, splines, surface roughness or scratches etc.

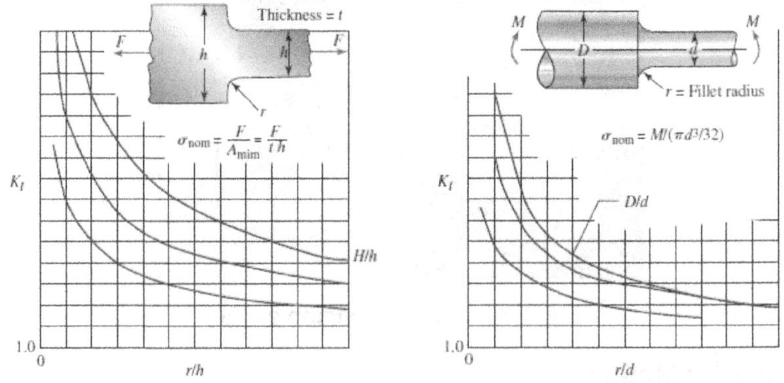

(a) Stepped flat plate in tension

(b) Round bar in bending

Fig. 1.23. Stress concentration

The presence of stress concentration can be attributed to several factors, including the abrupt change in geometry, the redistribution of forces, and the resulting stress concentration factors. Stress concentration factors (Kt) are dimensionless values that quantify the increase in stress at a specific location compared to the nominal stress. These factors depend on the geometry and material properties of the structure.

When external loads or forces are applied to a structure, the stress is distributed throughout the material. However, at locations where there is a sudden change in geometry, the stress tends to concentrate, leading to higher stress levels compared to the surrounding areas. This concentration of stress can result in premature failure, even when the overall stress levels are within the material's strength limits.

It is important to consider stress concentration when designing structures or components, as it can significantly affect their strength and durability. Engineers employ various techniques to mitigate stress concentration, such as using fillets or rounded edges to reduce sharp transitions, adding reinforcement or stiffening elements, or modifying the design to distribute the stress more evenly.

Theoretical Stress Concentration Factor

The theoretical or form stress concentration factor is defined as the ratio of the maximum stress in a member (at a notch or a fillet) to the nominal stress at the same section based upon net area. Mathematically, theoretical or form stress concentration factor,

$$K_t = \frac{\text{Maximum stress}}{\text{Nominal stress}}$$

The value of *Kt* depends upon the material and geometry of the part. In static loading, tress concentration in ductile materials is not so serious as in brittle materials, because in ductile materials local deformation or yielding takes place which reduces the concentration. In brittle materials, cracks may appear at these local concentrations of stress which will increase the stress over the rest of the section. It is, therefore, necessary that in designing parts of brittle materials such as castings, care should be taken. In order to avoid failure due to stress concentration, fillets at the changes of section must be provided.

In cyclic loading, stress concentration in ductile materials is always serious because the ductility of the material is not effective in relieving the concentration of stress caused by cracks, flaws, surface roughness, or any sharp discontinuity in the geometrical form of the member.

Stress Concentration due to Holes and Notches

Consider a plate with transverse elliptical hole and subjected to a tensile load as shown in Fig.1.20. We see from the stress-distribution that the stress at the point away from the hole is practically uniform and the maximum stress will be induced at the edge of the hole. The maximum stress is given by

$$\sigma_{max} = \sigma\left(1 + \frac{2a}{b}\right)$$

The theoretical stress concentration factor,

$$k_t = \frac{\sigma_{max}}{\sigma} = \left(1 + \frac{2a}{r}\right)$$

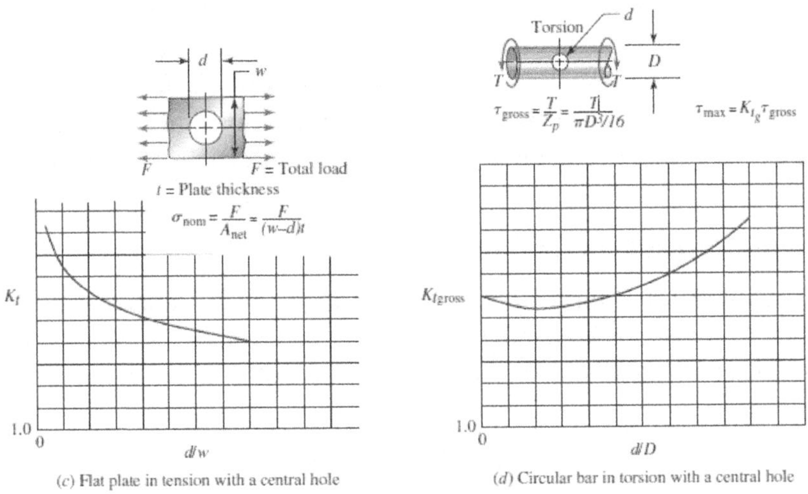

Fig. 1.24. Stress concentration due to holes.

Plane Stress

The element in Figure. 1.25a that is assumed to be aligned along some natural direction of a machine, such as the center of a shaft, or thick-walled cylinder, or along the axis of a beam that is modeling the machine, is rotated counter clockwise an angle (θ). A new set of normal and shear stresses will act on the plane stress element. This rotated element is shown in Fig. 1.25 b, where the new coordinate axes and stresses are denoted by (σ_{xx}), (σ_{yy}), and (τ_{xy}).

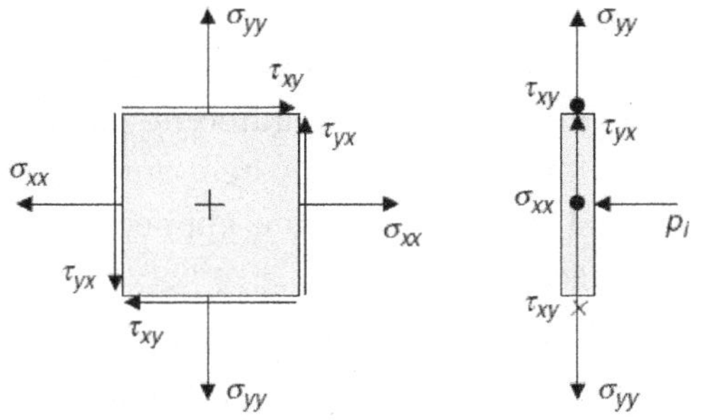

Fig. 1. 25. (a) Plane stress element

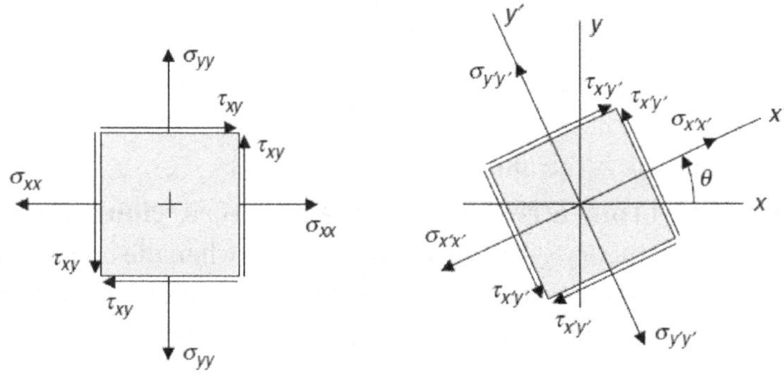

Fig. 1.25 (b) Rotated Plane stress element

The equation for principal stresses is used to determine the maximum and minimum normal stresses acting on a material or structural element. The principal stresses are the maximum and minimum values of normal stress that occur at specific orientations or planes within the material. The equation for principal stresses can be derived from the general stress transformation equations. For a two-dimensional stress state (in the x-y plane), the equation for principal stresses is given by:

$$\sigma_{1,2} = (\sigma_x + \sigma_y) / 2 \pm \sqrt{(\sigma_x - \sigma y)^2/4 + \tau_x y^2}$$

Where: $\sigma_{1,2}$ are the principal stresses, σ_x is the normal stress in the x-direction, σ_y is the normal stress in the y-direction, and τ_{xy} is the shear stress acting on the x-y plane. The plus and minus signs in the equation represent the two principal stress values. The principal stresses are typically ordered such that σ_1 is the maximum principal stress and σ_2 is the minimum principal stress.

1.15 Failure Theories

Failure theories are used in engineering to predict the failure or collapse of materials or structural elements under different loading conditions. These theories provide criteria or equations that help engineers determine when a material or structure will fail based on the applied stresses. Here are some commonly used failure theories:

- **Maximum Shear Stress Theory (Tresca Criterion):** The maximum shear stress theory states that failure occurs when the maximum shear stress in a material exceeds the shear strength of the material. This theory assumes that failure occurs when the shear stress reaches a critical value, regardless of the normal stresses present.

  The equation for the maximum shear stress can be expressed as:

  $$\tau_{max} = (\sigma_{max} - \sigma_{min}) / 2$$

  Where: τ_{max} is the maximum shear stress, σ_{max} is the maximum normal stress, and σ_{min} is the minimum normal stress.

- **Maximum Normal Stress Theory (Rankine Criterion):** The maximum normal stress theory states that failure occurs when the maximum normal stress in a material exceeds the tensile or compressive strength of the material. This theory assumes that failure occurs when the normal stress reaches a critical value, regardless of the shear stresses present.

  The equation for the maximum normal stress can be expressed as:

  $$\sigma_{max} = (\sigma_1 + \sigma_2) / 2 + \sqrt{(\sigma 1 - \sigma 2)^2 / 4 + \tau^2}$$

  Where: σ_{max} is the maximum normal stress, σ_1 is the principal stress with the higher magnitude, σ_2 is the principal stress with the lower magnitude, and τ is the shear stress.

- **Maximum Distortion Energy Theory (von Mises Criterion):** The maximum distortion energy theory, also known as the von Mises criterion, states that failure occurs when the distortion energy (also called von Mises stress or equivalent stress) in a material exceeds the yield strength of the material. This theory is commonly used for ductile materials and assumes that failure occurs when the combined effect of normal and shear stresses reaches a critical value. According to this theory, failure occurs when the distortion energy (also known as von Mises stress or equivalent stress) in a material exceeds the yield strength of the material. The equation for the von Mises stress can be expressed as:

$$\sigma_{\text{von Mises}} = \sqrt{(\sigma_1{}^2 - \sigma_1\sigma_2 + \sigma_2{}^2 + 3\tau_{12}{}^2)}$$

Where: $\sigma_{\text{von mises}}$ is the von Mises stress or equivalent stress, σ_1 and σ_2 are the principal stresses, and τ_{12} is the shear stress. In this theory, failure is predicted when the von Mises stress reaches or exceeds the yield strength of the material. The yield strength is typically determined through experimental testing or material specifications. The Maximum Distortion Energy Theory is often used for ductile materials because it takes into account both normal and shear stresses and provides a more accurate prediction of failure compared to other failure theories, such as the Maximum Shear Stress Theory or the Maximum Normal Stress Theory.

- **Mohr-Coulomb Theory:** The Mohr-Coulomb theory is used to analyse the failure of materials under both normal and shear stresses. It considers the strength parameters of the material, such as cohesion and angle of internal friction, to determine the failure criteria. This theory is commonly used for analyzing the stability of soil and rock masses.
- **Brittle Fracture Theory:** Brittle fracture theories are used to predict the failure of brittle materials, such as ceramics or some types of metals. These theories consider factors like stress concentration, crack propagation, and fracture toughness to determine the conditions under which brittle materials will fail.

Design Problems

1) A prismatic bar of circular section with 80 mm diameter is subjected to bending moment of 5 kN-m and a torque of 7 kN-m. Analyze the state of stress at the critical section.

Solution:

Moment of Inertia, $I = \frac{\pi D^4}{64} = \frac{\pi \times 80^4}{64} = 2.016 \times 10^6 \text{ mm}^4$

Polar moment of Inertia, $I = \frac{\pi D^4}{32} = \frac{\pi \times 80^4}{32} = 4.032 \times 10^6 \text{ mm}^4$

Moment of Inertia, $I = \frac{\pi D^4}{64} = \frac{\pi \times 80^4}{64} = 2.016 \times 10^6 \text{ mm}^4$

Maximum bending stress, $\sigma_x = \frac{M y_{max}}{I} = \frac{5X10^6 X40}{2.016X10^6} = 99.206 \text{ N/mm}^2$

We know that principal stress:

$$\sigma_{1,2} = \frac{99.206}{2} \pm \sqrt{\left(\frac{99.206^2}{2}\right) + (69.44)^2}$$

Thus we get

$$\sigma_1 = 134.944 \text{ N/mm}^2 \text{ and } \sigma_2 = -35.737 \text{ N/mm}^2$$

$$\tau_{max} = \frac{\sigma 1 - \sigma 2}{2} = 85.34 \text{ N/mm}^2$$

2) Figure 1.26 shows a crank loaded by a force F=2.5 kN. A circular rod AB is fixed to a plate at A and a rectangular lever BC is fixed to the rod at B. Design the diameter's' of the rod and the rectangular cross-section of lever BC. Assume $\frac{b}{t} =$ 5, Permissible tensile stress for crank material = 80 N/mm^2, Permissible shear stress for crank material =55 N/mm^2.

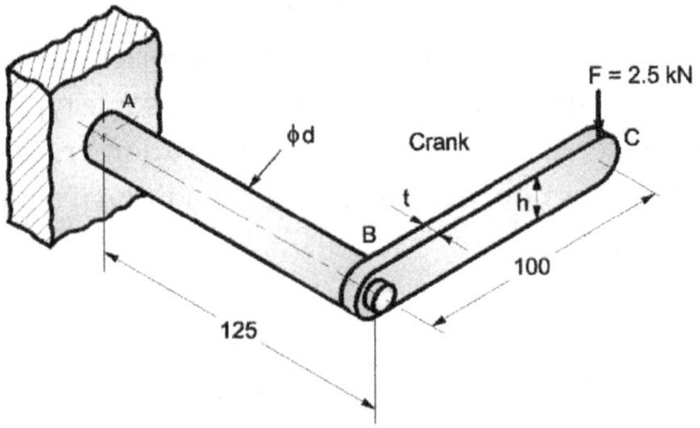

Fig. 1.26

Solution:

Design of Crank:

Maximum bending moment on crank at section A is

M = F× 125 = 2.5 × 10^3 × 125 = 312.5 × 10^3 N-mm

The torque on crank is,

$$T = F \times 100 = 2.5 \times 10^3 \times 100 = 250 \times 10^3 \text{ N-mm}$$

The bending stress and torsional shear stress induced in the crank are,

$$\sigma_x = \sigma_b = \frac{My}{I} = \frac{M(\frac{d}{2})}{\frac{\pi d4}{64}} = \frac{32M}{\pi d^3} = \frac{3183.099 \times 10^3}{d^3}, N/_{mm^2}$$

$$\tau_{xy} = \tau = \frac{Tr}{J} = \frac{T(\frac{d}{2})}{\frac{\pi d4}{32}} = \frac{16T}{\pi d^3} = \frac{1273.239 \times 10^3}{d^3}, N/mm^2$$

1. Maximum principal stress is

$$\sigma_1 = \left(\frac{\sigma x}{2}\right)^2 + \sqrt{\left(\frac{\sigma x}{2}\right)^2} + \tau xy^2$$

$$= \left(\frac{3183.099 \times 10^3}{2d^3}\right)^2 + \sqrt{\left(\frac{3183.099 \times 10^3}{2d^3}\right)^2} + \left(\frac{1273.239 \times 10^3}{d^3}\right)^2$$

Maximum shear stress is

$$\tau_{max} = \frac{2038.177 \times 10^3}{d^3} N/mm^2$$

According to Maximum shear stress theory:

$$\tau_{max} = \tau_{all}$$

$$\frac{2038.177 \times 10^3}{d^3} = 55$$

d = 33.34 mm

According to maximum normal stress theory

$$\sigma_1 = \sigma_{all}$$

$$\frac{3629.726 \times 10^3}{d^3} = 80$$

d = 35.67 mm

2. Design of lever

The maximum bending moment acting on lever is

$$M_L - F \times 100 - 2.5 \times 10^3 \times 100 - 250 \times 10^3 \text{ N-mm}$$

The section modulus for the lever cross section is,

$$Z = \frac{I_{xx}}{y} = \frac{(\frac{1}{12})th^3}{\frac{h}{2}} = \frac{1}{6}th^2 = \frac{1}{6}t(5t)^2 = \frac{25}{6}t^3 \; mm^3$$

The maximum bending stress induces in a lever is

$$\sigma_{bl} = \frac{ML}{Z} = \frac{250 \times 10^3}{(25d^3/6)} =$$

$$\therefore t = 9.08 \; mm$$

$$h = 5t = 5X9.1 = 45.5 \; mm$$

3) A cylindrical shaft made of steel of yield strength 700 MPa is subjected to static loads consisting of bending moment 10 kN-m and a torsional moment 30 kN-m. Determine the diameter of the shaft using two different theories of failure, and assuming a factor of safety of 2. Take E = 210 GPa and poison's ratio = 0.25.

We know that section modulus of the shaft

$$Z = \frac{\pi}{32} x\ d^3\ mm^3$$

Bending (tensile) stress due to the bending moment

$$\sigma_1 = \frac{M}{Z} = \frac{10 \times 10^6}{0.0982\ d^3} N/mm^2$$

Shear stress due to torsional moment

$$\tau = \frac{16T}{\pi d^3} = \frac{152.8\ X\ 10^6}{d^3} N/mm^2$$

1) According to maximum principal stress,

$$\sigma_{t1} = \frac{\sigma 1 + \sigma 2}{2} + \frac{1}{2}[\sqrt{(\sigma 1 - \sigma 2)^2 + 4\tau^2}$$

$$= \frac{50.9\ X\ 10^6}{d^3} + \frac{161\ X\ 10^6}{d^3} = \frac{211.9X\ 10^6}{d^3} N/mm^6$$

And minimum

$$\sigma_{t2} = \frac{\sigma 1 + \sigma 2}{2} - \frac{1}{2}[\sqrt{(\sigma 1 - \sigma 2)^2 + 4\tau^2}$$

$$= \frac{50.9\ X\ 10^6}{d^3} - \frac{161\ X\ 10^6}{d^3} = \frac{-110X\ 10^6}{d^3} N/mm^6$$

2) According to maximum shear stress theory

$$\tau = \frac{\sigma t1 - \sigma t2}{2} = \frac{1}{2}\left[\frac{211.9X\ 10^6}{d^3} + \frac{110X\ 10^6}{d^3}\right] = \frac{161X\ 10^6}{d^3} N/mm^2$$

We also know that according to maximum shear stress theory

$$\tau_{max} = \frac{\sigma yt}{2\ F.S} = \frac{161X\ 10^6}{d^3} = \frac{700}{2X2} = 175$$

$$d = 97.2mm$$

3) According to maximum strain energy theory

$$\frac{1}{2}[(\sigma_{t1})^2 + (\sigma_{t2})^2 - \frac{2\ \sigma_{t1}\ X \sigma_{t2}}{m}] = \frac{1}{2E}\left(\frac{\sigma_{yt}}{F.S}\right)^2$$

$$\frac{44902\ X\ 10^{12}}{d^3} + \frac{12122\ X\ 10^{12}}{d^3} + \frac{11665\ X\ 10^{12}}{d^3} = 122500$$

$$d = 90.8\ mm$$

4) A cantilever beam made of cold drawn carbon steel of circular cross-section as shown in Figure 1.27, is subjected to a load which varies from – F to 3 F. Determine the maximum load that this member can withstand for an indefinite life using a factor of safety as 2. The theoretical stress concentration factor is 1.42 and the notch sensitivity is 0.9. Assume Ultimate stress = 550 MPa, Yield stress = 470 MPa, Endurance limit = 275 MPa, Size factor = 0.85, Surface finish factor= 0.89.

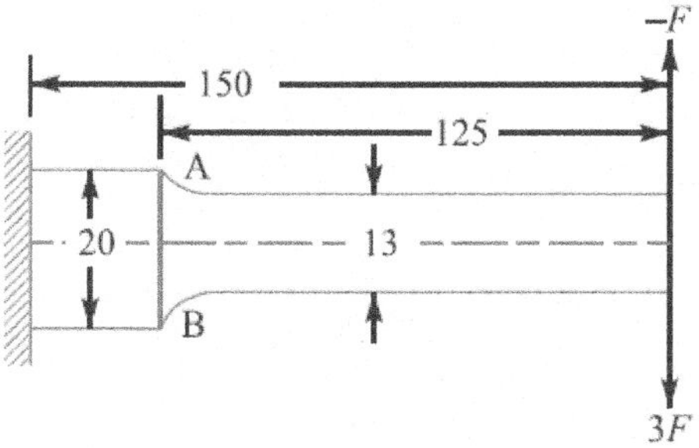

Fig. 1.27. Cantilever beam

Solution:

We know that maximum bending moment at point A

$$M_{max} = W_{max} \text{ X } 125 = 3\text{F x } 125 = 375 \text{ F N-mm}$$

Minimum bending moment at point A

$$M_{max} = W_{min} \text{ X } 125 = -\text{F x } 125 = -125 \text{ F N-mm}$$

Mean or average bending moment

$$M_m = \frac{M_{max}+M_{min}}{2} = \frac{375\ F+(-125\ \text{F})}{2} = 125 \text{ F N-mm}$$

Variable bending moment

$$M_v = \frac{M_{max} - M_{min}}{2} = \frac{375\ F-(-125\ \text{F})}{2} = 250 \text{ F N-mm}$$

Section modulus

$$\text{Z} = \frac{\pi}{32} \text{x } d^3 \text{ mm}^3 = 215.7 \text{ mm}^3$$

Mean bending stress

$$\sigma_1 = \frac{M_m}{Z} = \frac{125\ F}{215.7} = 0.58 \text{ F N/mm}^2$$

Variable bending stress

$$\sigma_1 = \frac{M_v}{Z} = \frac{250\ F}{215.7} = 1.16 \text{ F N/mm}^2$$

Fatigue stress concentration factor

$$K_f = 1 + q(K_t - 1) = 1 + 0.9(1.42 - 1) = 1.378$$

According to Goodman's formula

$$\frac{1}{F.S} = \frac{\sigma_m}{\sigma_u} + \frac{\sigma_v\ X\ K_f}{\sigma_e\ X\ K_{surf}\ X\ K_{size}}$$

$$\frac{1}{2} = \frac{0.58F}{550} + \frac{1.16\,F\,X\,1.378}{275\,X\,0.89X\,0.85}$$

$$F = \frac{1}{2X\,0.00873} = 57.3\text{ N}$$

According to Goodman's formula

$$\frac{1}{F.S} = \frac{\sigma_m}{\sigma_y} + \frac{\sigma_v\,X\,K_f}{\sigma_e\,X\,K_{surf}\,X\,K_{size}}$$

$$\frac{1}{2} = \frac{0.58F}{470} + \frac{1.16\,F\,X\,1.378}{275\,X\,0.89X\,0.85}$$

$$F = \frac{1}{2X\,0.00891} = 56\text{ N}$$

Taking larger of the two values, we have F = 57.3 N

5) A bar of circular cross-section is subjected to alternating tensile forces varying from a minimum of 200 kN to a maximum of 500 kN. It is to be manufactured of a material with an ultimate tensile strength of 900 MPa and an endurance limit of 700 MPa. Determine the diameter of bar using safety factors of 3.5 related to ultimate tensile strength and related to endurance limit and a stress concentration factor of 1.65 for fatigue load. Use Goodman straight line as basis for design.

Solution:

Mean or average bending moment

$$W_m = \frac{W_{max}+W_{min}}{2} = \frac{500+200}{2} = 350\text{ kN}$$

Mean bending stress

$$\sigma_m = \frac{W_m}{A} = \frac{350X\,10^3}{0.7854\,d^2} = \frac{446X\,10^3}{d^2}\text{N/mm}^2$$

Variable force,

$$W_v = \frac{W_{max}-W_{min}}{2} = \frac{500-200}{2} = 150\text{ kN}$$

Variable stress

$$\sigma_v = \frac{W_v}{A} = \frac{150\,10^3}{0.7854\,d^2} = \frac{191\,10^3}{d^2}\text{N/mm}^2$$

According to Goodman's formula

$$\frac{\sigma_v}{\frac{\sigma_e}{F.S_e}} = 1 - \frac{\sigma_m\,X\,K_f}{\sigma_u\,X\,F.S_u}$$

d = 63mm

Short Questions & Answers

1. **Define Factor of safety.**

   The ratio between maximum stresses to working stress is known as factor of safety.

   Factor of safety = $\frac{\text{Maximum stress}}{Working\ stress}$

2. **Define endurance limit.**

   Endurance limit is the maximum value of completely reversed stress that the standard specimen can sustain an infinite number (10^6) of cycles without failure.

3. **What is impact load?**

   If the time of load application is less than one third of the lowest natural period of vibration of the part, it is called an impact load.

4. **What are the various phases of design process?**

   1. Recognition of need.
   2. Definition of problem
   3. Synthesis
   4. Analysis and optimization
   5. Evaluation
   6. Presentation

5. **What are the different types of loads that can act on machine components?**

   1. Steady load.
   2. Variable load.
   3. Shock load
   4. Impact load.

6. **What are the factors affecting endurance strength?**

   Factors affecting endurance strength are

   1. Load
   2. Surface finish
   3. Size
   4. Temperature
   5. Impact
   6. Reliability

7. **What are the types of variable stresses?**

   1. Completely reversed or cyclic stresses
   2. Fluctuating stresses
   3. Repeated stresses

8. **Differentiate between repeated stress and reversed stress.**

   Repeated stress refers to a stress varying from zero to a maximum value of same nature.

Reversed stress of cyclic stress varies from one value of tension to the same value of compression.

9. What are the types of fracture?

1. Ductile fracture
2. Brittle fracture

10. Distinguish between brittle fracture and ductile fracture.

In brittle fracture, crack growth is up to a small depth of the material. In ductile fracture large amount of plastic deformation is present to a higher depth.

11. Define stress concentration and stress concentration factor.

Stress concentration is the increase in local stresses at points of rapid change in cross section or discontinuities. Stress concentration factor is the ratio of maximum stress at critical section to the nominal stress

12. Explain size factor in endurance strength.

Size factor is used to consider the effect of the size on endurance strength. A large size object will have more defects compared to a small one. So, endurance strength is reduced. If K is the size factor,

Actual endurance strength = Theoretical endurance limit × K

13. Explain Griffith theory. (Or) State the condition for crack growth.

A crack can propagate if the energy release rate of crack is greater than crack resistance.

14. What are the modes of fracture?

1. Mode I (Opening mode) – Displacement is normal to crack surface.
2. Mode II (Sliding mode) – Displacement is in the plane of the plate.
3. Mode III (Tearing mode) – Out of plane shear.

15. What are the factors to be considered in the selection of materials for a machine element?

1. Required material properties
2. Manufacturing ease
3. Material availability
4. Cost

16. What are various theories of failure?

1. Maximum principal stress theory
2. Maximum shear stress theory
3. Maximum principal strain theory.

17. List out the factors involved in arriving at factor of safety

1. Material properties
2. Nature of loads
3. Presence of localized stresses
4. Mode of failures

18. Give some methods of reducing stress concentration.

1. Avoiding sharp corners.
2. Providing fillets.
3. Use of multiple holes instead of single hole
4. Undercutting the shoulder parts.

19. Explain notch sensitivity. State the relation between stress concentration factor, fatigue stress concentration factor and notch sensitivity.

Notch sensitivity (q) is the degree to which the theoretical effect of stress concentration is actually reached.

The relation is, $K_f = 1 + q\,(K_t - 1)$

20. What are the factors that effect notch sensitivity?

1. Material
2. Notch radius
3. Size of component
4. Type of loading
5. Grain Structure

21. What is the use of Goodman & Soderberg diagrams?

They are used to solve the problems of variable stresses.

22. Define machinability

It is the property of the material, which refers to a relative case with which a material can be cut. It is measured in a number of ways such as comparing the tool life for cutting different material

23. What is an S-N Curve?

An S- N curve has fatigue stress on Y axis and number of loading cycles in X axis. It is used to find the fatigue stress value corresponding to a given number of cycles.

24. Define Ductility

It is the property of the material enabling it to be drawn into wire, with the application of tensile force. It must be both strong and plastic. It is usually measured in terms of percentage elongation and reduction in area. (eg) Ni, Al, Cu.

25. Define fatigue

When a material is subjected to repeated stress, it fails at stresses below the yield point stress; such type of failure of the material is called fatigue.

26. What is curved beam?

In curved beam the neutral axis does not coincide with the centroidal axis.

27. Give some example for curved beam.

C frame, crane hook.

28. What is principle stress and principle plane?

A plane which has no shear stress is called principle plane the corresponding stress is called principle stress.

29. Write the bending equation.

$$M/I = E/R = Fs/Y.$$

Where

M – Bending moment

I - Moment of inertia

E - Young's modulus

R - Radius of the shaft

Fs – Shear stress

Y - Distance from neutral axis

30. Write the torsion equation.

T/J = CØ/L = Fs/R

T – Torque

J - Polar moment of inertia

C- Rigidity modulus

Ø – Angle of twist

L – Length of the shaft

Fs – Shear stress

R - Radius of the shaft

2

Introduction to Bearings

A mechanical device that reduces friction between two surfaces. Plain bearings, also known as sleeve bearings or journal bearings, operate based on either rubbing contact between the bearing surfaces or the use of pressure to separate the surfaces. When there is a relative motion between two machine parts, one of which supports the others. The supporting member is called Bearing.

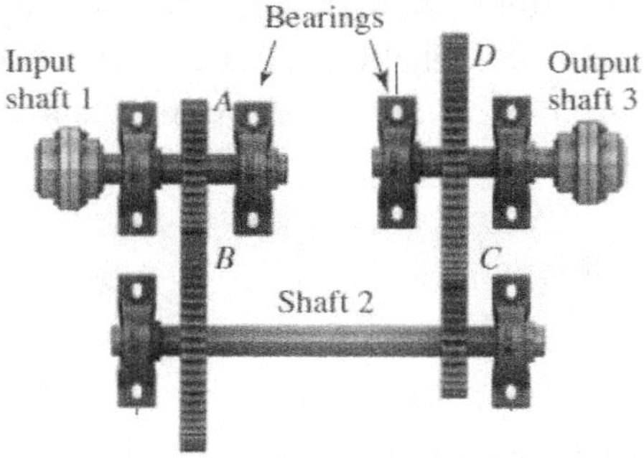

Fig. 2.1. Bearing applications

- **Rubbing contact:** Plain bearings rely on the rubbing contact between the bearing surfaces to support and guide the relative motion between two components. The surfaces may be made of different materials, such as metal or polymer, and are designed to minimize friction and wear.
- **Pressure separation:** In some cases, plain bearings utilize pressure to separate the bearing surfaces. This pressure can be generated by the movement of one component relative to another, creating a hydrodynamic effect that lifts the surfaces apart. Alternatively, an external supply of lubricant can be introduced under pressure to separate the surfaces.
- **Lubrication:** Proper lubrication is crucial for the smooth operation of plain bearings. Lubricants, such as oils or greases, are used to reduce friction, dissipate heat, and protect the bearing surfaces from wear.

Lubrication can be achieved through the movement of the components or by externally supplying lubricant to the bearing.

- **Availability:** Plain bearings are available from specialist bearing suppliers who offer a range of designs and materials to suit different applications. These suppliers provide expertise in selecting the appropriate plain bearing for specific requirements, ensuring optimal performance and longevity.
- **Cost-effectiveness:** Plain bearings can be more cost-effective compared to rolling element bearings. They typically involve fewer moving components, which can result in lower manufacturing and maintenance costs. Additionally, the absence of rolling elements reduces the complexity and potential failure points in the bearing system.

Plain bearings are commonly used in various applications, including machinery, automotive systems, industrial equipment, and appliances. They offer advantages such as simplicity, reliability, and cost-effectiveness, making them a suitable choice for many applications where rolling element bearings may not be necessary or practical.

2.1 Function of Bearing

- A bearing permits relative motion between two machine members while minimizing Frictional resistance.
- A bearing consists of an inner and outer member separated either by a thin film of Lubricant or a rolling element.
- A bearing bears the load.
- It locates the moving parts in correct position.
- It provides free motion to the moving part by reducing friction.

2.2 Selection of bearing

When selecting a bearing, several factors need to be considered to ensure optimal performance and reliability. Here are the key factors to consider:

- **Load:** The load on the bearing, including both radial and axial loads, is a critical factor in bearing selection. It is important to determine the magnitude, direction, and variability of the load to choose a bearing that can handle the specific load requirements.

- **Speed:** The rotational speed at which the bearing will operate is another crucial consideration. High-speed applications require bearings that can handle the resulting centrifugal forces, minimize friction, and maintain proper lubrication.
- **Location:** The operating environment and location of the bearing play a significant role in selecting the appropriate bearing type. Factors such as temperature, humidity, contamination, and exposure to corrosive substances need to be considered to ensure the bearing can withstand the conditions.
- **Size:** The size and dimensions of the bearing should be chosen to fit within the available space and accommodate the desired load and speed requirements. It is important to consider the shaft and housing tolerances to ensure proper fit and alignment.
- **Cost:** Cost considerations are important in bearing selection. The desired performance and reliability should be balanced with the available budget. It is essential to evaluate the long-term costs, including maintenance, replacement, and downtime, to make an informed decision.
- **Starting torque:** In applications where starting torque is a concern, such as electric motors, the bearing selection should consider factors that minimize friction and facilitate smooth starting and operation.
- **Noise:** Noise levels can be a critical factor in certain applications, such as precision machinery or noise-sensitive environments. Bearing selection should consider noise-reducing features and materials to minimize unwanted noise generation.
- **Lubrication supply:** The availability and method of lubrication supply should be considered. Some bearings require external lubrication systems, while others may be self-lubricating. The lubrication method should align with the application requirements and maintenance capabilities.

By carefully considering these factors, engineers and designers can select the most suitable bearing type, design, and material to ensure optimal performance, longevity, and cost-effectiveness in a given application. Collaboration with bearing manufacturers or suppliers can provide valuable expertise and guidance in the selection process.

2.3 Classification of Bearings

Bearings can be classified into several categories based on different criteria. Here are some common classifications of bearings:

1. Based on the type of load they can handle:

- Radial bearings: These bearings are designed to support primarily radial loads, perpendicular to the shaft axis.
- Thrust bearings: These bearings are designed to support axial loads, parallel to the shaft axis.

2. Based on the type of motion they allow:

- Plain bearings: Also known as sleeve bearings or journal bearings, these bearings facilitate sliding or rubbing motion between the bearing surfaces.
- Rolling element bearings: These bearings use rolling elements, such as balls or rollers, to enable smooth rolling motion between the bearing surfaces.

3. Based on the type of rolling elements used:

- Ball bearings: These bearings use balls as rolling elements to reduce friction and enable smooth motion.
- Roller bearings: These bearings use cylindrical, tapered, or spherical rollers as rolling elements to distribute the load over a larger surface area.

4. Based on the design and configuration:

- Deep groove ball bearings: These bearings have deep raceway grooves, allowing them to handle both radial and axial loads.
- Angular contact ball bearings: These bearings have contact angles that enable them to handle both radial and axial loads in a specific direction.
- Cylindrical roller bearings: These bearings have cylindrical rollers and are suitable for high radial load applications.

Fig. 2.2. Cylindrical roller bearings

- Tapered roller bearings: These bearings have tapered rollers and can handle both radial and axial loads in a specific direction.

Fig. 2.3. Tapered roller bearings

- Spherical roller bearings: These bearings have barrel-shaped rollers and can accommodate misalignment and heavy radial loads.

Fig. 2.4. Spherical roller bearings

- Needle roller bearings: These bearings have long, thin rollers and are suitable for applications with limited space and high radial loads.

Fig. 2.5. Needle roller bearings

5. Based on the type of lubrication:

- Grease-lubricated bearings: These bearings are pre-lubricated with grease and require little to no additional lubrication during their service life.
- Oil-lubricated bearings: These bearings require a continuous supply of oil for lubrication, typically through an external lubrication system.

These are just a few examples of the various classifications of bearings. Each type of bearing has its own advantages, limitations, and suitable applications. The selection of the appropriate bearing type depends on factors such as load, speed, operating conditions, and specific application requirements.

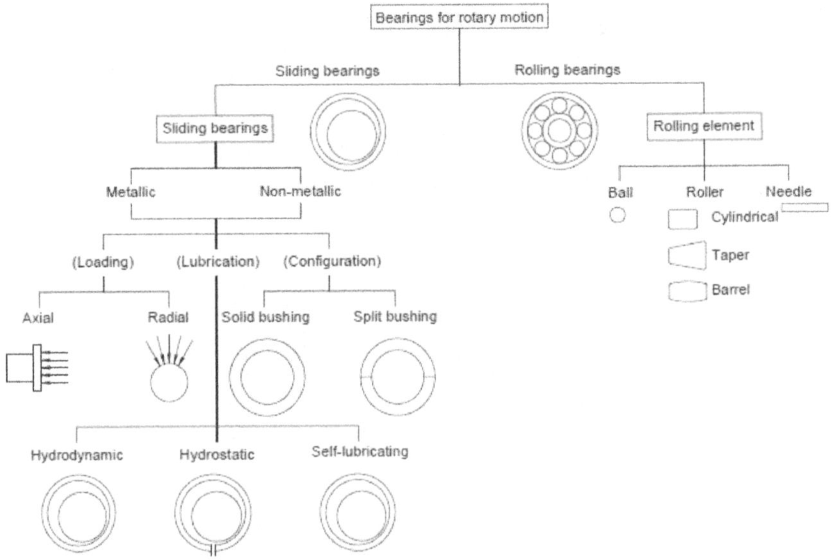

Fig. 2.6. Bearing classification

2.4 Roller Bearing

A roller bearing is a type of bearing that uses cylindrical, tapered, or spherical rollers as rolling elements to facilitate smooth motion and distribute the load over a larger surface area. Roller bearings are widely used in various applications to support radial and axial loads.

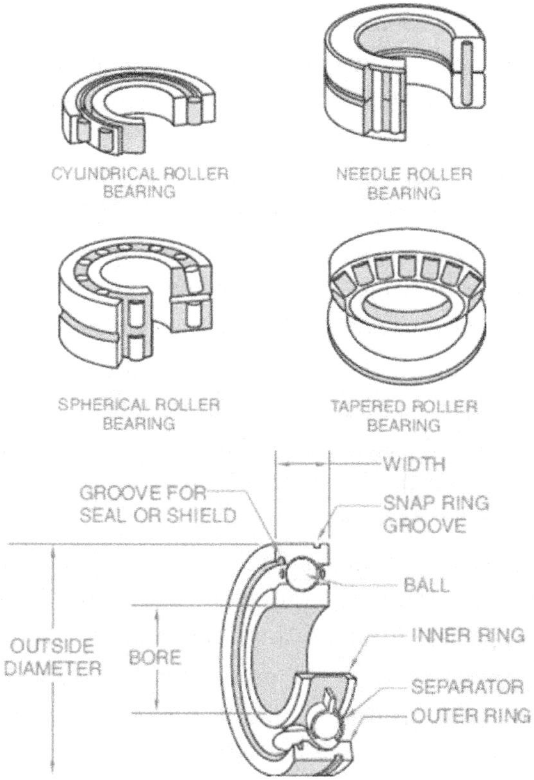

Fig.2.7. Types of roller bearing

Key features and characteristics of roller bearings:

- **Rolling elements:** Roller bearings use rollers as the rolling elements instead of balls. The rollers can be cylindrical, tapered, or spherical in shape, depending on the specific design and application requirements.
- **Load capacity:** Roller bearings have a higher load-carrying capacity compared to ball bearings due to the larger contact area between the rollers and the raceways. This allows them to handle heavier radial and axial loads.
- **Radial and axial load support:** Roller bearings can support both radial loads, which are perpendicular to the shaft axis, and axial loads, which are parallel to the shaft axis. The specific design and configuration of the roller bearing determine its ability to handle different types and directions of loads.

- **Misalignment compensation:** Some roller bearings, such as spherical roller bearings, are designed to accommodate misalignment between the shaft and the housing. This feature allows for smoother operation and reduced stress on the bearing.
- **Different types and configurations:** Roller bearings come in various types and configurations to suit different applications. Some common types include cylindrical roller bearings, tapered roller bearings, and spherical roller bearings. Each type has its own unique design and characteristics to meet specific load, speed, and application requirements.
- **Lubrication:** Proper lubrication is essential for the smooth operation and longevity of roller bearings. They can be lubricated with grease or oil, depending on the specific application and operating conditions. Lubrication helps reduce friction, dissipate heat, and protect the bearing surfaces from wear and corrosion.

Roller bearings are widely used in industries such as automotive, aerospace, industrial machinery, construction equipment, and more. They offer advantages such as high load capacity, durability, and the ability to handle both radial and axial loads.

The selection of the appropriate roller bearing type depends on factors such as load requirements, speed, operating conditions, and specific application needs.

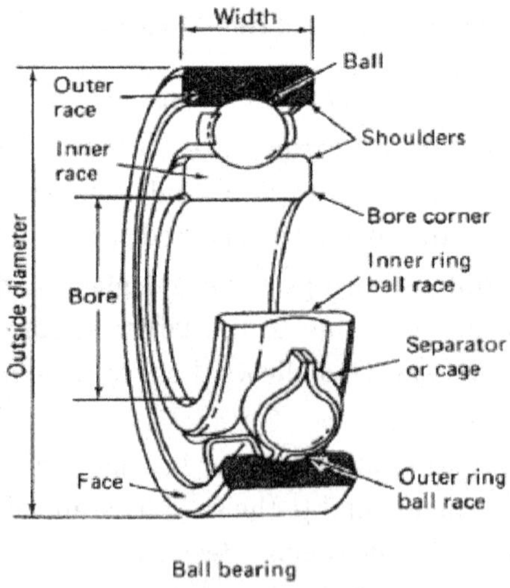

Fig. 2.8. Ball bearing

2.5 Sliding Bearing

A sliding bearing, also known as a plain bearing or a sleeve bearing, is a type of bearing that operates based on the principle of sliding or rubbing contact between the bearing surfaces. Unlike roller bearings, which use rolling elements, sliding bearings rely on a film of lubricant to separate the surfaces and reduce friction.

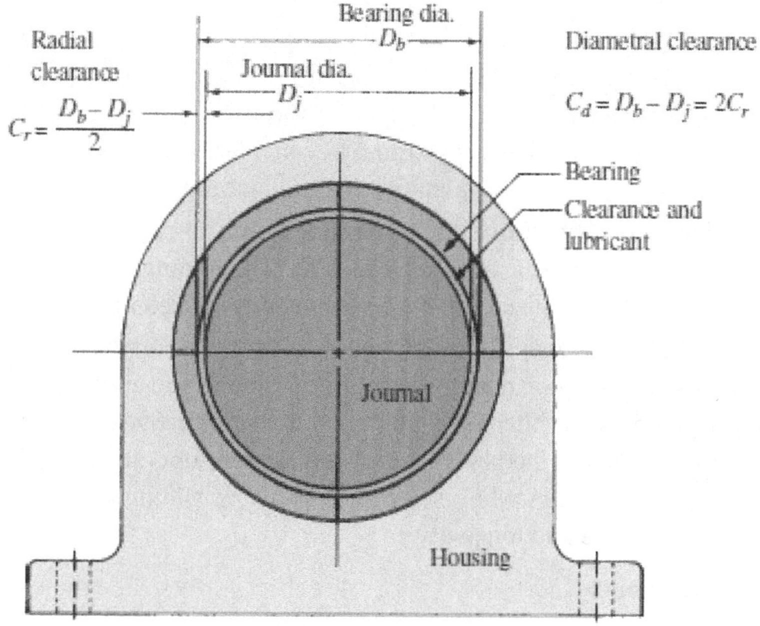

Fig. 2.9. Sliding contact bearing

Here are some key features and characteristics of sliding bearings:

- **Sliding contact:** Sliding bearings work by allowing the bearing surfaces to slide against each other. The surfaces can be made of different materials, such as metal, polymer, or composite materials, depending on the specific application requirements.
- **Lubrication:** Lubrication is crucial for the smooth operation of sliding bearings. A film of lubricant, such as oil or grease, is used to reduce friction, dissipate heat, and protect the bearing surfaces from wear. The lubricant is typically supplied either by the movement of the components or through an external lubrication system.

- **Load capacity:** Sliding bearings can handle both radial and axial loads, depending on their design and configuration. The load capacity of a sliding bearing is determined by factors such as the material properties, surface area, and lubrication conditions.
- **Low maintenance:** Sliding bearings generally require less maintenance compared to roller bearings. They have a simpler design with fewer moving parts, reducing the need for frequent inspections or replacements.
- **Cost-effectiveness:** Sliding bearings can be more cost-effective compared to roller bearings, especially in applications where high precision or high-speed operation is not required. They involve fewer components and are often less expensive to manufacture and maintain.
- **Noise and vibration:** Sliding bearings tend to generate less noise and vibration compared to roller bearings. The sliding motion between the surfaces results in smoother operation and reduced impact forces.

Sliding bearings are commonly used in various applications, including machinery, automotive systems, industrial equipment, and appliances. They offer advantages such as simplicity, reliability, and cost-effectiveness. However, it is important to consider factors such as load, speed, operating conditions, and lubrication requirements when selecting and using sliding bearings to ensure optimal performance and longevity.

Magnitude of Load

The magnitude of the load is one of the factors that usually determines the size of the bearing to be used. Generally, roller bearing are available to support heavier loads than similar size ball bearing and bearings having a full complement of rolling elements can accommodate heavier loads than the corresponding caged bearing.

Direction of Load

Radial load

The load which comes perpendicular on the shaft called redial load. Cylindrical roller bearing, needle roller bearing, and toroidal roller bearing can only support pure radial loads.

Axial load

The load which comes axis on the shaft called axial load. Thrust ball bearing and four point contact ball bearing are suitable for light or moderate loads that are purely axial.

Combined load

A combined load comprises a redial and an axial load acting simultaneously.

For combined loads, single and double row angular contact ball bearing, and single row taper roller bearing are most commonly used, although deep groove ball bearing and spherical roller bearing are suitable.

Advantages

1. Low coefficient of friction
2. High life.
3. Mounting is easy.
4. It is very clean compared to sliding contact bearing.
5. Accuracy is more.
6. Low maintenance cost.
7. Less lubrication compared to sliding contact bearings.
8. Occupies less space.
9. Very high radial as well as thrust load capacity.
10. High load bearing capacity.

Disadvantages:

1. More initial cost.
2. Design is complicated.
3. Less resistance to shock load.
4. Noise is more at very high speed.

Designation of Lubricating Oil

Lubricating oil is designated by its properties like.

1. Viscosity.
2. Density.
3. Flash point.
4. Fire point.

5. Oil lines.
6. Viscosity index.

2.6 Viscosity and Its Effect on the Performance of Bearing

Viscosity is a fundamental property of a lubricant that plays a crucial role in the performance of bearings. It refers to the resistance of a fluid to flow and is measured in units of centistokes (cSt) or square millimetres per second (mm^2/s).

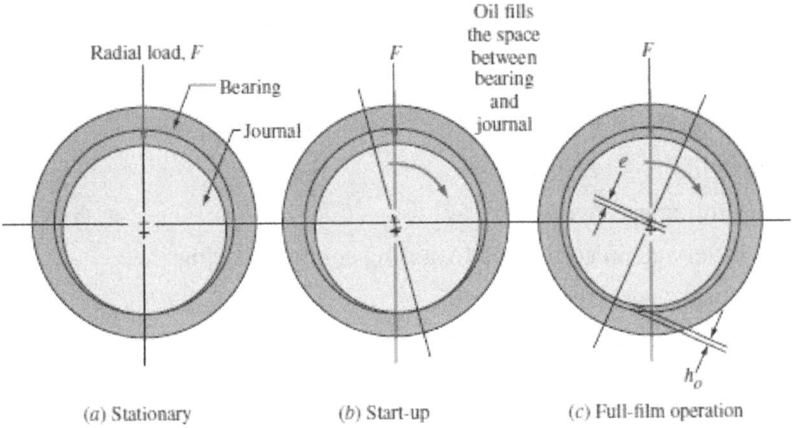

Fig. 2.10. Thin film contact bearing

The viscosity of a lubricant can have a significant impact on the performance of a bearing in the following ways:

- **Friction and wear reduction:** The viscosity of the lubricant affects the formation of a lubricating film between the bearing surfaces. A lubricant with appropriate viscosity forms a thicker film, reducing direct metal-to-metal contact and minimizing friction and wear. This helps to extend the bearing's service life and improve its overall performance.
- **Load-carrying capacity:** The viscosity of the lubricant influences the load-carrying capacity of the bearing. A lubricant with higher viscosity can better support and distribute the load across the bearing surfaces, reducing the risk of excessive stress and premature failure.
- **Temperature control:** Viscosity also plays a role in temperature control within the bearing. As the bearing operates, friction generates heat, and the lubricant's viscosity affects its ability to dissipate this heat. A lubricant

with appropriate viscosity can help maintain the bearing within the desired temperature range, preventing overheating and potential damage.

- **Sealing effectiveness:** In some applications, the lubricant also acts as a sealant to prevent contaminants from entering the bearing. The viscosity of the lubricant affects its ability to form an effective seal, reducing the risk of contamination and maintaining the bearing's performance and reliability.
- **Lubricant flow and distribution:** The viscosity of the lubricant influences its flow and distribution within the bearing. A lubricant with suitable viscosity ensures proper lubrication to all critical areas, reducing the risk of inadequate lubrication and associated issues such as increased friction, wear, and potential bearing failure.

It is important to note that the viscosity requirements for a bearing depend on various factors, including the bearing type, load, speed, operating conditions, and ambient temperature. Manufacturers often provide guidelines and specifications regarding the recommended viscosity range or specific lubricants for optimal bearing performance. Regular monitoring and maintenance of the lubricant's viscosity are essential to ensure the bearing operates within the desired parameters and to prevent potential issues related to inadequate lubrication.

According to Newton's law of viscosity shear stress is proportion to the fluid.

$$\therefore \left(\frac{P}{A}\right) \propto \left(\frac{V}{n}\right)$$

$$where\ \left(\frac{P}{A}\right)\ shear\ stress$$

$$\left(\frac{V}{n}\right)\ rate\ of\ shear.$$

$$P = \mu A\left(\frac{V}{n}\right)$$

$$\mu = absolute\ viscosity. -Ns/mm^2$$

1) Static equivalent load:

$$W_{OR} = XW_R + YW_A.$$

$$W_R = Radical\ load.$$

$$W_A = Radical\ load.$$

$$X = Radial\ load\ factor.$$

$$Y = Axial(or)\ thrust\ load\ factor.$$

2) Life of rolling contact bearing:

$$L = \left(\frac{C}{W}\right)^P$$

Where

L= bearing life(in million revolution)

C= dynamic load rating.

W = Equivalent dynamic load.

P = 3 (for ball bearing)

= 10/3 (for roller bearing).

The relationship between life in million revolutions and life in working hours is given by.

$$L = \frac{60NLH}{10^6}$$

LH = bearing life.

N = Speed of Rotation (rpm).

3) Dynamic equivalent load

$W = X.V.W_R + YW_A$

V = A rotation factor.

V = 1 for all types of bearing where inner race is rotating

V = 1 for self-aligning bearing where inner race is stationary

V = 1.5 For all types of bearing except self-aligning where inner race is stationary

Code For Bearing

0	Double row angular contact ball bearing
1	Self aligning ball bearing
2	Spherical roller bearing
	Spherical roller thrust bearing
3	Taper roller bearing
4	Double row deep groove ball bearing
5	Thrust ball bearing
6	Single row deep groove ball bearing
7	Single row angular contact ball

8 Cylindrical roller thrust bearing
C CARB toroidal roller bearing
N Cylindrical roller bearing
QJ Four point contact ball bearing
T Taper roller bearings according to ISO355-1997

2.7 Bearing Life

If a bearing is clean, properly lubricated and mounted and is operating at reasonable temp., failure is due to fatigue caused by repeated contact stresses.

Life – number of revolution or hours of operation, at constant speed, required for the failure criterion to develop.

Rating life: defines the number of revolution or hours of operation, at constant speed, in such a way that of the bearings tested (from the same group) will complete or exceed before the first evidence of failure develops. This is known as L_{10} life.

For ball bearings and spherical bearings:

L_{10} = 500 (hours) x 33.33 (rpm) x 60 = 10^6 = 1 million revolutions

For tapered bearings manufactured by Timken:

L_{10} = 3000 (hours) x 500 (rpm) x 60 = 90 x 10^6 = 90 million revolutions

Basic Dynamic load rating (C): constant radial load that a group of bearings can carry for L_{10} life.

$L_{10} = (C / F)^a$, a = 3 for ball bearings and a = 10/3 for roller bearings

F = applied radial load

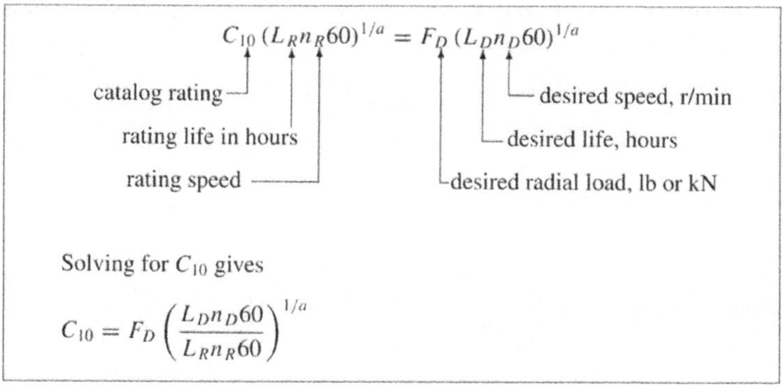

Fig. 2.11. Bearing life

Design Problems

1) A roller bearing is selected to with stand a radial load of 40 KN and life of 1200 hours at 600 rpm. What load rating would you look for in searching from manufactures catalogue if it specifies load at speed 500 rpm and life 3000 hrs.

Solution

Given data:

W=40 KN = $40 \times 10^3\ N$, L = 1200 hrs =1200×60×N

L = 1200 60 ×600 =43.2× 10^6 , W = 600 rpm

Load rating $C = W[\frac{l}{10^6}]^{1/k}$

$$= 40 \times 10^3\ (\frac{43.2\times 10^6}{10^6})^{\frac{1}{10/3}}$$

$$C = 123795.57N$$

$$C = 123.795KN$$

$$\therefore C = W[\frac{l}{10^6}]^{1/k}$$

L = 3000×60×500 =90 ×10^6 $rev.$

Substitute c=123.79 × $10^3 N$.

$$123.79\times 10^3 = w(\frac{90\times 10^6}{10^6})^{\frac{1}{10/3}}$$

$$W = 32093KW$$

2) A 6203 single row deep groove ball bearing has a basic static load rating of 4500 N and basic dynamic load rating of 7350N. If it is subjected to a radial load of 1350N and axial load of 1260N, what is the rated life with outer ring stationary?

Solution:

Bearing number 6203 (DB pg.no 340)

Given data:

$C_o = 4500\ N,\ C = 7350\ N, W_R = 1350\ N, W_A = 1260\ N$

Solution:

w.k.t $C = W[\frac{l}{10^6}]^{1/k}$

$W = XVW_R + YW_A$

$\frac{W_A}{W_R} = \frac{1260}{1350} = 0.93$

$\frac{W_A}{C_o} = \frac{1260}{4500} = 0.28$

From table 16.1 page no 330.

$\frac{W_A}{W_R} = 0.93 \ and \ \frac{W_A}{C_o} = 0.28$

We get

$X = 0.56\,, Y = 1.15 = 1.2$

$X = 1 \qquad y = 0 \qquad\qquad psa$

Assume V=1

$\therefore W = XVW_R + YW_A$

$= 0.56 \times 1 \times 1350 + 1.2 \times 1260$

$W = 2268N = 1350N \ psa$

$\therefore C = W[\frac{l}{10^6}]^{1/k}$

$7350 = 2268[\frac{l}{10^6}]^{1/k}$

$\because K = 3 6or \ ball \ bearing \ (c = 7350 \ given)$

L = 34 ×10^6 *rev.*

Life of bearing = L= 34 ×10^6 *rev.*

L= 161.3 ×10^6 *rev.*

3) Select a single row deep- groove ball bearing for a radial load of 4000N and an axial load of 5000 N, operating at a speed of 1600rpm for an average life of 5 years at 10 hours per day. Assume uniform and steady load.

Solution:

Given data:

$W_R = 4000 \ N$

$W_A = 5000 \ N$

$N \ = 1600\, rpm$

Since the average life of bearing in 5 years at 10 hours per say

$$\therefore Life\ of\ bearing\ a\ hours = LH = 5 \times 300 \times 10 \ = 15{,}000\ Hours$$

$(300\ \ Working\ days\ per\ year)$

Life of bearing in resolutions.

$L = 60N \times LH$

$L = 60 \times 1600 \times 15000 = 1440 \times 10^6\ rev.$

w.k.t

Dynamic Equivalent road

$W = XVW_R \ + YW_A$

$\frac{W_A}{W_R} = \frac{5000}{4000} = 1.25\ (e > 1)$

$\frac{W_A}{C_o} = unknown$

Assume $\frac{W_A}{C_o} = 0.5$

V=1 and X=0.56 , Y= 1.00.

$\therefore W \ = XVW_R \ + YW_A$

$W \ = 0.56 \times 1 \times 4000 + 1 \times 5000 = 7240N.$

Ks for ball bearing

$C = W[\frac{l}{10^6}]^{1/ks}$

(K=3 for ball bearing steady load)

$C = 7240(\frac{1440 \times 10^6}{10^6})^{\frac{1}{3}}$

$C = 81760N = 81.76KN$

Select 6315 table 16.9h page no.342

$C_O \ = 11.100\ KN, C \ = 89.280\ KN$

$\frac{W_A}{C_o} = \frac{5000}{71100} = 0.07$

From table 16.1 page no.330

$(0.084) \times -0.56 \qquad Y = 1.55 = 1.6$

$W = XVW_R + YW_A$

$W = 0.56 \times 1 \times 4000 + 1.6 \times 5000$

$W = 10{,}240N.$

$\therefore$ Basic dynamic rating

$$C = 10240(\frac{1440 \times 10^6}{10^6})^{\frac{1}{3}}$$

$C = 115635N.$

$C = 115.635KN.$

Table No 16.9 b page no: 342

C= 117680

Corresponding Bearing No.6319 may be selected.

4) Select a deep groove ball bearing to carry a radial load of 5KN and an axial load of 1.5KN. The shaft is of 130mm diameter and relates at 2500 rpm. Expected life of the bearing is 20,000hrs.

Solution:

Given data:

$W_R = 5\ N, W_A = 1.5\ N, d = 130mm, N = 2500\ rpm,\ LH = 20{,}000\ hrs$

$L = 60N \times LH$

$L = 60 \times 2500 \times 20000 = 3 \times 10^9\ rev.$

Dynamic equivalent radial load

$W = XVW_R + YW_A$

$$\frac{W_A}{W_R} = \frac{1500}{5000} = 0.3\ (e < 1)$$

Since C_O is not given

Assume $\frac{W_A}{C_O} = 0.5$

From table X=1, Y=0

Assume V=1

$\therefore W = 1 \times 1 \times 5000 \times 0 \times 1500 = 5000N$

$\therefore C = W[\frac{l}{10^6}]^{1/k}$

$C = 5000(\frac{3 \times 10^9}{10^6})^{\frac{1}{3}}$

$C = 72.112KN.$

From table 16.9b (DB)

C=71100, so 6313 may be selected or (6218) 341 page No

Short Questions and Answers

1. **What is bearing?**

   Bearing is a stationery machine element which supports a rotating shafts or axles and confines its motion.

2. **Classify the types of bearings.**

   i. Depending upon the type of load coming upon the shaft:

      a. Radial bearing

      b. Thrust bearings.

   ii. Depending upon the nature of contact:

      a. Sliding contact

      b. Rolling contact bearings or Antifriction bearings.

3. **What are the required properties of bearing materials?**

   Bearing material should have the following properties.

   a. High compressive strength

   b. Low coefficient of friction

   c. High thermal conductivity

   d. High resistance to corrosion v.Sufficient fatigue strength

   e. It should be soft with a low modulus of elasticity

   f. Bearing materials should not get weld easily to the journal material.

4. **What is a journal bearing?**

   A journal bearing is a sliding contact bearing which gives lateral support to the rotating shaft.

5. **What are the types of journal bearings depending upon the nature of contact?**

   1. Full journal bearing

   2. Partial bearing

   3. Fitted bearing.

6. What are the types of journal bearing depending upon the nature of lubrication?

1. Thick film type
2. Thin film type
3. Hydrostatic bearings
4. Hydrodynamic bearing.

7. What is known as self – acting bearing?

The pressure is created within the system due to rotation of the shaft, this type of bearing is known as self – acting bearing.

8. What is the nature of contact involved in a ball bearing element?

Instead of sliding, the contact between the bearing elements is rolling.

9. Define antifriction bearing?

The contact between the bearing elements is rolling, this type has very small friction.

10. What are the types of rolling contact bearing?

i. Depending upon the type of rolling element,

a. Ball bearing

b. Roller bearing

ii. Depending upon the load to be carried,

a. Radial

b. Angular contact

c. Trust bearing

11. State the components of rolling contact bearings?

a. Outer race
b. Inner race
c. Rolling element
d. Seperator.

12. What are the several types of radial ball bearing?

a. Deep groove ball bearing
b. Self aligning ball bearing
c. Angular contact ball bearing
d. Filling notch bearing
e. Double row bearing.

13. What are the types of trust ball bearings?

a. One directional flat race

b. One directional Grooved race

c. Two directional Grooved race.

14. What is load rating?

The load carrying capacity of a rolling element bearing is called load rating.

15. What is basic static load rating?

It is defined as load acting on a non rotating bearing under which permanent deformation is 0.0001 times the ball of roller diameter.

16. Explain the term dynamic load carrying capacities of rolling contact bearing?

Dynamic load rating is defined as the radial load in radial bearing that can be carried for a minimum life of one million revolution.

17. List the types of bearing materials?

a. Lead base babbit
b. Tin base babbit
c. Leaded bronze
d. Copper laed alloy
e. Gun metal
f. Phosphor bronze.

18. State the theory of lubrication?

a. Hydrostatic theory of lubrication.
b. Hydrodynamic theory of lubrication.

19. Define Kinematic viscosity?

The kinematic viscosity is defined as the ratio of absolute viscosity to the density of oil.

3

Design of Shafts and Keys

Shafts are mechanical components used to transmit power and rotational motion between different parts of a machine or system. They are typically cylindrical in shape and can be found in various applications, such as engines, gearboxes, pumps, and conveyor systems.

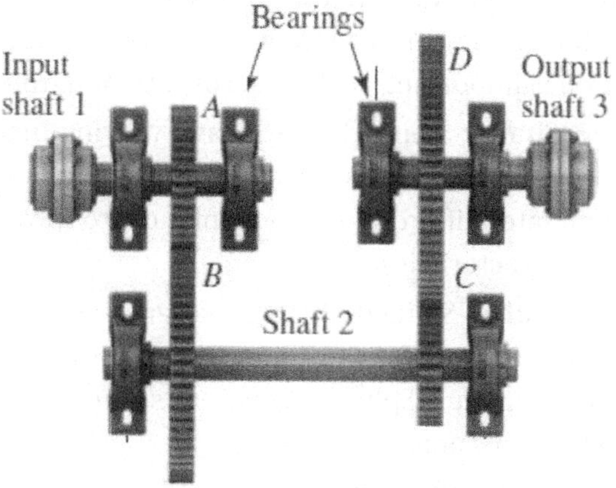

Fig. 3.1 Shafts applications

Key aspects related to shafts:

1. **Function:** The primary function of a shaft is to transmit torque and rotational motion from a power source to other components within a machine or system. Shafts can also provide support and alignment for rotating elements, such as gears, pulleys, or couplings.
2. **Material Selection:** Shaft materials are chosen based on factors such as the required strength, stiffness, durability, and resistance to wear or corrosion. Common materials used for shafts include steel (such as carbon steel, alloy steel, or stainless steel), aluminum, titanium, and various types of alloys or composites.

3. **Shaft Design:** Shaft design involves determining the appropriate dimensions, geometry, and features based on the specific application requirements. Factors to consider include the torque to be transmitted, rotational speed, axial and radial loads, and environmental conditions. Shaft design also considers factors such as keyways, splines, threads, and surface finishes.
4. **Shaft Types:** Shafts can be classified into different types based on their specific design and application. Some common types include:
   - **Solid Shafts:** These are solid cylindrical shafts with a consistent diameter along their length. They are used in applications where high strength and rigidity are required.
   - **Hollow Shafts:** Hollow shafts have a hollow interior, which reduces weight and allows for the passage of fluids, wires, or other components. They are commonly used in applications where weight reduction is important, such as aerospace or automotive industries.
   - **Stepped Shafts:** Stepped shafts have varying diameters along their length, with distinct steps or changes in diameter. They are used to accommodate different components or to provide specific load-bearing characteristics.
   - **Splined Shafts:** Splined shafts have grooves or splines along their length, which allow for the connection of other components, such as gears or couplings. Splines provide a secure and precise method of torque transmission.
5. **Shaft Alignment and Support:** Proper alignment and support of shafts are crucial for their efficient operation and longevity. Misalignment or inadequate support can lead to excessive vibration, increased wear, and premature failure. Techniques such as precision machining, bearing selection, and alignment procedures are employed to ensure proper shaft alignment and support.
6. **Shaft Couplings:** Shaft couplings are used to connect two shafts together, allowing for the transmission of torque and motion. Couplings can compensate for misalignment, absorb shock and vibration, and provide flexibility in the system. Common types of couplings include rigid couplings, flexible couplings, and universal joints.
7. **Shaft Maintenance and Inspection:** Regular maintenance and inspection of shafts are important to ensure their continued performance

and reliability. This includes lubrication, monitoring for wear or damage, and periodic inspection for signs of misalignment or fatigue.

3.1 Classification of Shafts

Shafts can be classified into different types based on their specific design, application, and features. Here are some common types of shafts:

- **Solid Shafts:** Solid shafts are cylindrical shafts with a consistent diameter along their entire length. They are typically used in applications where high strength, rigidity, and torque transmission are required. Solid shafts are commonly found in machinery, automotive components, and power transmission systems.
- **Hollow Shafts:** Hollow shafts have a hollow interior, which reduces weight and allows for the passage of fluids, wires, or other components. They are often used in applications where weight reduction is important, such as aerospace, automotive, and robotics industries. Hollow shafts can provide a balance between strength and weight savings.
- **Stepped Shafts:** Stepped shafts have varying diameters along their length, with distinct steps or changes in diameter. These steps can be used to accommodate different components or to provide specific load-bearing characteristics. Stepped shafts are commonly used in applications where different parts need to be mounted or supported at different locations along the shaft.
- **Splined Shafts:** Splined shafts have grooves or splines along their length, which allow for the connection of other components, such as gears, couplings, or sprockets. Splines provide a secure and precise method of torque transmission. Splined shafts are commonly used in automotive transmissions, industrial machinery, and power transmission systems.
- **Flexible Shafts:** Flexible shafts are designed to transmit rotary motion between two misaligned components. They consist of a series of interlocking helical coils enclosed in a protective casing. Flexible shafts are used in applications where there is a need for remote or flexible power transmission, such as in rotary tools, automotive steering systems, and remote control mechanisms.
- **Crankshafts:** Crankshafts are specialized shafts used in internal combustion engines. They convert the reciprocating motion of the pistons into rotary motion. Crankshafts have multiple journals and throws to

accommodate the connecting rods and provide the necessary crank angles for proper engine operation.

- **Camshafts:** Camshafts are another specialized type of shaft used in engines. They have specially shaped lobes or cams that actuate the valves in an engine, controlling the intake and exhaust processes. Camshafts are typically driven by the crankshaft and are critical for proper engine timing and performance.
- **Drive Shafts:** Drive shafts, also known as propeller shafts or cardan shafts, are used to transmit torque and rotational motion between the engine or power source and the driven wheels or other components in vehicles or machinery. Drive shafts are commonly found in automobiles, trucks, and industrial equipment.

These are just a few examples of the different types of shafts used in various applications.

3.2 Stresses in Shaft

Shafts are subjected to various types of stresses due to the loads and forces acting on them during operation. Understanding the stresses in shafts is crucial for their design and ensuring their structural integrity. Here are some common types of stresses that occur in shafts:

- **Torsional Stress:** Torsional stress is the primary stress experienced by shafts due to the twisting or torsional forces applied to them. It is caused by the torque transmitted through the shaft. Torsional stress is highest at the outer surface of the shaft and decreases towards the center. The maximum torsional stress is typically calculated using the formula T/J, where T is the applied torque and J is the polar moment of inertia of the shaft cross-section.
- **Bending Stress:** Bending stress occurs in shafts when they are subjected to bending moments or forces that cause them to deflect. Bending stress is highest at the outer surface of the shaft, known as the tensile side, and lowest at the inner surface, known as the compressive side. The maximum bending stress is typically calculated using the formula M*c/I, where M is the bending moment, c is the distance from the neutral axis to the outer surface, and I is the moment of inertia of the shaft cross-section.

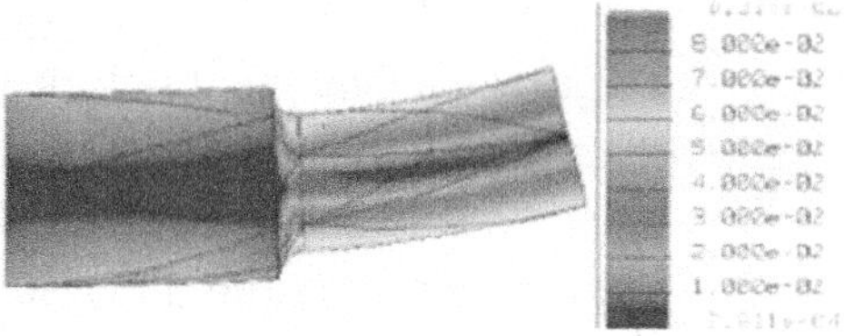

Fig. 3.2. Bending stress

- **Shear Stress:** Shear stress is the stress that occurs parallel to the cross-sectional area of the shaft. It is caused by the shear forces acting on the shaft. Shear stress is highest at the outer surface of the shaft and decreases towards the center. The maximum shear stress is typically calculated using the formula V/A, where V is the shear force and A is the cross-sectional area of the shaft as shown in figure 3.3.

Fig. 3.3. Torsional stress

- **Axial Stress:** Axial stress occurs in shafts when they are subjected to axial loads or forces along their length. Axial stress is calculated by dividing the axial force by the cross-sectional area of the shaft. Axial stress is typically lower compared to torsional, bending, and shear stresses in most shaft designs.
- **Combined Stresses:** In many cases, shafts experience a combination of torsional, bending, shear, and axial stresses simultaneously. These combined stresses need to be considered in the design to ensure that the shaft can withstand the applied loads without failure. Various theories and methods, such as the maximum shear stress theory or the von Mises criterion, can be used to evaluate the combined stresses and determine the safety factor of the shaft.

3.3 Shaft Subjected to Twisting Moment Only

When a shaft is subjected to a twisting moment only, it experiences torsional stress. Torsional stress is the primary stress in this case and is caused by the torque applied to the shaft. The stress distribution in the shaft is typically non-linear, with the maximum stress occurring at the outer surface and decreasing towards the center.

To analyse the stresses in a shaft subjected to a twisting moment only, the following factors need to be considered:

- **Torsional Moment (Torque):** The torsional moment or torque applied to the shaft is the primary factor that determines the magnitude of the torsional stress. It is typically denoted by the symbol T and is measured in units of force multiplied by distance (e.g., Nm or lb-ft).
- **Shaft Geometry:** The geometry of the shaft, including its length, diameter, and cross-sectional shape, affects the distribution of stresses. The shaft's cross-section is often assumed to be circular, but it can also be non-circular in some cases.
- **Material Properties:** The material properties of the shaft, such as its modulus of rigidity (G) and shear modulus, determine its ability to resist torsional deformation. The material's shear strength is also important in assessing the shaft's resistance to failure.
- **Polar Moment of Inertia:** The polar moment of inertia (J) is a property of the shaft's cross-section that quantifies its resistance to torsional deformation. It depends on the shape and dimensions of the cross-section and is used to calculate the maximum torsional stress.

The maximum torsional stress (τ_{max}) in a shaft subjected to a twisting moment can be calculated using the formula:

$$\tau_{max} = \frac{Tr}{J}$$

where r is the radial distance from the shaft's center to the outer surface.

To ensure the shaft's safety and prevent failure, the calculated maximum torsional stress should be compared to the allowable stress or the material's shear strength. A safety factor is typically applied to account for uncertainties in the applied loads, material properties, and other factors.

3.4 Shaft Subjected to Bending Moment Only

When a shaft is subjected to a bending moment only, it experiences bending stress. Bending stress is the primary stress in this case and is caused by the bending moment applied to the shaft. The stress distribution in the shaft is typically highest at the outer surface on the tensile side and lowest at the inner surface on the compressive side.

To analyse the stresses in a shaft subjected to a bending moment only, the following factors need to be considered:

1. **Bending Moment:** The bending moment applied to the shaft is the primary factor that determines the magnitude of the bending stress. It is typically denoted by the symbol M and is measured in units of force multiplied by distance (e.g., Nm or lb-ft).
2. **Shaft Geometry:** The geometry of the shaft, including its length, diameter, and cross-sectional shape, affects the distribution of stresses. The shaft's cross-section is often assumed to be circular, but it can also be non-circular in some cases.
3. **Material Properties:** The material properties of the shaft, such as its modulus of elasticity (E) and yield strength, determine its ability to resist bending deformation. The material's tensile and compressive strengths are also important in assessing the shaft's resistance to failure.
4. **Moment of Inertia:** The moment of inertia (I) is a property of the shaft's cross-section that quantifies its resistance to bending deformation. It depends on the shape and dimensions of the cross-section and is used to calculate the maximum bending stress.

The maximum bending stress (σ_{max}) in a shaft subjected to a bending moment can be calculated using the formula:

$$\sigma_{max} = \frac{MC}{I}$$

Where c is the distance from the neutral axis to the outer surface of the shaft.

To ensure the shaft's safety and prevent failure, the calculated maximum bending stress should be compared to the allowable stress or the material's yield strength. A safety factor is typically applied to account for uncertainties in the applied loads, material properties, and other factors.

3.5 Design Procedure for Parallel Keys

Key: The keyway in the shaft is milled in a curved shape whereas the keyway in the hub is usually straight. The main advantage of this key is that it will align itself in the keyway as shown in figure 3.4.

Fig. 3.4. Key applications

3.6 Types of Sunk Keys

1. Rectangular sunk key

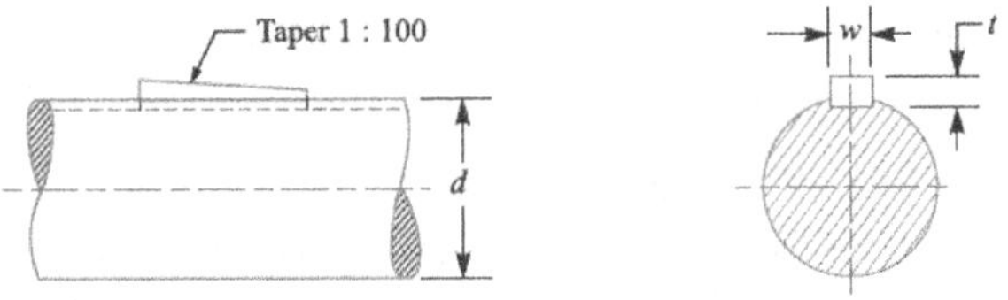

Fig. 3.5. Rectangular Key

2. Square sunk key

The only difference from the rectangular sunk key is the width and thickness is equal

3. Parallel sunk key

The parallel sunk key may be of rectangular or square cross section. The cross section is uniform in width and thickness throughout length.

4. Gib head key

A gib head key is similar to a square or rectangular key but it has a head at one end, generally at the larger end of the taper sunk key. The gib head is used for driving the key while assembling or disassembling.

5. Feather key

Feather key is used where it is necessary to slide a keyed gear, pulley assembly along the shaft. Keys are tight fitted or screwed on the shaft.

6. Woodruff key

A woodruff key is used to transmit small amount of torque in automotive and machine tool industries.

Keyseats

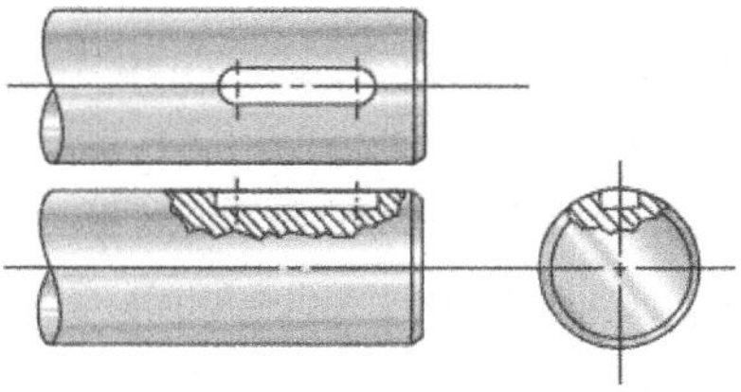

Fig. 3.6. Key seats

- Complete the design of the shaft into which the key will be installed, and specify the actual diameter at the location of the key seat.
- Select the size of the key from DB Table.
- Specify a suitable design factor, N. In typical industrial applications, $N = 3$ is adequate to accommodate accidental overloads and shock.
- Specify the material for the key, usually SAE 1018 steel. A higher-strength material can be used.
- Determine the yield strength of the materials for the key, the shaft, and the hub.
- If a square key is used and the key material has the lowest strength, compute the minimum required length of the key. This length will be satisfactory for both shear and bearing stress.
- If a rectangular key is used, or if either the shaft or the hub has a lower strength than the key, compute the minimum required length of the key based on bearing stress. The larger of the two computed lengths governs the design. Check to be sure that the computed length is shorter than the hub length. If not, a higher-strength material must be selected and the design process repeated. Alternatively, two keys or a spline can be used instead of a single key.

- Specify the actual length of the key to be equal to or longer than the computed minimum length. A convenient standard size should be specified using the preferred basic sizes
- Complete the design of the key seat in the shaft and the keyway in the hub

3.7 Design of Coupling

Shaft couplings are used in machinery for several purposes

1. To provide for connection of shaft of units those are manufactured separately.
2. To provide for misalignment of the shaft or to introduce mechanical flexibility.
3. To reduce the transmission of shock loads from one shaft to another.
4. To introduce protection against over loads.

Requirement of a Good Shaft Coupling

1. It should be easy to connect or disconnect.
2. It should transmit the full power from one shaft to the other shaft without losses.
3. It should hold the shaft in perfect alignment.
4. It should have no projecting parts.

3.8 Types of Shaft Coupling

1. Rigid coupling

- It is used to connect two shafts which are perfectly aligned. The types are
- Sleeve (or) muff coupling
- Clamp (or) split muff (or) compression coupling
- Flange coupling

2. Flexible coupling

It is used to connect two shafts having lateral and angular misalignments. The types are

- Bushed pin type coupling
- Universal coupling
- Oldham coupling

Sleeve or Muff Coupling

It is made of cast iron. It consists of a hollow cylinder whose inner diameter is that same as that of the shaft. It is fitted over the ends of two shafts by means of a gib head key. The power transmitted from one shaft two other shafts by means of a key and a sleeve.

3.9 Flange Coupling

A flange coupling usually applied to a coupling having two separate cast iron flanges. Each flange is mounted on the shaft and keyed to it. The faces are turned up at right angle to the axis of the shaft. One of the flange has a projected portion and the other flange has a corresponding recess. This helps to bring the shaft into line and to maintain alignment. The two flanges are coupled together by means of bolt and nuts.

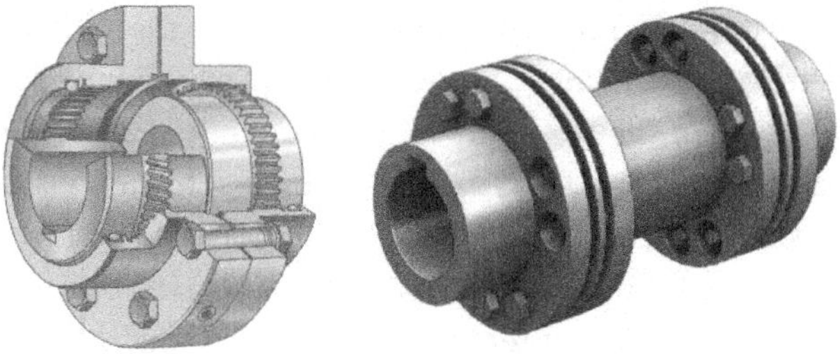

Fig. 3.7. Rigid coupling

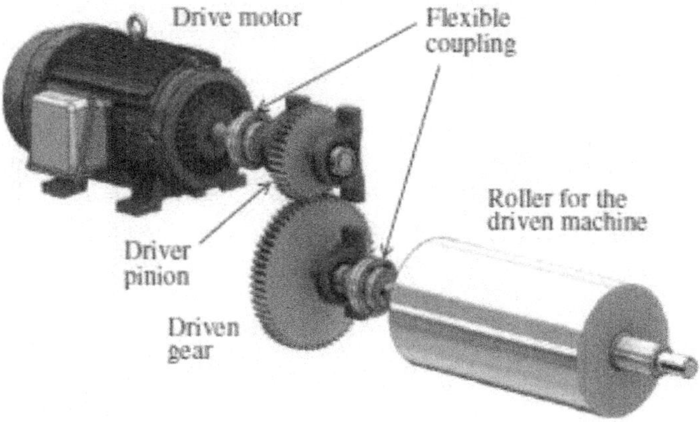

Fig. 3.8. Flexible couplings

Design Problems

1) Compute the angle of twist of a 10-mm-diameter shaft carrying 4.10 N m of torque if it is 250 mm long and made of steel with G = 80 GPa.

Solution

Over the length of 250 mm, the shaft twists 0.75°.

Compute the angle of twist in the shaft.

Given Torque = T = 4.10 N #m; length = L = 250 mm.

Shaft diameter = D = 10 mm; G = 80 GPa.

$$\theta = \frac{TL}{GJ} = \frac{4.10X\ 10^3 X\ 250}{8010^3 X\ 982} = 0.013 \text{ rad}$$

$$\theta = (0.013)\left(\frac{180}{\pi}\right) = 0.75^{\circ}$$

2) A hoisting drum of 0.5 m diameter is keyed to a shaft which is supported in two bearings and driven through a reduction gear pair having a reduction ratio of 12:1 is shown in fig. 3. The gear, having pitch circle diameter of 450 mm, is mounted at the end of the shaft such that it overhangs the nearest bearing by 150 mm (Assume pressure angle 20°). The load to be hoisted is 8 kN at the speed of 50 m/min. The efficiency of drive is 80 %. The shaft is made of steel, for which the working stresses are 115 Mpa in tension and 50 Mpa in shear. If the combined shock and fatigue factors for bending and torsion are 2 and 1.5 respectively, determine:

(i) The power and speed of electric motor; and

(ii) The diameter of shaft

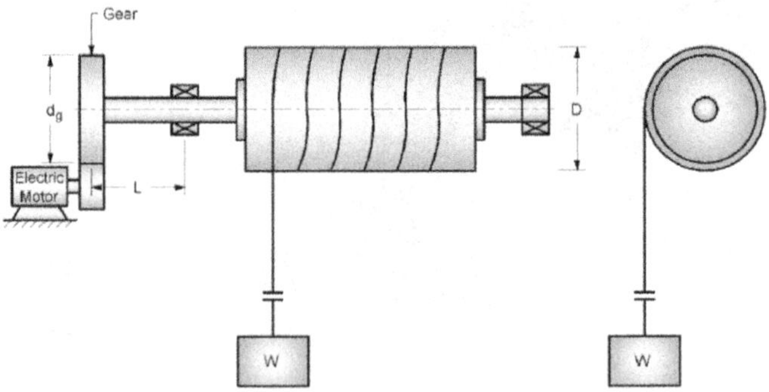

Fig. 3.9 Hoisting drum

Solution:

$T = \frac{WD}{2} = \frac{8 \times 10^3 \times 500x}{2}$ = 2000x 10^3 N-mm = 2000 N-m

W.K.T $V = \frac{\pi D N}{60 \times 1000}$

$$\frac{50}{60} = \frac{\pi \times 500 \times N}{60 \times 1000}$$

N = 31.83 r.p.m

N= GN

= 12 x 31.83

= 381.98 r.p.m

Power P = $\frac{2 \pi NT}{60 \times 1000 \times \eta_m} = \frac{2 \pi \times 31.83 \times 2000}{60 \times 1000 \times 0.8}$

= 8.33 kW

Taangential force on gear $F_t = \frac{T}{\frac{d_g}{2}} = \frac{2000 \times 10^3}{450/2}$ = 8888.88 N

Radial force on Gear $F_r = F_t \tan \phi$ = 3235.29 N

Resultant force on Gear $F = \sqrt{Ft^2 + Fr^2}$

= 9459.35N

Maximum bending moment on shaft M = F_g x L = 9459.35 x 150

= 1418.9 x 10^3

Equivalent torque on shaft $T_e = \sqrt{(K_b M)^2 + (K_t T)^2}$

= 4129.54 x 10^3 N-mm

Equivalent bending moment on shaft $M_e = \frac{1}{2} \lfloor K_b M \rfloor + \sqrt{(K_b M)^2 + (K_t T)^2}$

= 3483.67x 10^3 N-mm

Diameter of shaft by maximum shear stress theory

$\tau_{max} = \frac{16 T_e}{\pi d^3}$

= 75 mm

Diameter of shaft by maximum principal stress theory

$\sigma_{max} = \frac{32 M_e}{\pi d^3}$

D = 68 mm

Short Questions and Answers

1. **Define the term critical speed.**

   The speed, at which the shaft runs so that the additional deflection of the shaft from the axis of rotation becomes infinite, is known as critical or whirling speed.

2. **Factor is considered to design a shaft?**

   i. strength

   ii. stiffness

3. **What is a shaft?**

   A shaft is a rotating machine element,which transmits power from one point to another point.

4. What are the types of shafts?

   i. Line shaft — ii. Spindle

   iii. Stub shaft — iv. Counter shaft

5. **What is key?**

   A key is device, which is used for connecting two machine parts for preventing relative motion of rotation with respect to each other.

6. **What is key?**

   Key is a device which is used for connecting tow machine parts for preventing relative motion of rotation with respect to each other.

7. **What are the types of keys?**

   i. Saddle key — ii. Tangent key

   iii. Sunk key — iv. Round key and taper pins.

8. **How are sunk key designed?**

   Sunk keys are designed to fit in a sunk key way. Whose bed is parallel to the axis of the shaft.

9. **What is the main use of woodruff keys?**

   A woodruff key is used to transmit small value of torque in automotive and machine tool industries. The keyway in the shaft is milled in a curved shape whereas the key way in the hub is usually straight.

10. **List the various failures occurred in sunk keys.**

    1. Shear failure

    2. Crushing failure

11. **What is simple torsion?**

    When a shaft is subjected to pure torsional moment M, the shaft diameter can be found from torsional shear strength equation.

    Shear strength = $16M/3.14d^3$

12. **What is simple bending moment?**

    When a shaft is subject to a pure bending load,the principal stress induced in the shaft are tension and compression.The maximum stress induced in the shaft can be determined by the theory of simple bending moment relation.

13. What are the types of rigidity?

i. Torsional rigidity

ii. Lateral rigidity.

14. What are the different measures followed to control the lateral deflection?

i. Reducing the span length

ii. Increasing the number of supports

iii. Selecting the cross-section in which the area moment of inertia as in case of hollow shaft.

15. Define the term critical speed?

The speed at which the shaft runs so that the additional deflection of the shaft from the axis of rotation becomes infinite, is known as critical speed.

16. What is the function of a coupling between two shafts?

Couplings are used to connect sections of long transmission shafts and to connect the shaft of a driving machine to the shaft of a driven machine.

Exercises

1) A hollow shaft is subjected to a maximum torque of 1.5 kN-m and a maximum bending moment of 3 kN-m. It is subjected, at the same time, to an axial load of 10 kN. Assume that the load is applied gradually and the ratio of the inner diameter to the outer diameter is 0.5. If the outer diameter of the shaft is 80 mm, find the shear stress induced in the shaft.
2) A hollow shaft of 0.5 m outside diameter and 0.3 m inside diameter is used to drive a propeller of a marine vessel. The shaft is mounted on bearings 6 metre apart and it transmits 5600 kW at 150 r.p.m. The maximum axial propeller thrust is 500 kN and the shaft weighs 70 kN.

   Determine:

   a. The maximum shear stress developed in the shaft, and

   b. The angular twist between the bearings
3) A steel spindle transmits 4 kW at 800 r.p.m. The angular deflection should not exceed 0.25° per metre of the spindle. If the modulus of rigidity for the material of the spindle is 84 GPa, find the diameter of the spindle and the shear stress induced in the spindle.
4) Compare the weight, strength and stiffness of a hollow shaft of the same external diameter as that of solid shaft. The inside diameter of the hollow shaft being half the external diameter. Both the shafts have the same material and length.

4

Design of Fasteners and Joints

The design of fastening elements, such as bolts, screws, and rivets, is crucial in ensuring the integrity and reliability of assembled structures.

Factors Considered for Selection of Fasteners

- Strength: Will it hold the loads and pressures?
- Security: Will it remain attached?
- Cost: Realistic?
- Installation: Appropriate for situation?
- Skill: Is specialized training needed?
- Equipment: Is specialized equipment needed and available?
- Appearance: If the fastener shows, which kind looks best?

4.1 Screws

Mechanical devices for fastening things together. Essentially a cylindrical or conical piece of metal threaded evenly around its outside surface with an advancing spiral ridge and commonly having a slotted head, it penetrates only by being turned, as with a screwdriver.

The most common types of screws are:

1. Wood screws
2. Machine screws
3. Sheet metal screws
4. Set screws

Wood Screws

1. Serve much the same purpose as a nail, but:
    - Provide greater holding power than a nail.
    - Screws can be easily removed and replaced.

- Screws are neater in appearance and offer more decorative possibilities.

2. In addition to fastening pieces of wood together – the most common use of wood screws would be to anchor objects (hardware) to a wood surface.

Sheet-Metal Screws

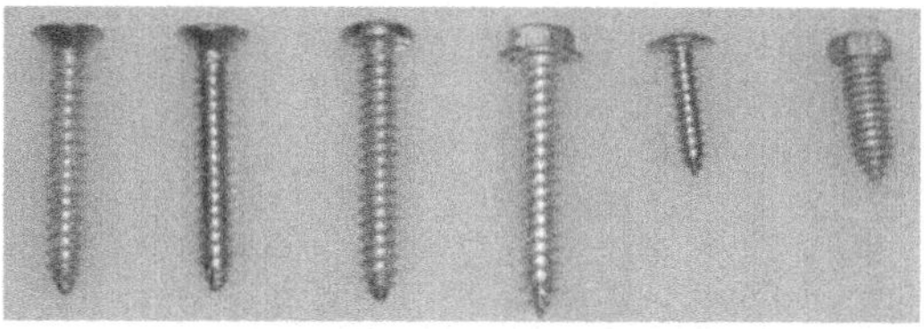

Fig. 4.1. Sheet metal screws

1. Also called "Tapping Screws" or "Self-Threading Screws".
2. Used to fasten light pieces of metal together or to attach covers, panels and other light parts.
3. These screws have sharp threads that can cut their own grooves into metal.
4. They come with "coarse" or "fine" threads and are usually case hardened to cut threads and withstand hard twisting forces.
5. Distinguishable from wood screws in that they are threaded all the way from the point to the head.

Machine Screws

Machine screws are used for the assembly of metal parts and usually are driven into "threaded" holes rather than drawn tight with nuts.

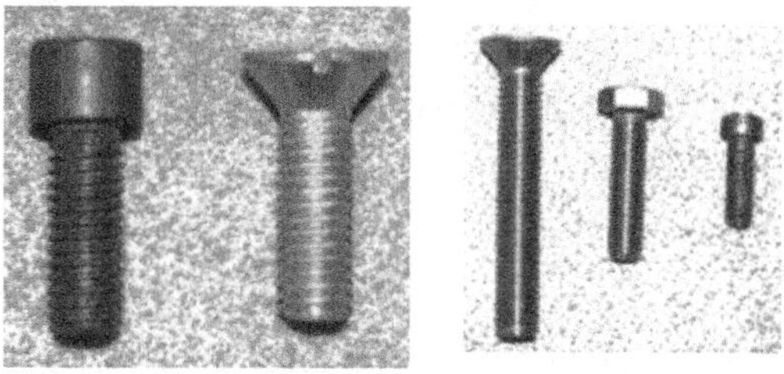

Fig. 4.2. Machine screws

1. Like all screws, there are many head designs to choose from.

2. Machine screw threads are also designated by the number of threads per inch, just like bolt threads:
   - A 6-32 machine screw has a #6 body diameter and 32 threads per inch of length.
   - Most machine screws are fully threaded to the head.

Set Screws

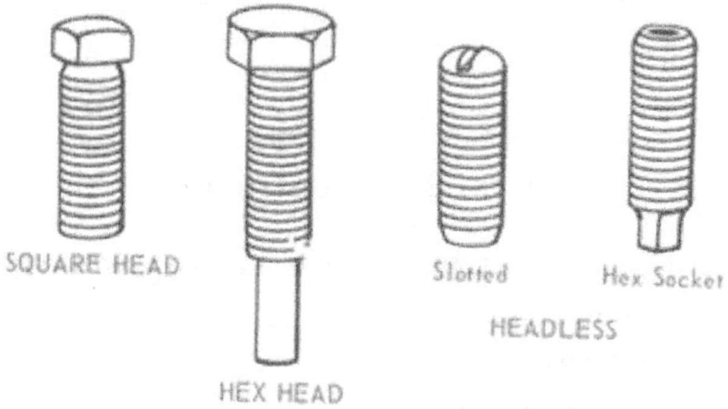

Fig. 4.3. Set screws

Set screws are used to hold a knob, collar, pulley or gear to a rotating shaft.

1. There are a variety of "head" or "point" styles, each best suited for its job.
2. Generally made of high-strength material and are heat treated.
3. Not an especially strong type of fastening – depend on friction and "shear" to hold parts together.

American Screw Gauge

- Sizes are designated by length in inches (millimeters).
- Diameters less than ¼ inch (6 mm) use gauge number.
- Diameters greater than ¼ inch use fractions of an inch.

Wire Gauge Number	0	2	4	6	8	10	12	14	16	18	20
Decimal Size	.060"	.086"	.112"	.138"	.164"	.190"	.203"	.242"	.268"	.294"	.320"
Fractional Size	1/16"	3/32"	1/8"	9/64"	11/64"	13/64"	7/32"	1/4"	9/32"	19/64"	21/64"

Fig. 4.4.

4.2 Bolts, Cap Screws, Nuts and Washers

Bolts are usually used in plain holes drilled through the parts being fastened.

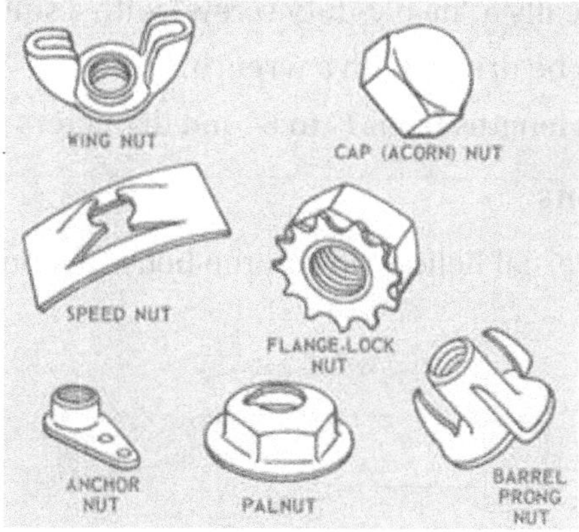

Fig. 4.5. Bolts

- Bolts are generally held in place with a mating nut.
- When the nut for any bolt is turned down on wood, always use a flat washer under the nut.
- Cap screws are normally used in threaded holes, without a nut.

Machine Bolts/Cap Screws

Machine bolts have square or hexagonal heads.

- Installed with a wrench.
- Usually used if the parts to be joined are made of metal.

Round-Head Bolts

- Commonly used to fasten wood parts.
- Most have a square neck under the head.
    - Also used to fasten steel parts with square punched holes.
- A Carriage Bolt is the most common type of round-headed bolt to be used when working with wood.
- A Plow Bolt has a flat, tapered head that fits into a countersunk hole – primarily used with metal parts.
- Used in the marine industry for attaching cutters and other parts to dredges.

Other "Bolts"

- Some fasteners are referred to as bolts but are actually screws.
- A **Lag Bolt** is really a "heavy-duty screw" with a square or hex head.
  - Designed to be driven with a wrench.
  - Available in lengths from 1" to 6" and diameters from 1/4" to 1/2".

Sizes and Descriptions

- **Threads** – External helical ribs on the body of a bolt at the end opposite the head.

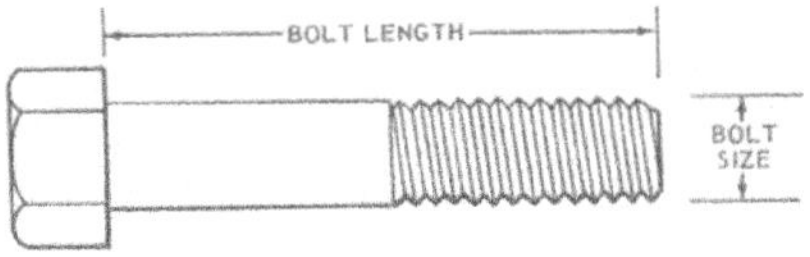

Fig. 4.6. Bolt descriptions

- The **diameter** of a bolt is determined by the diameter of the crest of the threads.
- The **length** of most bolts (or machine screws) is determined by the measuring from the bottom of the head to the end of the threads.
  - Flat head bolts are measured from the threaded end to the top of the head.
  - The **Head Size** determines what size wrench or socket must be used to turn or hold the bolt or nut.
  - A square or hexagonal bolt head is measured across the "flats".
  - Example – A ¾" wrench is needed to turn a ½" diameter bolt head.

Threads

- **Threads – External** helical ribs on the body of a bolt. Usually a bolt "mates" with **internal** threads of a nut.

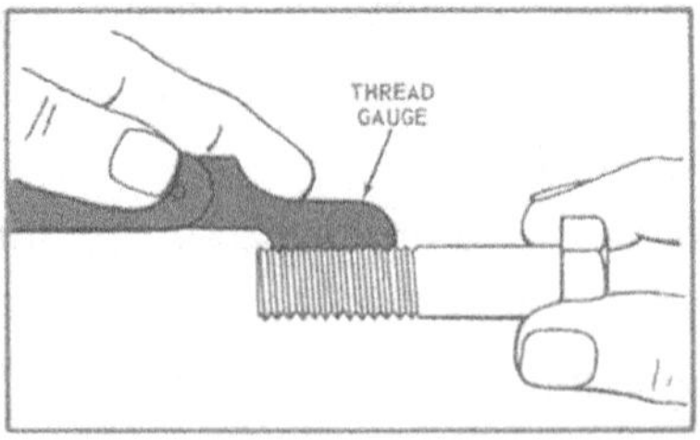

Fig. 4.7. Thread gauge

- The top of the rib is called the **crest**, or thread tip.
- Bottom of the groove is called the thread **root**.
- Threads are measured by counting the **number per inch**. (Metric threads are measured by the distance between threads - **pitch** - in mm)

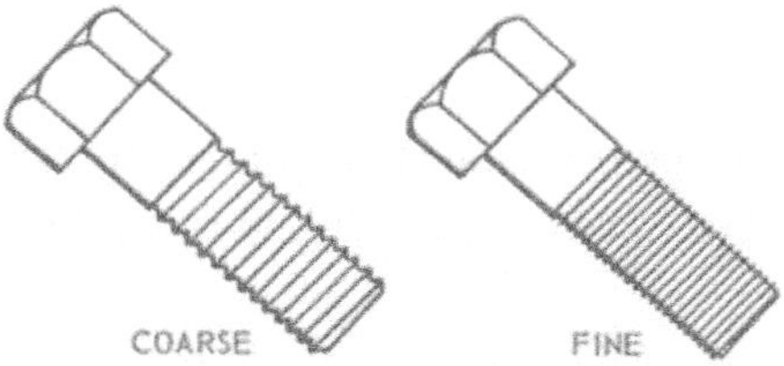

Fig. 4.8. Types of threads

- The type of threads that are used for most applications are coarse with deep grooves.
- Some threads are finer, with shallower grooves.
  - Bolts with fine threads are used only under special conditions - such as when the parts being fastened have thin walls.
  - Bolts and screws normally have **right-hand threads.**
  - Turned to the right (clockwise) when tightened.
- Occasionally, bolts, screws and nuts with **left-hand threads** are needed.
  - Turned to the left (counter-clockwise) when tightened.

American National Standards Institute (ANSI)

- There are carefully controlled standards for threading bolts and nuts.

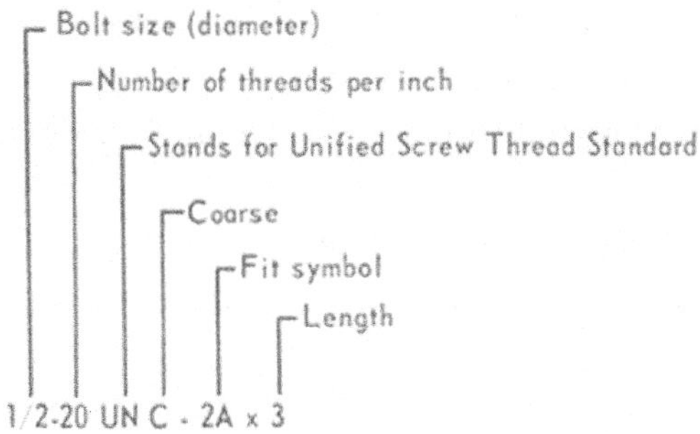

Fig. 4.9. Bolt description

- ANSI establishes such things as the angle of threads, the depth of the root and the manufacturing tolerances (fit) which are referred to as the *"Unified Screw Thread Standards"*.

4.3 Nuts and Washers

Nut

Nuts have coarse or fine **internal threads** that correspond to the threads of a bolt and are designed to "screw" onto the bolt to fasten it in place.

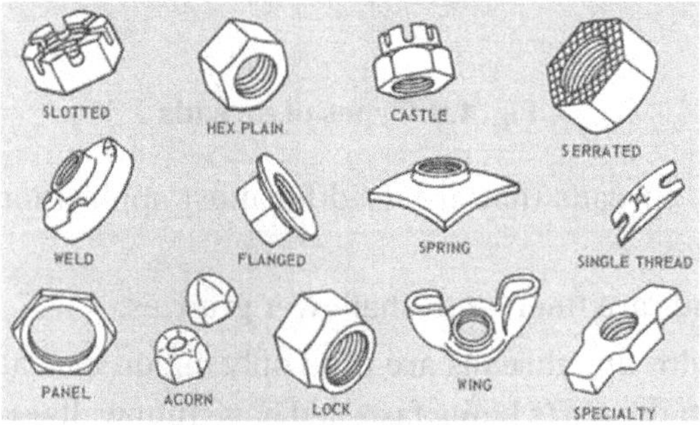

Fig. 4.10. Types of nuts

- A great variety of shapes and sizes for standard and special applications.
- Threads per inch or distance between threads can be determined with a thread gauge just like bolt threads.
- Nuts have three important dimensions:
  - Thickness
  - Distance across the flats
  - Inside diameter (same as that of the bolt with which it is to be used).
- **Jam Nuts** – Used to lock a threaded part in place.
- **Castellated and Slotted Nuts** – Secure a nut in place so it can't possibly come loose.
- **Self-Locking Nuts** – Stay firmly in place even with constant vibration.
- Many other types of nuts available for special uses.

Washer

- A plain **washer** is simply a steel disk with a hole through the center.
  - Like bolts and nuts the may be manufactured with a variety of different materials

    - They help distribute the load over an area larger than the head of the bolt or nut, thus reducing the stresses that would otherwise exist.
    - Plain washers are identified by their outside diameter and the diameter of the hole, which is the bolt size rather than the actual diameter of the hole.
    - The washer thickness varies with the size of the washer.
- Lock washers are frequently used to keep nuts and bolts tight, especially when they are subject to vibration.
    - **Helical Spring Washers** – Made of tough spring steel. They are split and one end of the split is bent up. When the nut is tightened, the section of the washer that is bent up "bites" into the nut and the fastened part.
    - **Toothed Lock Washers** – Has many sharp, heat-treated teeth to dig into the surfaces pressing against it.
    - Many other types of washers are available for special uses.

Key Considerations in the Design of Fastening Elements

1. **Material Selection:** The choice of material for fastening elements is important to ensure sufficient strength, corrosion resistance, and durability. Common materials include steel, stainless steel, aluminium, and titanium. The material selection should consider factors such as the load-bearing capacity, environmental conditions, and compatibility with the materials being joined.
2. **Strength and Load Capacity:** Fastening elements must be designed to withstand the anticipated loads and forces. This involves determining the required strength and load capacity based on factors such as the applied loads, joint configuration, and safety factors. Design calculations should consider factors such as tensile strength, shear strength, and fatigue resistance.
3. **Thread Design:** For threaded fasteners, the design of the threads is critical. The thread profile, pitch, and engagement length should be carefully considered to ensure proper load distribution, thread strength, and ease of assembly. Threaded fasteners may have different thread types, such as metric, unified, or specialty threads, depending on the application requirements.

4. **Head Design:** The head of a fastening element should be designed to facilitate proper installation and provide sufficient bearing area. The head design may vary depending on the type of fastener, such as hexagonal, Phillips, or socket head. The head should be designed to resist stripping, provide adequate torque transfer, and allow for easy tightening or loosening.
5. **Preload and Tightening:** Achieving the proper preload or clamping force is essential for the performance of fastening elements. The design should consider the required preload and the method of tightening, such as torque-controlled or tension-controlled methods. Proper tightening procedures and torque specifications should be provided to ensure consistent and reliable clamping force.
6. **Joint Design:** The design of the joint or connection where the fastening element is used is critical. Factors such as joint type, clearance, alignment, and surface preparation should be considered to ensure proper load transfer, alignment, and stability. The joint design should also account for potential factors such as thermal expansion, vibration, and dynamic loads.
7. **Corrosion Protection:** Fastening elements may be exposed to corrosive environments, which can compromise their integrity. Proper corrosion protection measures, such as coatings, plating's, or the use of corrosion-resistant materials, should be considered to ensure long-term performance and prevent premature failure.
8. **Testing and Validation:** Fastening elements should undergo testing and validation to ensure their performance and reliability. This may involve testing for strength, fatigue resistance, corrosion resistance, and other relevant factors. Compliance with industry standards and specifications should be considered during the design and testing process.

The design of fastening elements requires careful consideration of various factors to ensure the integrity and reliability of assembled structures.

The Fastenings may be classified into the following two groups:

1. The Permanent Fastenings are those fastenings which cannot be disassembled without destroying the connecting components. Examples: Welded joint, Rivet joint.
2. The Temporary or Detachable Fastenings are those fastenings which can be disassembled without destroying the connecting components.

Examples:

1. Thread Joints
   a. Bolted Joints
   b. Screws Joints
2. Keys
3. Coupling
4. Pins Joints
   a. Cotters Joints
   b. Knuckle Joints
5. Pipe Joints

4.4 Welded Joint

Welding can be defined as a process of joining metallic parts by heating to a suitable temperature with or without the application of pressure. Welding is an economical and efficient method for obtaining a permanent joint of metallic parts.

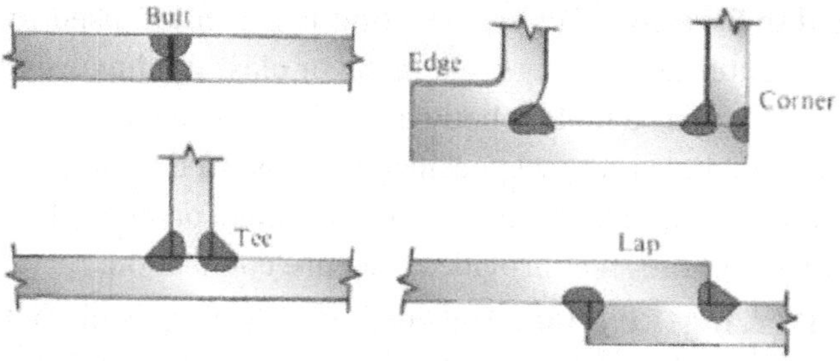

Fig. 4.11. Types of welded joints

Two distinct application of welding

1. It can be used as a substitute for a riveted joint
2. Welded structure as an alternative method for casting or forging.

4.5 Riveted Joint

The rivets are used to make permanent fastening between the two or more plates such as in structural work, ship building, bridges, tanks and boiler shells. The riveted joints are widely used for joining light metals. A rivet is a short cylindrical bar with a head integral to it. The cylindrical portion of the rivet is called shank or body and lower portion of shank is known as tail.

Riveting is a method of joining two or more materials together using a rivet, which is a cylindrical fastener with a head on one end. The rivet is inserted through aligned holes in the materials to be joined, and then deformed or "set" to create a permanent connection. Here are some common methods of riveting:

1. **Solid Riveting:** Solid riveting is the traditional method of riveting and involves using a solid rivet. The process begins by heating the rivet and placing it through the aligned holes in the materials. The protruding end of the rivet is then hammered or mechanically compressed to deform it, creating a head on the opposite side. The deformation of the rivet creates a tight and secure joint.
2. **Blind Riveting:** Blind riveting, also known as pop riveting, is a method used when access to both sides of the joint is limited. It involves using a blind rivet, which has a mandrel or stem attached to it. The rivet is inserted through the aligned holes, and a specialized tool is used to pull the mandrel, causing the blind end of the rivet to expand and create a head on the blind side of the joint. The mandrel is then snapped off, leaving a secure connection.
3. **Tubular Riveting:** Tubular riveting is a method used for joining thin-walled materials, such as sheet metal or plastic. It involves using a tubular rivet, which has a hollow body and a head. The rivet is inserted through the aligned holes, and a specialized tool is used to deform the end of the rivet, causing it to flare out and create a head on one side of the joint. The flared end of the rivet provides a secure connection.
4. **Self-Piercing Riveting:** Self-piercing riveting is a method used for joining materials that are difficult to drill or punch holes into, such as high-strength steel or aluminum. It involves using a self-piercing rivet, which has a sharp point and a hollow body. The rivet is driven through the materials using a specialized tool, which simultaneously pierces the materials and deforms the rivet to create a head on one side of the joint. The self-piercing rivet forms a strong and reliable connection.
5. **Impact Riveting:** Impact riveting is a method used for joining materials that are difficult to deform, such as hardened steel or composite materials. It involves using a solid rivet and a specialized tool that delivers a high-velocity impact force to deform the rivet and create a head on one side of the joint. The impact force causes the rivet to plastically deform and create a secure connection.

Material of Rivets

The material of the rivets must be tough and ductile. They are usually made of steel (low carbon steel or nickel steel), brass, aluminum or copper, but when strength and a fluid tight joint is the main consideration, then the steel rivets are used. The rivets for general purposes shall be manufactured from steel conforming to the following Indian Standards:

- IS: 1148–1982 (Reaffirmed 1992) – Specification for hot rolled rivet bars (up to 40 mm diameter) for structural purposes; or
- IS: 1149–1982 (Reaffirmed 1992) – Specification for high tensile steel rivet bars for structural purposes.
- The rivets for boiler work shall be manufactured from material conforming to IS: 1990 – 1973 (Reaffirmed 1992) – Specification for steel rivets and stay bars for boilers.

4.6 Types of Riveted Joints

1. According to purpose
2. According to position of plates connected
3. According to arrangement of rivets

Types of Rivets

1. Button Head
2. Counter sunk Head
3. Oval counter Head
4. Pan Head
5. Conical Head

4.7 Important terms of Riveted Joints

- **Pitch (p):** The Distance between two adjacent rivet holes in a row.
- **Back pitch (P_b):** The Distance between two adjacent rows of rivets.
- **Diagonal pitch (P_d):** The smallest distance between centers of two rivet holes in adjacent rows of ZIG-Zag riveted joints.
- **Margin (m):** It is the distance between center of a rivet hole and nearest edge of the plate.

Design Problems

1) A steel bolt of M 16 x 2 is 300 mm long carries an impact load of 5000 N-m. If the threads stop adjacent to the nut and e = 2.1x 10 [5] Mpa.

i. Find the stress in the root area.

ii. Find the stress if the shank area is reduced to root area.

Solution:

Given data:

Shank diameter of the bolt, d = 16 mm, Length of the bolt, l = 300 mm

Impact load, U = 5000 N-mm, Modulus of elasticity, E = 2.1×10^5 MPa

Stress in the root area of shank, $A = \frac{\Pi}{4} d^2$

$= \frac{\Pi}{4} 16^2 = 201 \text{ mm}^2$

Root diameter, $d_c = 0.84d$

$= 0.84 \times 16$

$= 13.44$ mm

Area of cross section at the root, $A_c = \frac{\Pi}{4} 13.44^2$

$= 142 \text{ mm}^2$

Strain energy stored in the bolt, $U = \frac{1}{2} \frac{P^2}{AE} l$

Tensile force, $P = \sqrt{\frac{Ux2AE}{l}}$

$= \sqrt{\frac{5000 \ x \ 2 \ x \ 2.1x10^5}{300}}$

$= 37510$ N

Stress in the root area, $\sigma = \frac{P}{A_c} = \frac{37510}{142} = 264.15 \frac{N}{mm^2}$

Stress, if the Shank area is reduced to root area

i.e., shank area, $A = A_m$, Then

Tensile force on the bolt

$$P = \sqrt{\frac{U2AE}{l}}$$

$$= 31527.76 \frac{N}{mm^2}$$

$$\sigma = \frac{P}{A_c} = \frac{31527.76}{300} = 222 \frac{N}{mm^2}$$

2) The cylinder head of a steam engine is held in position by 12 bolts. The effective diameter of cylinder is 320 mm and steam pressure is 0.9 Mpa. Assuming that the bolts are not initially stressed, find the size of bolts if the tensile stress is not to exceed 23 Mpa.

Solution:

Given data:

Number of bolts, n= 12

Effective diameter of cylinder, D =320 mm

Pressure of steam, p= 0.9 Mpa

Permissible tensile stress, σ_t = 23 Mpa

W.k.t

$$P = \frac{\Pi}{4} d^2 p$$

$$= \frac{\Pi}{4} 320^2 \text{ x } 0.9$$

$$P = 72382.295 \, N$$

Let, d_c be the core diameter of studs.

Resisting force offered by 'n' number of studs is,

$$P = \frac{\Pi}{4} {d_c}^2 \sigma_t \text{ x n}$$

$$72382.295 = \frac{\Pi}{4} {d_c}^2 \, x \, 23 \, x \, 12$$

$$72382.295 = 216.77 \, {d_c}^2$$

$${d_c}^2 = 333.913$$

$$d = 18.273 \text{ mm}$$

3) Figure below shows a cylindrical rod of 50 mm diameter welded to a flat plate. The cylindrical fillet weld is loaded eccentrically by a force of 10 kN acting at 200 mm from the welded end. If the size of the weld is 20 mm, determine the maximum normal stress in the weld.

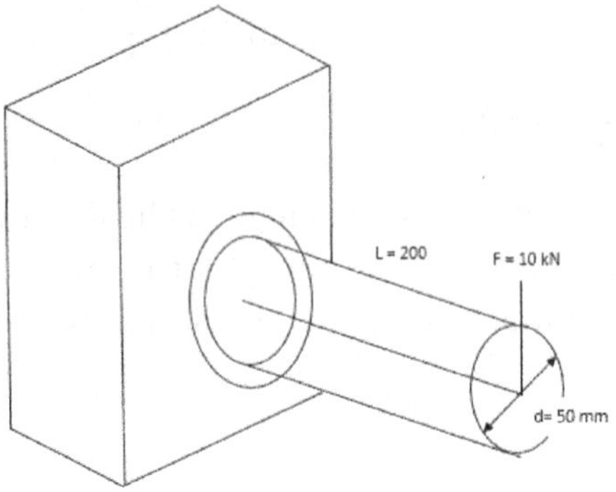

Fig. 4.12. Welded joint

Solution:

Given data:

Diameter, d = 50 mm, Length, f = 200 mm, Load, F= 10 kN, Size of weld, S = 20 mm

W.k.t

$$A = t \times \pi \times d$$

$$= 0.707S\ \pi \times d$$

$$= 0.707 \times 20 \times \pi \times 50$$

$$= 2221.106\ mm^2$$

Bending moment, M = F x L

$$= 10 \times 10^3 \times 200$$

$$= 2 \times 10^6\ N\text{-}mm$$

Section modulus of the weld,

$$Z = \frac{\pi t}{4} d^2$$

$$= \frac{\pi}{4}(0.707 \times 20) \times 50^2$$

$$= 27763.82\ mm^3$$

Bending stress, $\sigma_b = \frac{M}{Z} = \frac{2 \times 10^6}{27763.82} = 72\ N/mm^2$

Direct shear stress, $\tau = \frac{F}{A} = \frac{10 \times 10^3}{2221.106} = 4.5\ N/mm^2$

Maximum shear stress,

$$\tau_{max} = \frac{1}{2}\sqrt{\sigma_b{}^2 + 4\,\tau^2}$$

$$= \frac{1}{2}\sqrt{72^2 + 4 \times 4.5^2}$$

$$= 36.28 \text{ N/mm}^2$$

Maximum normal stress

$$\sigma_{t\,max} = \frac{1}{2}\,\sigma_b + \frac{1}{2}\sqrt{\sigma_b{}^2 + 4\,\tau^2}$$

$$= \frac{1}{2}\,x\;72 + \frac{1}{2}\sqrt{72^2 + 4 \times 4.5^2}$$

$$= 72.28 \text{ N/mm}^2$$

4) A 65 mm diameter solid shaft is to be welded to a flat plate by a fillet weld around the circumference of the shaft. Determine the size of the weld if the torque on the shaft is 3kN-m and the allowable shear stress in the weld is 70 MPa.

Solution:

Given data:

Diameter of the shaft, d = 65 mm

Torque on the shaft, T = 3 kN-m

= 3×10^6 N-mm

Allowable shear stress, τ_{max} = 70 MPa

= 70 N/mm^2

The maximum shear stress for a circular fillet weld is given by

$$\tau_{max} = \frac{2.83}{\pi\, d^2} \times \frac{T}{S}$$

$$= \frac{2.83}{\pi\, x\, 65^2} \times \frac{3x\,10^6}{S}$$

$$70 = \frac{639.633}{S}$$

S = 10 mm

The size of the weld, S = 10 mm

Short Questions and Answers

1. **How is a bolt designated?**

   A bolt is designated by a letter M followed by nominal diameter and pitch in mm.

2. **What factors influence the amount of initial tension?**

   i. External load

   ii. Material used

   iii.Bolt diameter

3. **What is bolt of uniform strength?**

   A bolt of uniform strength has equal strength at the thread and shank portion.

4. **What are the ways to produce bolts of uniform strength?**

   i. Reducing shank diameter equal to root diameter.

   ii. Drilling axial hole

5. **What stresses act on screw fastenings?**

   i. Initial stresses due to screwing up

   ii. Stresses due to external forces iii.Combined stresses.

6. **What are the different applications of screwed fasteners?**

   The different applications of screwed fasteners are

   a.For readily connecting & disconnecting machine parts with out damage

   b.The parts can be rigidly connected

   c.Used for transmitting power

7. **What are the advantages of screwed fasteners?**

   The advantages of screwed fasteners are

   a. They are highly reliable in operation

   b. They are convenient to assemble & disassemble

   c. A wide range of screws can be used for various operating conditions

   d. They are relatively cheap to produce.

8. **Define pitch.**

   Pitch is defined as the distance from appoint on one thread to the corresponding on the adjacent thread in the same axis plane.

9. **Define lead.**

   Lead is defined as the distance, which a screw thread advances axially in one rotation of the nut.

10. **What are the different types of metric thread?**

    1. BSW (British standard Whit worth)

    2. BSE (British standard End

11. **Define welding.**

    Welding can be defined as a process of joining two similar or dissimilar metals with or without application of pressure along with or without addition of filler material.

12. What are the types of welded joints?

i. Butt joint   ii. Lap joint

iii. T – joint   iv.Corner joint   v. Edge joint.

13. What are the two types of stresses are induced in eccentric loading of loaded joint?

1. Direct shear stress.
2. Bending or torsional shear stress.

14. Define butt and lap joint

1. Butt joint:

   The joint is made by welding the ends or edges of two plates.

2. Lap joint:

   The two plates are overlapping each other for a certain distance. Then welded. Such welding is called fillet weld.

15. When will the edge preparation need?

If the two plates to be welded have more than 6mm thickness, the edge preparation should be carried out.

16. What are the two types of fillet weld?

i. Longitudinal or parallel fillet weld

ii. Transverse fillet weld

17. State the two types of eccentric welded connections.

i. Welded connections subjected to moment in a plane of the weld.

ii. Welded connections subjected to moment in a plane normal to the plane of the weld.

18. What are the practical applications of welded joints?

It has employed in manufacturing of machine frames, automobile bodies, aircraft, and structural works.

19. What is Tee-joint?

The two plates are arranged in T shape which means the plates are located at right angles to each other.

20. What is corner joint?

Two plates are arranged at right angles such that it forms an angle.

21. What are types of fillet weid?

i. Longitudinal or parallel fillet weld.

ii. Transverse fillet weld.

22. When will the weld deposit be weaker?

When the components are made of high carbon steel or alloy steel, the weld becomes weaker.

23. Define eccentrically loaded welded joints?

The external loaded where applied may not pass through the geometric centre in structural joints are called as eccentrically loaded joints.

24. What are the two types of stress are induced in eccentric loading of loaded joint?

i. Direct shear stress

ii. Bending shear stress.

25. State the two types of eccentric welded connections.

i. Welded connections subjected to moment in a plane of the weld.

ii. Welded connections subjected to moment in a plane normal to the plane of the weld.

26. Under what circumstances flexible couplings are used?

They are used to join the abutting ends of shafts when they are not in exact alignment. They are used to permit an axial misalignment of the shafts without under absorption of the power, which the shafts are transmitting.

27. What are the purposes in machinery for which couplings are used?

1. To provide the connection of shafts of units those are manufactured separately such as motor and generator and to provide for disconnection for repairs or alterations.
2. To provide misalignment of the shafts or to introduce mechanical flexibility.
3. To reduce the transmission of shock from one shaft to another.
4. To introduce protection against over load.

28. What are the types of Rigid coupling?

i. Sleeve, ii. Flange, iii. Clamp coupling.

29. What are the types of Flexible coupling?

i. Universal, ii. Oldham's, iii. Pushed pin type coupling.

30. What are the main functions of the knuckle joints?

It is used to transmit axial load from one machine element to other.

31. What material used for flange coupling?

Cast iron

Exercises

1. Design and make a neat dimensioned sketch of a muff coupling which is used to connect two steel shafts transmitting 40 kW at 350 r.p.m. The material for the shafts and key is plain carbon steel for which allowable shear and crushing stresses may be taken as 40 MPa and 80 MPa respectively. The material for the muff is cast iron for which the allowable shear stress may be assumed as 15 MPa.
2. Design a cast iron protective type flange coupling to transmit 15 kW at 900 r.p.m. from an electric motor to a compressor. The service factor may be assumed as 1.35. The following permissible stresses may be used:

   Shear stress for shaft, bolt and key material = 40 MPa

   Crushing stress for bolt and key = 80 MPa

   Shear stress for cast iron = 8 MPa

5

Design of Spring

Springs are elastic bodies (generally metal) that can be twisted, pulled, or stretched by some force. They can return to their original shape when the force is released. In other words it is also termed as a resilient member. The design of a spring involves several considerations to ensure it meets the desired requirements and functions effectively.

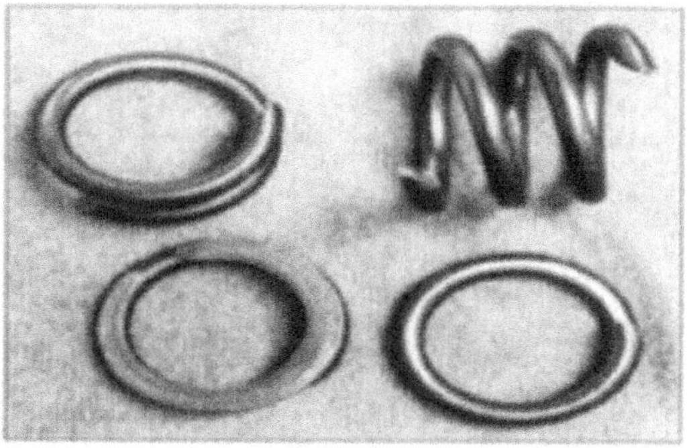

Fig. 5.1. Springs

Important Functions and Applications of Spring

1. Springs are used to absorb shocks and vibrations eg: vehicle suspension springs, railway buffers to control energy, buffer springs in elevators and vibration mounts for machinery.
2. Measuring forces : Spring balances, gages
3. Storing of energy in clocks, toys, movie cameras, circuit breakers ,starters
4. Springs are used to apply force and control motion.

5.1 Commonly Used Spring Materials

One of the important considerations in spring design is the choice of the spring material. Some of the common spring materials are given below.

- **Hard-drawn wire:** This is cold drawn, cheapest spring steel. Normally used for low stress and static load. The material is not suitable at subzero temperatures or at temperatures above 120°C.
- **Oil-tempered wire:** It is a cold drawn, quenched, tempered, and general purpose spring steel. However, it is not suitable for fatigue or sudden loads, at subzero temperatures and at temperatures above 180°C. When we go for highly stressed conditions then alloy steels are useful.
- **Chrome Vanadium:** This alloy spring steel is used for high stress conditions and at high temperature up to 220°C. It is good for fatigue resistance and long endurance for shock and impact loads.

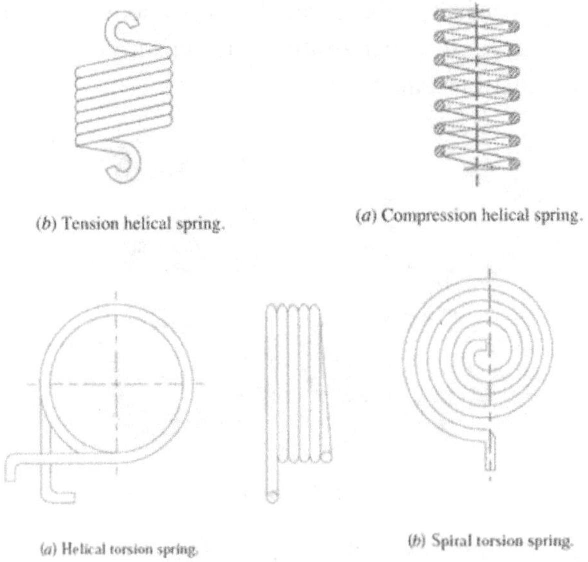

Fig. 5.2. Types of springs

- **Chrome Silicon:** This material can be used for highly stressed springs. It offers excellent service for long life, shock loading and for temperature up to 250°C.
- **Music wire:** This spring material is most widely used for small springs. It is the toughest and has highest tensile strength and can withstand repeated loading at high stresses. However, it can not be used at subzero temperatures or at temperatures above 120°C. Normally when we talk about springs we will find that the music wire is a common choice for springs.

- **Stainless steel:** Widely used alloy spring materials.
- **Phosphor Bronze / Spring Brass:** It has good corrosion resistance and electrical conductivity. That's the reason it is commonly used for contacts in electrical switches. Spring brass can be used at subzero temperatures.

5.2 Classification of Springs

1. Helical springs:
    a. Tension helical spring
        1) Open coil helical spring
        2) Closed coil helical spring
            i. Compression helical spring
            ii. Torsion spring
            iii. Spiral spring
2. Leaf springs

Tension Helical Spring

It has some means of transferring the load from the support to the body by means of some arrangement. It stretches apart to create load. The gap between the successive coils is small. The wire is coiled in a sequence that the turn is at right angles to the axis of the spring. The spring is loaded along the axis. By applying load the spring elongates in action.

5.3 Types of Springs

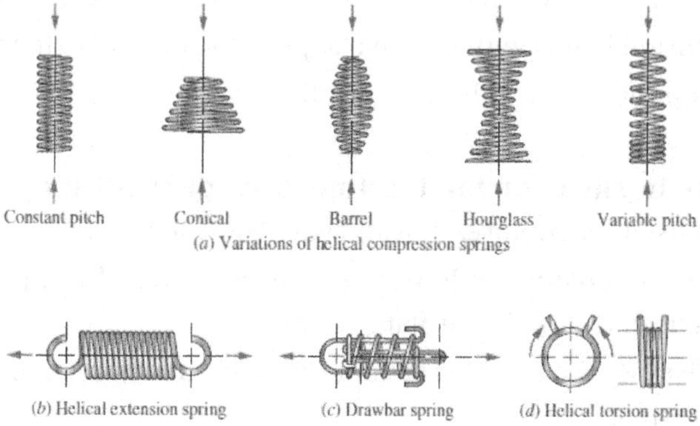

Fig. 5.3. Types of helical springs

5.4 Spring Terminologies

- **Active coils:** those coils which are free to deflect under load.
- **Buckling:** bowing or lateral displacement of a compression spring; this effect is related to slenderness ratio L/D.
- **Closed and ground ends:** same as *closed ends,* except that the first and last coils are ground to provide a flat bearing surface.
- **Closed ends:** compression spring ends with coil pitch angle reduced so that they are square with the spring axis and touch the adjacent coils.
- **Close-wound:** wound so that adjacent coils are touching.
- **Deflection:** motion imparted to a spring by application or removal of an external load.
- **Elastic limit:** maximum stress to which a material may be subjected without permanent set.
- **Endurance limit:** maximum stress, at a given stress ratio, at which material will operate in a given environment for a stated number of cycles without failure.
- **Free angle:** angular relationship between arms of a helical torsion spring which is not under load.
- **Free length:** overall length of a spring which is not under load.
- **Helical springs:** springs made of bar stock or wire coiled into a helical form; this category includes compression, extension, and torsion springs.
- **Initial tension:** a force that tends to keep coils of a close-wound extension spring closed and which must be overcome before the coils start to open.
- **Loops:** formed ends with minimal gaps at the ends of extension springs.
- **Mean diameter:** in a helical spring, the outside diameter minus one wire diameter.
- **Modulus in shear or torsion (modulus of rigidity *G*):** coefficient of stiffness used for compression and extension springs.
- **Modulus in tension or bending (Young's modulus *E*):** coefficient of stiffness used for torsion or flat springs.
- **Pitch:** distance from center to center of wire in adjacent coils in an open-wound spring.
- **Plain ends:** end coils of a helical spring having a constant pitch and with the ends not squared.

- **Plain ends, ground:** same as *plain ends,* except that wire ends are ground square with the axis.
- **Rate:** spring gradient, or change in load per unit of deflection.
- **Residual stress:** stress mechanically induced by such means as set removal, shot peening, cold working, or forming; it may be beneficial or not, depending on the spring application.

Compression helical spring

Among the four types, the plain end type is less expensive to manufacture. It tends to bow sideways when applying a compressive load.

Torsion spring

It is also a form of helical spring, but it rotates about an axis to create load. It releases the load in an arc around the axis. Mainly used for torque transmission. The ends of the spring are attached to other application objects, so that if the object rotates around the center of the spring, it tends to push the spring to retrieve its normal position.

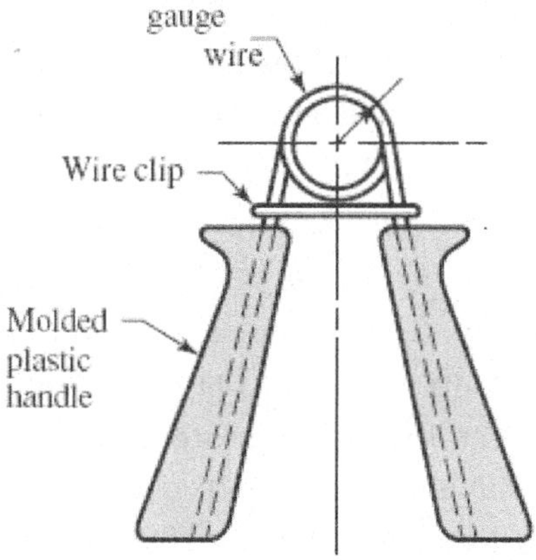

Fig. 5.4. Torsion spring

Spiral Spring

It is made of a band of steel wrapped around itself a number of times to create a geometric shape. Its inner end is attached to an arbor and outer end is attached to a retaining drum. It has a few rotations and also contains a thicker band of steel. It releases power when it unwinds.

Design Procedure of Spring

The design of a helical compression spring involves the following considerations:

- Modes of loading : whether the spring is subjected to static or infrequently varying
- load or alternating load.
- The force deflection characteristic requirement for the given application.
- Is there any space restriction.
- Required life for springs subjected to alternating loads.
- Environmental conditions such as corrosive atmosphere and temperature.
- Economy desired.

Considering these factors the designer select the material and specify the wire size, spring diameter, number of turns spring rate, type of ends, free length and the surface condition. A helical compression spring, that is too long compared to the mean coil diameter, acts as a flexible column and may buckle at comparatively low axial force.

Springs which cannot be designed buckle- proof must be guided in a sleeve or over an arbour. This is undesirable because the friction between the spring and the guide may damage the spring in the long run.

Key factors to consider when designing a spring:

1. **Load requirements:** Determine the load or force that the spring needs to support or apply. This includes considering the maximum load, minimum load, and any variations in load during operation.
2. **Spring type:** Select the appropriate type of spring based on the application requirements. Common types include compression springs, extension springs, torsion springs, and flat springs. Each type has its own characteristics and is suitable for specific applications.
3. **Material selection:** Choose a material that provides the necessary strength, durability, and resistance to fatigue and corrosion. Common spring materials include steel alloys, stainless steel, phosphor bronze, and titanium. The material selection should consider factors such as load requirements, temperature range, and environmental conditions.
4. **Wire diameter and coil dimensions:** Determine the appropriate wire diameter and coil dimensions based on the load requirements, available

space, and desired spring characteristics. The wire diameter affects the spring's strength and flexibility, while the coil dimensions determine the overall length and diameter of the spring.

5. **Spring rate:** Calculate the spring rate, also known as the spring constant, which represents the relationship between the applied force and the resulting deflection or displacement of the spring. The spring rate is determined by the material properties, wire diameter, coil dimensions, and the number of active coils.
6. **Stress and deflection analysis:** Perform stress and deflection analysis to ensure that the spring can handle the expected load without exceeding its elastic limits or causing permanent deformation. This analysis involves considering factors such as stress concentration, buckling, and fatigue life.
7. **End configurations:** Determine the appropriate end configurations for the spring, such as closed and ground ends, open ends, or various types of hooks or loops. The end configurations affect how the spring is attached or connected to other components in the system.
8. **Surface finish and treatment:** Consider the surface finish and treatment options to enhance the spring's performance and durability. This may include processes such as shot peening, heat treatment, or coating to improve fatigue resistance, corrosion resistance, or reduce friction.
9. **Testing and validation:** Conduct testing and validation to ensure that the designed spring meets the desired specifications and performance requirements. This may involve load testing, deflection testing, stress analysis, or fatigue testing.

It is important to note that designing a spring requires expertise and knowledge of engineering principles. Consulting with a professional spring manufacturer or engineer can provide valuable guidance and assistance in the design process to ensure a safe and effective spring design for the intended application.

5.5 Leaf Spring

To meet the need of natural resources conservation, automobile manufacturers are attempting to reduce the weight of vehicles in recent years. Weight reduction can be achieved primarily by the introduction of better material, design optimization and better manufacturing processes. The suspension leaf spring is one of the potential items for weight reduction in automobiles unsprang weight. This achieves the vehicle with more fuel efficiency and improved riding qualities. The introduction of composite materials was made it possible to reduce the weight of leaf spring without any reduction on load carrying capacity and stiffness Weight reduction has been the main focus of automobile manufacturers in the present scenario. The replacement of steel with optimally designed composite leaf spring can provide 92% weight reduction. Moreover the composite leaf spring has lower stresses compared to steel spring.

Sometimes it is also called as a semi-elliptical spring, as it takes the form of a slender arc shaped length of spring steel of rectangular cross section. The center of the arc provides the location for the axle, while the tie holes are provided at either end for attaching to the vehicle body. Heavy vehicles, leaves are stacked one upon the other to ensure rigidity and strength. It provides dampness and springing function.

Merits of leaf spring

- Reduced weight.
- Due to laminate structure and reduced thickness of the mono composite leaf spring, the overall weight would be less.
- Due to weight reduction, fuel consumption would be reduced.
- They have high damping capacity; hence produce less vibration and noise.
- They have good corrosion resistance

Fig. 5.5. Leaf spring

Demerits of leaf spring

- They have less specific modulus and strength. Increased weight.
- Conventional leaf springs are usually manufactured and assembled by using number of leafs made of steel and hence the weight is more.

- Its corrosion resistance is less compared to composite materials.
- Steel leaf springs have less damping capacity.

5.6 Applications of Leaf Spring

- The leaf spring acts as a linkage for holding the axle in position and thus separate linkage are not necessary. It makes the construction of the suspension simple and strong.
- As the positioning of the axle is carried out by the leaf springs so it makes it disadvantageous to use soft springs i.e. a spring with low spring constant.
- Therefore, this type of suspension does not provide good riding comfort. The inter-leaf friction between the leaf springs affects the riding comfort.
- Acceleration and braking torque cause wind-up and vibration. Also wind-up causes rear-end squat and nose-diving.
- The inter-leaf friction damps the spring's motion and reduces rebound, which until shock absorbers were widely adopted was a great advantage over helical springs.

5.7 Stresses in Helical Springs of Circular Wire

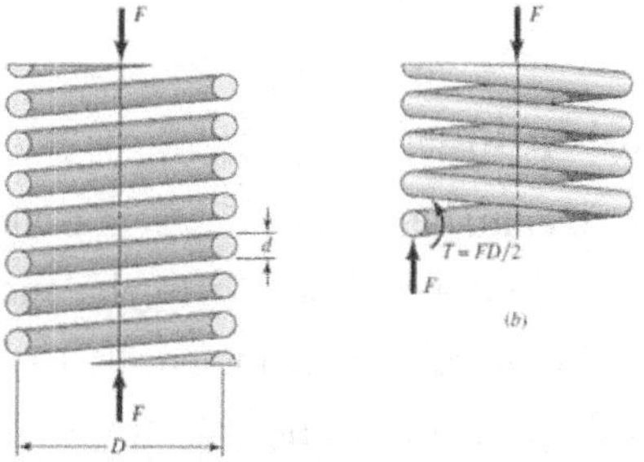

Fig. 5.6. Helical spring

$$\tau = K_S \times \frac{8WD}{\pi d^3}$$ (DB page no 7.100)

$$K_S = 1 + \frac{1}{2C}$$

$$C = \frac{D}{d}$$

Deflection of the spring 'y'

$$\delta = \frac{8wD^3n}{Gd^4}$$

D = Mean diameter of the spring coil,

d = Diameter of the spring wire,

n = Number of active coils,

G = Modulus of rigidity for the spring material,

W = Axial load on the spring,

τ = Maximum shear stress induced in the wire,

C = spring index = D/d,

p = Pitch of the coils, and

δ = Deflection of the spring, as a result of an axial load W.

Wahl's stress factor $K = \frac{4C-1}{4C-4} + \frac{0.615}{C}$ (DB page no 7.100)

Maximum shear stress induced

$$\tau = K_S \times \frac{8W.C}{\pi d^2}$$ (Take P=w)

Stiffness of the spring can be denoted by q

$\frac{W}{\delta} = \frac{G.d^4}{8D^3.n} = \frac{G.d}{8c^3.n}$ = constant

Applications of Helical Springs

- To apply forces and controlling motion, as in brakes and clutches.
- Measuring forces, as in the case of a spring balance.
- Storing energy, as in the case of springs used in watches and toys.
- Reducing the effect of shocks and vibrations in vehicles and machine foundations.

Design Problems

1) A helical spring is made from a wire of 6 mm diameter and has outside diameter of 75 mm, if the permissible shear stress is 350 Mpa and modulus of rigidity is 84 kN/mm², find the axial load which the spring can carry and the deflection per active turn.

Solution:

Given data:

Diameter of wire, d = 6 mm

Outside diameter of spring coil, D_0 = 75 mm

Shear stress, τ = 350 MPa = 350 N/mm^2

Modulus of rigidity, G = 84 kN/mm^2

Let D be the mean coil diameter

Then $D + d = D_0$

$D = D_0 - d$

$= 75 - 6$

Mean coil diameter, D= 69 mm

1) Axial Load:

$$\text{Shear stress induced in wire, } \tau = \frac{8W_1.D}{\pi d^3}\left[1 + \frac{d}{2D}\right]$$

$$350 = \frac{8W_1.69}{\pi 6^3}\left[1 + \frac{6}{2x\ 69}\right]$$

$$W_1 = \frac{350}{0.848}$$

$$= 412.735 \text{ N}$$

Axial load on spring neglecting the effect of curvature is 412.735 N

$$\text{Wahl's stress factor } K = \frac{4C-1}{4C-4} + \frac{0.615}{C}$$

$$= \frac{4x\ 11.5-1}{4x\ 11.5-4} + \frac{0.615}{C} \quad (C = \frac{D}{d} = 11.5)$$

K= 1.124

Also shear stress induced in wire

$$\tau = K \times \frac{8W_2.D}{\pi d^3}$$

$$350 = 1.124 \text{ x} \frac{8W_2.69}{\pi 6^3}$$

$$W_2 = \frac{350}{0.914} = 412.735\text{N}$$

2) Deflection per active turn $\left(\frac{\delta}{n}\right)$

Deflection per active turn, neglecting effect of curvature is given by

$$\frac{\delta}{n} = \frac{8W_2.D^3}{Gd^4}$$

$$= \frac{8x\ 382.932\ x\ (69)^3}{84\ x\ 10^3 x\ 6^4}$$

$$= 9.244 \text{ mm}$$

2) Design a leaf spring for a truck to the following specifications:

Maximum load on the springs	= 200 kN
Number of springs	= 5
Material for springs	= Chromium Vanadium steel
Permissible tensile stress	= 650 N/mm^2
Maximum number of leaves	= 11
Span of spring	= 1100 mm
Permissible deflection	= 80 mm
Young's Modulus of the spring	= 2*10^5 N/mm^2

Solution:

Bending stress on the spring = $6\ Fl \div nbt2\ \leq\ 650$

Where F=1/2 x Load on each spring

$= \frac{1}{2} \times \frac{200}{4} = 20\ kN$

$$l = \frac{1}{2} \times span = 550\ mm$$

$$nbt^2 > \frac{6Fl}{600} = \frac{6 \times 20 \times 10^3 \times 550^3}{650} = 10.154 \times 10^4$$

Deflection $\delta = \frac{6Fl}{Enbt^3} \leq 80$

i.e. $nbt^3 > \frac{6Fl^{\ 3}}{600} = \frac{6{\times}20{\times}10^3{\times}550^3}{80{\times}2{\times}10^5}$

$$nbt^3 > 1.248\ \times\ 10^6$$

$$t = \frac{nbt^3}{nbt^2} = \frac{1.248 \times 10^6}{10.154 \times 10^4} = 12.3\ mm$$

Take thickness of the leaf = 12 mm

From stress consideration, $nb > \frac{10.154 \times 10^4}{12^2} = 705$

From deflection consideration, $nb > \frac{81.248 \times 10^6}{12^3} = 722$

Solution:

Take number of leaves = 11

And breadth of leaves = 70 mm

Table 5.1: Proportions for leaf springs

Breadth of leaf mm	Diameter of centre bolt mm	Cross section of clip mm X mm	Diameter of rivet mm	Diameter of bolt mm
32 41 45 50	8 to 10	20 X 4	6	6
55 60	8 to 10	20 X 4	8	8
65 70 75 80	12 to 16	25 X 6	10	10
90 110 125	12 to 16	32 X 6	10	10

Diameter of centre bolt = 13 mm

Clip section = 25 X 6 mm

Diameter of bolt/rivet for the clip = 10 mm

3) A truck spring has 12 leaves and is supported at a span length of 1.5 metre, with a central band of 80 mm wide. A load of 7 kN is applied at the centre of spring whose permissible stress is 400 N/mm^2. The spring has a ratio of total depth of width of about 2.5. Determine the width, thickness, deflection and length of all leaves.

Solution:

Given data

Central load W = 2P = 7 KN = 7000 N , P = 3500N, Span length, $2l_1$ = 1.5 m = 1000 mm

Central band width, a = 80 mm

Effective length, 2l= $2l_1$-a = 1500 - 80 = 1420 mm

l = 1420/2 = 710 mm

Total number of leaves, n=12

Among these ten leaves, let the number of full length

Leaves, n_r = 3 and the number of graduated leaves n_g=9

Permissible stress,(σ_b) =400 N/mm²

Let t = Thickness of each leaf

b = Width of each leaf

Then, total depth/width, $\frac{nt}{b} = \frac{12t}{b} = 2.5$

$$b = \frac{12t}{2.5} = 4.8\,t$$

Assume that the leaves are not initially stressed. For such conditions usually, the full length leaves are stressed more than graduated leaves, and hence design is based on stress induced in full length leaves, which is given by

$$\sigma_{hf} = \frac{18Pl}{b\ t^2(3n_f + 2n_g)} \leq (\sigma_b)$$

$$i.e.\ \frac{18\times 3500\times 710}{4.8\ t.t^2[(3\times 3)+(2\times 9)]} \leq 400$$

$$t \geq \left[\frac{18\times 3500\times 710}{4.8\times 27\times 400}\right]^{1/3} \geq 9.52\ mm$$

Let t = 10 mm (standard thickness)

Then b = 4.8 t = 4.8 × 10 = 48 mm (standard width)

The deflection of leaf spring is given by

$$\delta = \frac{12\ Pl^3}{Eb\ t^3(3n_f+2n_g)}$$ (Assume E = Youngs modulus = 2×10^5 N / mm²)

$$= \frac{12 \times 3500 \times 710^3}{2 \times 10^5 \times 48 \times 10^3 \times [(3 \times 3) + (2 \times 9)]} = 57.99\, mm = 58\, mm$$

The length of all leaves are determined as follows

For leaf spring having 'n' leaves of which two are full length leaves and others of graduated leaves including the master leaf, the length of rth leaf from the smallest leaf is given by

Length of rth leaf = Effective length / (n-2) X r + Ineffective length

Where 'r' varies from 1 to (n-2) and (n-1)th leaf is another extra full length leaf and nth leaf be master leaf

Now length of smallest leaf , $L_1 = \frac{2l}{n-2} \times 1 + a = \frac{920}{12-2} \times 1 + 80 = 222\, mm$

Length of 2nd leaf, $L_2 = \frac{2l}{n-2} \times 1 + a = \frac{920}{12-2} \times 2 + 80 = 364\, mm$

Length of 3rd leaf, $L_3 = \frac{2l}{n-2} \times 1 + a = \frac{920}{12-2} \times 3 + 80 = 506\, mm$

Length of 4th leaf, $L_4 = \frac{2l}{n-2} \times 1 + a = \frac{920}{12-2} \times 4 + 80 = 648\, mm$

Length of 5th leaf, $L_5 = \frac{2l}{n-2} \times 1 + a = \frac{920}{12-2} \times 5 + 80 = 790\, mm$

Length of 6th leaf, $L_6 = \frac{2l}{n-2} \times 1 + a = \frac{920}{12-2} \times 6 + 80 = 932\, mm$

Length of 7th leaf, $L_7 = \frac{2l}{n-2} \times 1 + a = \frac{920}{12-2} \times 7 + 80 = 1074\, mm$

Length of 8th leaf, $L_8 = \frac{2l}{n-2} \times 1 + a = \frac{920}{12-2} \times 8 + 80 = 1216\, mm$

Length of 9th leaf, $L_9 = \frac{2l}{n-2} \times 1 + a = \frac{920}{12-2} \times 9 + 80 = 1358\, mm$

Length of 10th leaf, $L_{10} = \frac{2l}{n-2} \times 1 + a = \frac{920}{12-2} \times 10 + 80 = 1500\, mm$

Length of 11th leaf, $L_{11} = L_{10} = 1500\, mm$

Length of 12th leaf, $L_{12} = span\ length + \Pi(d + t)2$

i.e. (Master leaf) = $2l_1 + \Pi(d + t)2 = 1500 + \Pi\ (20 + 10)2$

$$= 1690\, mm$$

Where,

d = inside diameter of eye = 20 mm (assume)

t = thickness of leaf = 10 mm

Resulting design dimensions

1. Type of spring	= Leaf spring
2. Number of leaves	= 12
3. Number of full length leaves	= 3
4. Number of graduated leaves	= 9
5. Width of each leaf	= 44 mm
6. Thickness of each leaf	= 10 mm
7. Deflection of spring	= 58 mm
8. Length of leaves from smallest leaf to master leaf	= 222, 364, 506, 648, 790, 932,

(i.e. for 10 leaves)1074, 1216, 1358, 1500, 1500, 1690 mm respectively.

4) A car is provided with four leaf springs each having 10 leaves. The span length of the spring is 1.2 metre. The cross-section of the spring is 44 X 6 mm. The full load is 8500 N. The rear axle takes 62% of the load. Find the stiffness of the springs.

Solution:

Given data:

Total load acting on four springs	= 8500 N
Load shared by rear axle	= 0.62 X 8500 = 5270 N
Load shared by front axle	= 8500-5270 = 3230 N
Number of leaves in each spring, n	= 10
Width of spring, b	= 44 mm
Thickness of spring, t	= 6 mm
Span length, $2l_1$ = 1.2 m	= 1200 mm

Now, load acting on each spring of the rear axle,

$$W_\gamma = \frac{5270}{2} = 2635\ N$$

and the deflection produced in each spring of rear axle is given by,

$$\delta_\gamma = \frac{12\ P_\gamma l^3}{Eb\ \ t^3(3n_f+2n_g)}$$

where,

Pr = Load acting on each eye of the rear spring $= \frac{2635}{2} = 1317.5\ N$

l = Half of effective length, $\frac{2l_1 - a}{2}$

$= \frac{1200-80}{2} = 560mm$ (Assume, a=band width = 80 mm)

E = $2.1X10^5$ N/mm² (Assumed)

n_f = No. of extra full length leaves = 2 (Assumed)

n_g = No. of graduated leaves including master leaf $= n - n_f = 10 - 2 = 8$

Stiffness of each spring of rear axle,

$$k_\gamma = \frac{P_\gamma}{\delta_\gamma} = \frac{Ebt^3(3n_f + 2n_g)}{12l^3}$$

$$= \frac{2.1 \times 10^5 \times 44 \times 6^3 \times (3 \times 2 + 2 \times 8)}{12 \times 560^3} = 21\ N/mm$$

Similarly, the deflection produced in each spring of front axle,

$$\delta_f = \frac{12\ P_f l^3}{Eb\ \ t^3(3n_f + 2n_g)}$$

Or, the stiffness of each spring of front axle,

$$k_f = \frac{P_f}{\delta_f} = \frac{Ebt^3(3n_f + 2n_g)}{12l^3}$$

Since the spring dimensions are same for both axles, we get $k_\gamma = k_f = 21\ N/mm$

Assignment Questions

(1) A helical spring made from 6.3mm diameter steel wire has an outside diameter of 57.3mm with squared & ground ends and has 12 coils. The allowable shear stress is 827MPa. Determine the following

(i) Spring rate

(ii) Free length

(iii) Pitch

(2) The following data refers to the valve of a petrol engine

Length of the spring when the valve is open - 40mm

Length of the spring when the valve is closed - 48mm

Spring load when the valve is closed - 350N

Spring load when the valve is open - 220N

Spring index - 6.8

(3) The maximum shear stress allowed is 150MPa & the modulus of rigidity is 84GPa. The ends are squared & ground and the gap between the adjacent coils is 0.1 times the wire diameter. Determine the following

(i) Wire dia

(ii) Mean dia

(iii) Number of coils

(iv) Free length

(v) Pitch

(4) A concentric spring for an aircraft engine valve is to exert a maximum for of 5000N under an axial deflection of 40mm. Both springs have same free length and same solid length and are subjected to equal maximum shear stress of 850 MPa. If the spring index for both the spring is 6 find the load shared by each spring

i) Maximum dimension of springs

ii) No of active coils in each.

Assume G= 80 and dimensional clearance is equal to difference between the wire diameter.

(5) A semi elliptical leaf spring consists of extra length leaves and 15 graduated length leaves including the master leaf. The centre to centre distance between the 2 eyes of the spring is 1m. The maximum force that can act on the spring is 75 kN. For each leaf the ratio of width to thickness is 9:1. The modulus of elasticity of leaf material is 2x105 N/mm2. The leaves are pre-stressed in such a way that when the force is maximum the stress induced in both leaves is 450 MPa. Determine the width and thickness of leaves, the initial nip, The initial pre load required to close the gap between the extra full length and graduated leaves.

Short Questions and Answers

1. **What is a spring?**

   A spring is an elastic member, which deflects, or distorts under the action of load and regains its original shape after the load is removed.

2. **State any two functions of springs.**

   i. To measure forces in spring balance, meters and engine indicators.

   ii.To store energy.

3. **What are the various types of springs?**

   i. Helical springs ii.Spiral springs

   iii. Leaf springs iv.Disc spring or Belleville springs

4. **Classify the helical springs.**

   a. Close – coiled or tension helical spring.

   b. Open –coiled or compression helical spring.

5. **Define : Leaf springs**

   A leaf spring consists of flat bars of varying lengths clamped together and supported at both ends, thus acting as a simply supported beam.

6. **Define : Belleville Springs**

   They are made in the form of a cone disc to carry a high compressive force. In order to improve their load carrying capacity, they may be stacked up together. The major stresses are tensile and compressive.

7. **What is spring index (C)?**

   The ratio of mean or pitch diameter to the diameter of wire for the spring is called the spring index.

8. **What is pitch?**

   The axial distance between adjacent coils in uncompressed state.

9. **What is solid length?**

   The length of a spring under the maximum compression is called its solid length. It is the product of total number of coils and the diameter of wire.

   Ls = nt x d

   Where, nt = total number of coils.

10. **What are the requirements of spring while designing?**

    a. Spring must carry the service load without the stress exceeding the safe value.

    b. The spring rate must be satisfactory for the given application.

11. **What are the end conditions of spring?**

    a. Plain end. b. Plain and ground end

    c. Squared end d. Squared and ground end.

12. **What is buckling of springs?**

    The helical compression spring behaves like a column and buckles at a comparative small load when the length of the spring is more than 4 times the mean coil diameter.

13. **What is surge in springs?**
    The material is subjected to higher stresses, which may cause early fatigue failure. This effect is called as spring surge.
14. **What is a laminated leaf spring?**
    In order to increase, the load carrying capacity, number of flat plates are placed and below the other.
15. **What semi – elliptical leaf springs?**
    The spring consists of number of leaves, which are held together by U- clips. The long leaf fastened to the supported is called master leaf. Remaining leaves are called as graduated leaves.
16. **What is nipping of laminated leaf spring?**
    Prestressing of leaf springs is obtained by a difference of radii of curvature known as nipping.
17. **What are the various application of springs?**
    The springs are used in various applications, they are
    a. Used to absorb energy or shocks (e.g. shock absorbers, buffers, e.t.c.)
    b. To apply forces as in brakes clutches, spring-loaded valves, e.t.c.
    c. To measure forces as in spring balances and engine indicators
    d. To store energy as in watches
18. **Define free length.**
    Free length of the spring is the length of the spring when it is free or unloaded condition. It is equal to the solid length plus the maximum deflection or compression plus clash allowance.
    Lf = solid length + Ymax + 0.15 YMax
19. **Define spring index.**
    Spring index (C) is defined as the ratio of the mean diameter of the coil to the diameter of the wire. C =D/d
20. **Define spring rate (stiffness).**
    The spring stiffness or spring constant is defined as the load required per unit deflection of the spring.
    K= W/y Where W-load y-deflection
21. **Define pitch.**
    Pitch of the spring is defined as the axial distance between the adjacent coils in uncompressed state. Mathematically Pitch = free length/ n-1
22. **What are the points to be taken into consideration while selecting the pitch of the spring?**
    The points taken into consideration of selecting the pitch of the springs are
    a. The pitch of the coil should be such that if the spring is accidentally compressed the stress does not increase the yield point stress in torsion.
    b. The spring should not be close up before the maximum service load is reached.

23. Define active turns.

Active turns of the spring are defined as the number of turns, which impart spring action while loaded. As load increases the no of active coils decreases.

24. Define inactive turns.

Inactive turns of the spring is defined as the number of turns which does not contribute to the spring action while loaded. As load increases number of inactive coils increases from 0.5 to 1 turn.

25. What are the different kinds of end connections for compression helical springs?

The different kinds of end connection for compression helical springs are

a. Plain ends
b. Ground ends
c. Squared ends
d. Ground & square ends

26. Write about the eccentric loading of springs?

If the load acting on the spring does not coincide with the axis of the spring, then spring is said to be have eccentric load. In eccentric loading the safe load of the spring decreases and the stiffness of the spring is also affected.

27. Explain about surge in springs?

When one end of the spring is resting on a rigid support and the other end is loaded suddenly, all the coils of spring does not deflect equally, because some time is required for the propagation of stress along the wire. Thus a wave of compression propagates to the fixed end from where it is reflected back to the deflected end this wave passes through the spring indefinitely. If the time interval between the load application and that of the wave to propagate are equal, then resonance will occur. This will result in very high stresses and cause failure. This phenomenon is called surge.

28. What are the methods used for eliminating surge in springs?

The methods used for eliminating surge are

a. By using dampers on the center coil so that the wave propagation dies out

b. By using springs having high natural frequency.

29. What are the disadvantages of using helical spring of non-circular wires?

a. The quality of the spring is not good

b. The shape of the wire does not remain constant while forming the helix. It reduces the energy absorbing capacity of the spring.

c. The stress distribution is not favorable as in circular wires. But this effect is negligible where loading is of static nature.

30. Why concentric springs are used?

a. To get greater spring force with in a given space

b. To insure the operation of a mechanism in the event of failure of one of the spring

31. **What is the advantage of leaf spring over helical spring?**
    The advantage of leaf spring over helical spring is that the end of the spring may be guided along a definite path as it deflects to act a structural member in addition to energy absorbing device.
32. **Write notes on the master leaf & graduated leaf?**
    The longest leaf of the spring is known as main leaf or master leaf has its ends in the form of an eye through which bolts are passed to secure the spring. The leaf of the spring other than master leaf is called the graduated leaves.
33. **What is meant by nip in leaf springs?**
    By giving greater radius of curvature to the full length leaves than the graduated leaves, before the leaves are assembled to form a spring thus a gap or clearance will be left between the leaves. This initial gap is called nip.
34. **What is the application of leaf spring?**
    The leaf springs are used in automobiles as shock absorbers for giving suspension to the automobile and it gives support to the structure.
35. **Define flat spiral spring.**
    A flat spiral spring is a long thin strip of elastic material wound like a spiral. These springs are frequently used in watch springs, gramophones, e.t.c

6

Introduction to Belt Drives

Belt drives are a type of power transmission system that use belts to transmit rotational motion and power between two or more rotating shafts. They are commonly used in various applications, including machinery, vehicles, and industrial equipment.

- Belts are used to connect two rotating item. Usages are as source of motion (conveyors system) or as a high efficiency power transmission
- a conveyor belt is one application where the belt is adapted to continually carry a load between two points
- power transmission is achieved by specially designed belts and pulleys. The demands on a belt drive transmission system are large and this has led to many variations on the theme

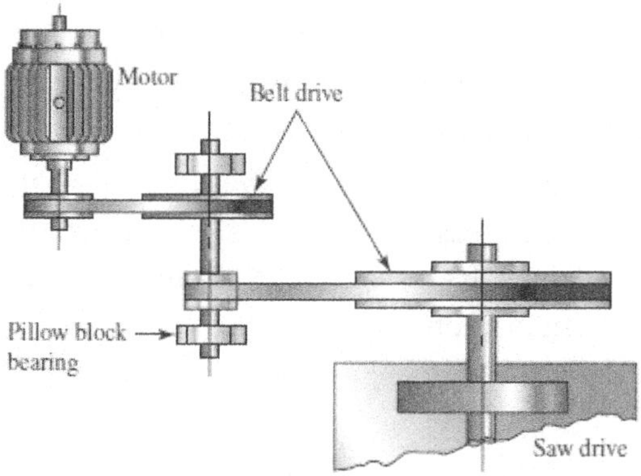

Fig. 6.1. Belt drive system

Key Aspects of Belt Drives

1. **Belt types:** Belt drives can use different types of belts, such as V-belts, flat belts, timing belts, and ribbed belts. Each type has its own design and

characteristics, making them suitable for specific applications based on factors like load, speed, and environmental conditions.

2. **Pulleys:** Belt drives consist of two or more pulleys, which are wheels with a grooved or smooth surface that the belt wraps around. The driving pulley is connected to the power source, while the driven pulley is connected to the driven shaft. The pulleys provide the necessary grip and traction to transmit power from the driving pulley to the driven pulley.
3. **Tensioning:** Proper tensioning of the belt is crucial for efficient power transmission and to prevent slippage. Belt tension can be adjusted using various methods, such as manual adjustment, spring-loaded tensioners, or automatic tensioning systems.
4. **Speed ratio:** Belt drives allow for speed ratio adjustments between the driving and driven shafts by using pulleys of different sizes. By changing the pulley diameters, the rotational speed and torque can be modified to suit the specific requirements of the application.
5. Belt drive efficiency: The efficiency of a belt drive refers to the percentage of input power that is effectively transmitted to the output. Factors such as belt type, tension, pulley design, and operating conditions can affect the overall efficiency of the belt drive system.
6. **Belt drive maintenance:** Regular maintenance is important to ensure the proper functioning and longevity of belt drives. This includes checking and adjusting belt tension, inspecting for wear or damage, and replacing worn-out belts or pulleys as needed.

Belt drives are widely used in various industries due to their versatility, ease of use, and cost-effectiveness. Proper design, selection, installation, and maintenance of belt drives are essential to ensure optimal performance and reliability in different applications.

6.1 Selection of a Belt Drives

When selecting a belt drive for a specific application, several factors need to be considered to ensure optimal performance and reliability. Here are some key factors to consider:

1. **Power requirements:** Determine the power requirements of the application, including the required torque and rotational speed. This will help determine the appropriate belt size and type that can handle the power transmission effectively.

2. **Load characteristics:** Consider the load characteristics, such as the magnitude and type of load (constant or variable), shock loads, and any potential overloads. This will help determine the required belt strength and durability.
3. **Speed ratio:** Determine the desired speed ratio between the driving and driven shafts. This will help determine the appropriate pulley sizes and belt length to achieve the desired speed ratio.
4. **Space limitations:** Consider any space limitations or constraints in the application. This includes the available space for the belt drive system, the required distance between the shafts, and any obstructions that may affect the installation or operation of the belt drive.
5. **Environmental conditions**: Evaluate the environmental conditions in which the belt drive will operate. Consider factors such as temperature, humidity, dust, chemicals, and exposure to oils or other contaminants. Select a belt material and type that can withstand these conditions without significant degradation or failure.
6. **Maintenance requirements:** Consider the maintenance requirements of the belt drive system. Some belt types may require more frequent maintenance, such as tension adjustments or periodic replacement, while others may require less maintenance. Assess the available resources and maintenance capabilities to ensure the selected belt drive is compatible with the maintenance practices of the application.
7. **Cost considerations:** Evaluate the cost-effectiveness of the belt drive system. Consider factors such as the initial cost of the belt drive components, the expected lifespan of the system, and the cost of maintenance and replacement parts. Balancing the upfront cost with the long-term reliability and performance can help determine the most cost-effective solution.
8. **Manufacturer recommendations:** Consult the manufacturer's recommendations and specifications for the specific belt drive system. Manufacturers often provide guidelines and technical information regarding the suitable belt types, pulley sizes, tensioning methods, and other considerations for different applications.

By considering these factors and consulting with belt drive manufacturers or experts, can select a belt drive system that meets the specific requirements of your application, ensuring efficient power transmission, reliability, and longevity.

The selection of a belt drive depends on several important factors, including:

1. **Speed of the driving and driven shaft:** The speed ratio between the driving and driven shafts is a crucial factor in selecting the appropriate belt drive. It determines the required pulley sizes and belt length to achieve the desired speed ratio.
2. **Power to be transmitted:** The power requirements of the application, including the required torque and rotational speed, are essential in selecting a belt drive. It helps determine the appropriate belt size and type that can handle the power transmission effectively.
3. **Space available:** The available space for the belt drive system is an important consideration. It includes factors such as the distance between the shafts, any obstructions or constraints in the application, and the overall size of the belt drive components.
4. **Centre distance between shafts:** The centre distance between the driving and driven shafts is a critical factor in selecting the appropriate belt drive. It affects the required belt length and the size of the pulleys.
5. **Service condition:** The service conditions in which the belt drive will operate play a significant role in the selection process. Factors such as temperature, humidity, dust, chemicals, and exposure to oils or other contaminants need to be considered to select a belt material and type that can withstand these conditions without significant degradation or failure.

Considering these factors will help ensure that the selected belt drive is suitable for the specific application, providing efficient power transmission, reliability, and longevity.

6.2 Types of Belts

There are several types of belt drives commonly used in various applications. Here are some of the most common types:

1. **Flat Belt Drive:** This type of belt drive uses a flat, rectangular cross-section belt to transmit power between pulleys. It is simple, cost-effective, and suitable for applications with varying center distances between shafts.
    - Simple construction
    - Low cost
    - High flexibility
    - High tolerance to overload

- Good resistance in abhrasive environments
- Sliding is possible
- Low efficiency at low speeds
- Tensioning is required

2. **V-Belt Drive:** V-belt drives use a trapezoidal cross-section belt that wedges into V-shaped grooves on the pulleys. They offer high power transmission capacity and are commonly used in automotive systems, industrial machinery, and HVAC systems.The "V" shape of the belt tracks in a mating groove in the pulley (or sheave), with the result that the belt cannot slip off.

   The belt also tends to wedge into the groove as the load increases — the greater the load, the greater the wedging action — improving torque transmission and making the vee belt an effective solution.

   For high-power requirements, two or more vee belts can be joined side-by-side in an arrangement called a multi-V, running on matching multi-groove sheaves.

   Advantages

   - Good resistance to overloads
   - Timing between sheaves may not be accurate

3. **Timing Belt Drive:** Timing belt drives use toothed belts that engage with toothed pulleys. They are used in applications that require precise synchronization of shafts, such as in engines, robotics, and conveyor systems.
4. **Ribbed Belt Drive:** Ribbed belt drives, also known as serpentine belt drives, use a belt with multiple longitudinal ribs that engage with corresponding grooves on the pulleys. They are commonly used in automotive engines to drive multiple accessories like the alternator, power steering pump, and air conditioning compressor.
5. **Round Belt Drive:** Round belt drives use round belts made of materials like rubber or urethane. They are flexible and commonly used in applications that require low power transmission, such as in light-duty machinery, conveyors, and printers.
6. **Chain Drive:** While not technically a belt drive, chain drives are often included in discussions of power transmission systems. They use a chain with interlocking links that engage with sprockets on the shafts. Chain

drives are known for their high power transmission capacity and durability, making them suitable for heavy-duty applications.

Each type of belt drive has its own advantages, limitations, and specific applications. The selection of the appropriate belt drive depends on factors such as power requirements, speed ratio, center distance between shafts, available space, and service conditions. Consulting with belt drive manufacturers or experts can provide valuable guidance in selecting the most suitable belt drive for a specific application.

Flat Belt

A flat belt is a type of belt used in belt drive systems that has a flat, rectangular cross-section. It is typically made of materials such as rubber, leather, or synthetic materials like nylon or polyurethane. Flat belts are commonly used in various applications, including industrial machinery, agricultural equipment, and automotive systems.

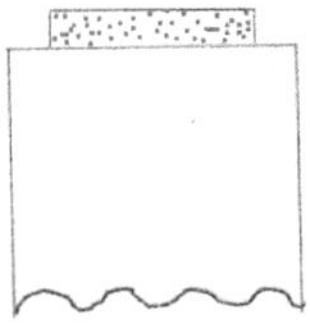

Fig. 6.2. Flat belt

Here are some key aspects of flat belts:

1. **Advantages:** Flat belts offer several advantages, including high flexibility, ease of installation, and cost-effectiveness. They can be easily adjusted and aligned, making them suitable for applications with varying center distances between shafts. Flat belts also provide smooth and quiet operation, with minimal vibration and noise.
2. **Power transmission:** Flat belts transmit power between two or more pulleys by frictional contact. The driving pulley imparts rotational motion to the belt, which then transfers the power to the driven pulley. The grip and traction between the belt and pulleys allow for efficient power transmission.
3. **Pulleys:** Flat belts require pulleys with a flat, smooth surface to ensure proper contact and grip. The pulleys are typically made of materials like cast iron, steel, or aluminum. The size and diameter of the pulleys

determine the speed ratio and power transmission capabilities of the belt drive system.

4. **Tensioning:** Proper tensioning of flat belts is crucial for efficient power transmission and to prevent slippage. Belt tension can be adjusted using methods such as manual adjustment, spring-loaded tensioners, or automatic tensioning systems. Maintaining the correct tension is important to ensure optimal performance and prevent premature wear or failure.
5. **Limitations:** Flat belts have some limitations, including limited power transmission capacity compared to other belt types like V-belts or timing belts. They are also more prone to slipping under high loads or when the tension is not properly maintained. Additionally, flat belts may require periodic replacement due to wear and fatigue.
6. **Maintenance:** Regular maintenance is important to ensure the proper functioning and longevity of flat belts. This includes checking and adjusting belt tension, inspecting for wear or damage, and replacing worn-out belts or pulleys as needed.

When selecting a flat belt, factors such as the power requirements, speed ratio, center distance between shafts, available space, and service conditions should be considered. Consulting with belt manufacturers or experts can provide valuable guidance in selecting the appropriate flat belt for a specific application.

V Belt

A V-belt, also known as a V-belt drive, is a type of belt drive system that uses a trapezoidal cross-section belt to transmit power between two or more pulleys. V-belts are commonly used in various applications, including industrial machinery, automotive systems, and HVAC systems.

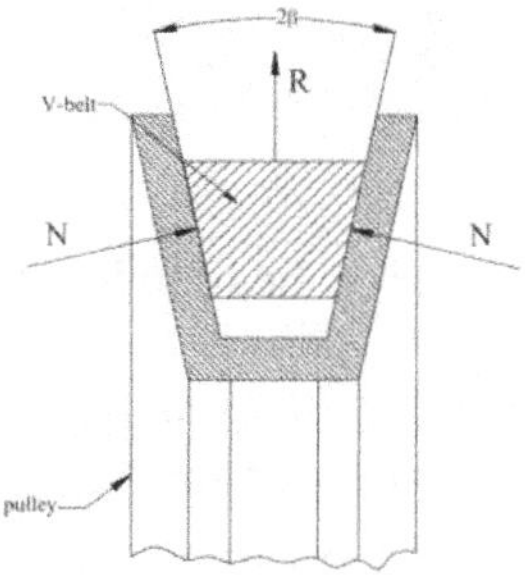

Fig. 6.3. V belt

Here are some key aspects of V-belts:

1. **Advantages:** V-belts offer several advantages, including high power transmission capacity, efficiency, and reliability. The V-shaped cross-section of the belt allows for increased contact area with the pulleys, resulting in better grip and traction. This enables V-belts to transmit higher torque and power compared to flat belts.
2. **Power transmission:** V-belts transmit power between two or more pulleys by frictional contact. The driving pulley imparts rotational motion to the belt, which then transfers the power to the driven pulley. The V-shaped cross-section of the belt wedges into the pulley grooves, creating a larger contact area and enhancing power transmission efficiency.
3. **Pulleys:** V-belts require pulleys with a V-shaped groove that matches the belt's cross-section. The pulleys are typically made of materials like cast iron, steel, or aluminum. The size and diameter of the pulleys determine the speed ratio and power transmission capabilities of the V-belt drive system.
4. **Tensioning:** Proper tensioning of V-belts is crucial for efficient power transmission and to prevent slippage. Belt tension can be adjusted using methods such as manual adjustment, spring-loaded tensioners, or automatic tensioning systems. Maintaining the correct tension is important to ensure optimal performance and prevent premature wear or failure.

Fig. 6.4. Bead belt drive

5. **Limitations:** While V-belts have high power transmission capacity, they may not be suitable for applications with high shock loads or high-speed requirements. In such cases, alternative belt types like timing belts or specialty belts may be more appropriate. Additionally, V-belts may require periodic replacement due to wear and fatigue.

6. **Maintenance:** Regular maintenance is important to ensure the proper functioning and longevity of V-belts. This includes checking and adjusting belt tension, inspecting for wear or damage, and replacing worn-out belts or pulleys as needed.

When selecting a V-belt, factors such as the power requirements, speed ratio, center distance between shafts, available space, and service conditions should be considered. Consulting with belt manufacturers or experts can provide valuable guidance in selecting the appropriate V-belt for a specific application.

Fig. 6.5. V belt

6.3 Open Belt Drive

An open belt drive is a type of belt drive system where the belt is not enclosed or covered. It consists of a belt that runs over two or more pulleys, transmitting power from the driving pulley to the driven pulley(s).

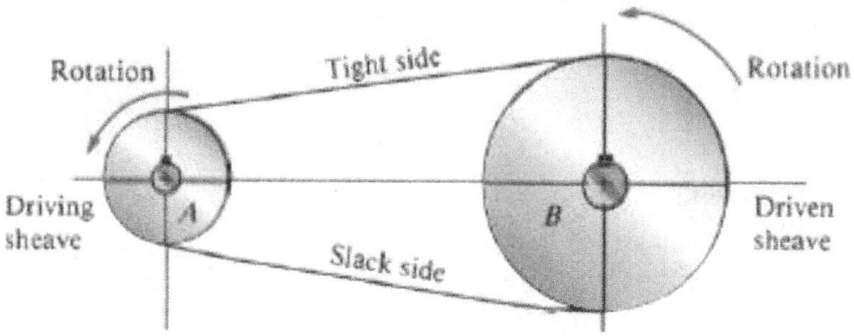

Fig. 6.6. Open belt drive

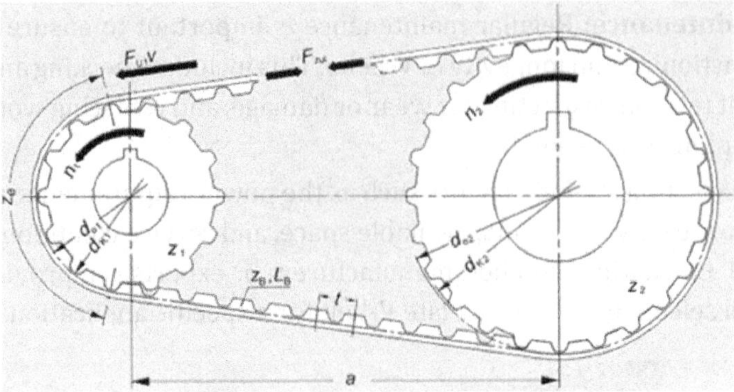

Fig. 6.7. Synchronous belt

Belts – Dynamic Considerations

The variation of the tension of a belt along the driving pulley can be expressed by the following formula:

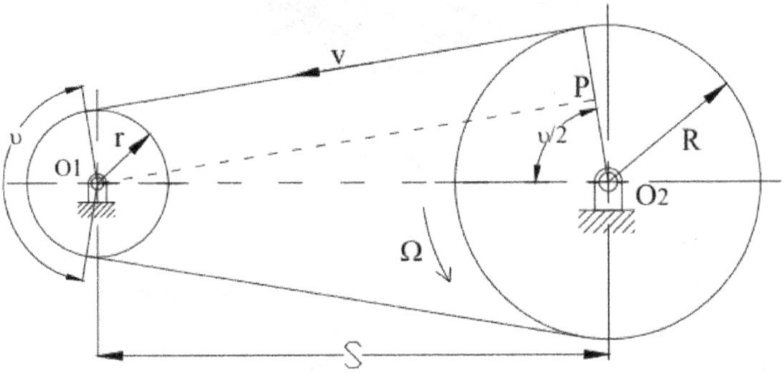

Fig. 6.8. Belt dynamics

$$\frac{T_1}{T_2} = e^{f\theta}$$

Where

T_1 = Tension at pulley entrance

T_1 = Tension at pulley exit

f = friction factor

θ = winding angle

1. **Belt and pulleys:** The open belt drive system consists of a flexible belt and two or more pulleys. The belt is typically made of materials like

rubber, leather, or synthetic materials, while the pulleys are usually made of materials such as cast iron, steel, or aluminum. The belt runs over the pulleys, creating frictional contact that allows for power transmission.

2. **Power transmission:** The driving pulley imparts rotational motion to the belt, which then transfers the power to the driven pulley(s). The grip and traction between the belt and pulleys enable the transfer of torque and power. The speed ratio between the driving and driven pulleys determines the speed and torque relationship in the system.
3. **Tensioning:** Proper tensioning of the belt is crucial for efficient power transmission and to prevent slippage. Belt tension can be adjusted using methods such as manual adjustment, spring-loaded tensioners, or automatic tensioning systems. Maintaining the correct tension is important to ensure optimal performance and prevent premature wear or failure.
4. **Advantages:** Open belt drives offer several advantages, including simplicity, ease of installation, and cost-effectiveness. They are relatively easy to adjust and align, making them suitable for applications with varying center distances between shafts. Open belt drives also provide visual inspection of the belt condition, allowing for easier maintenance and replacement.
5. **Limitations:** Open belt drives have some limitations. They are more prone to slipping compared to enclosed belt drives, especially under high loads or when the tension is not properly maintained. Open belt drives are also more susceptible to environmental factors such as dust, debris, and moisture, which can affect their performance and lifespan.
6. **Maintenance:** Regular maintenance is important for open belt drives. This includes checking and adjusting belt tension, inspecting for wear or damage, and replacing worn-out belts or pulleys as needed. Regular cleaning and lubrication may also be necessary to ensure smooth operation and prevent premature wear.

When considering an open belt drive, factors such as the power requirements, speed ratio, center distance between shafts, available space, and service conditions should be taken into account. Consulting with belt drive manufacturers or experts can provide valuable guidance in selecting and maintaining the appropriate open belt drive for a specific application.

6.4 Crossed or Twist Belt Drive

A crossed or twist belt drive is a type of belt drive system where the belt crosses over itself between the driving and driven pulleys. In this configuration, the belt forms an "X" or twist shape as it wraps around the pulleys.

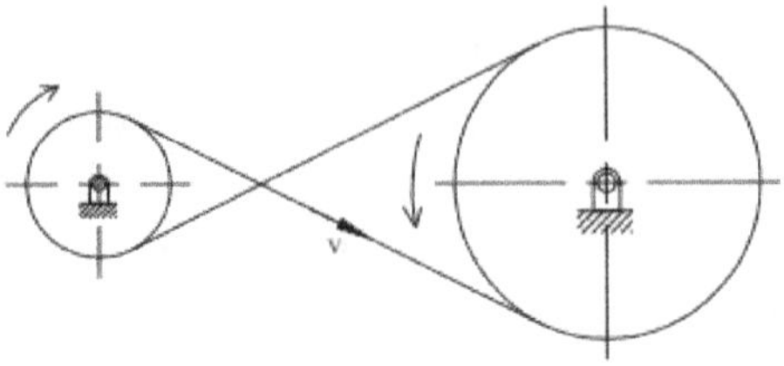

Fig. 6.9. Crossed belt drive

1. **Belt and pulleys:** The crossed or twist belt drive system consists of a flexible belt and two pulleys. The belt is typically made of materials like rubber, leather, or synthetic materials, while the pulleys are usually made of materials such as cast iron, steel, or aluminum. The belt crosses over itself between the pulleys, creating the crossed or twist configuration.
2. **Power transmission:** The driving pulley imparts rotational motion to the belt, which then transfers the power to the driven pulley. The crossed or twist configuration allows for power transmission in opposite directions, depending on the rotational direction of the driving pulley. This can be useful in certain applications where bidirectional power transmission is required.
3. **Tensioning:** Proper tensioning of the belt is crucial for efficient power transmission and to prevent slippage. Belt tension can be adjusted using methods such as manual adjustment, spring-loaded tensioners, or automatic tensioning systems. Maintaining the correct tension is important to ensure optimal performance and prevent premature wear or failure.
4. **Advantages:** Crossed or twist belt drives offer several advantages, including bidirectional power transmission capability and compact design. They can be useful in applications where the driving and driven pulleys need to rotate in opposite directions. The crossed or twist configuration also allows for a more compact layout, which can be advantageous in space-constrained environments.

5. **Limitations:** Crossed or twist belt drives have some limitations. They may have slightly lower power transmission efficiency compared to straight belt drives due to the increased bending and frictional losses at the crossover point. The crossed or twist configuration may also introduce additional stress and wear on the belt, requiring more frequent maintenance and replacement.
6. **Maintenance:** Regular maintenance is important for crossed or twist belt drives. This includes checking and adjusting belt tension, inspecting for wear or damage, and replacing worn-out belts or pulleys as needed. Regular cleaning and lubrication may also be necessary to ensure smooth operation and prevent premature wear.

When considering a crossed or twist belt drive, factors such as the power requirements, speed ratio, center distance between shafts, available space, and service conditions should be taken into account. Consulting with belt drive manufacturers or experts can provide valuable guidance in selecting and maintaining the appropriate crossed or twist belt drive for a specific application.

6.5 Belt Drive with Idler Pulley

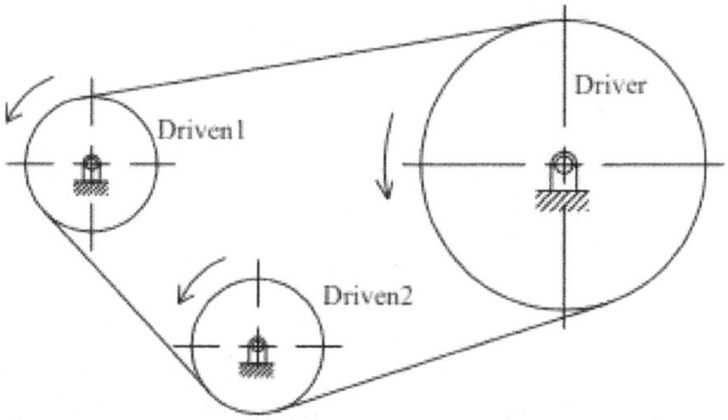

Fig. 6.10. Belt drive with idler pulley

It is the ratio between the velocities of the driver and the follower or driven. Let

D1=Diameter of the driver

D2=Diameter of the follower

N1=speed of the driver in rpm

N2=speed of the follower in rpm

$\therefore$ Length of the belt that process over the driver in one minute=$\pi d_1 N_1$

Similarly length of the belt that process over the follower in one minute=$\pi d_1 N_2$

$$\therefore L_1 = L_2$$

$$\pi D_1 N_1 = \pi D_2 N_2$$

$$\therefore Velocity\ ratio = \frac{N2}{N1} = \frac{d1}{d2}$$

When the thickness of the belt is considered, the velocity ratio $\frac{N2}{N1} = \frac{d1+t}{d2+t}$

Where `t' is thickness of the belt.

$\therefore$ Peripheral velocity of the belt on the driving pulley = v1 = $\frac{\pi d1N2}{60}$ m/s

And peripheral velocity of the belt on the driven pulley = v2 = $\frac{\pi d2N2}{60}$ m/s

$$v_{1=w_1}\ r1$$

Where w_1 =angular velocity of driven pulley

$$W_1 = \frac{\pi d2n2}{60}\ W_{2=}\frac{2\pi N2}{60}$$

If there is no slip v1=v2

$$\frac{\pi d1\ N1}{60} = \frac{\pi d2N2}{60} \text{ or } \frac{N2}{N1} = \frac{d1}{d2}$$

$$\text{ie velocity ratio} = \frac{speed\ of\ driven\ shaft}{speed\ of\ driver\ shaft}$$

$$= \frac{diameter\ of\ driver\ pulley}{diameter\ of\ driven\ pulley}$$

6.6 Slip of the Belt

Sometimes the frictional sap becomes in belt drives. This may cause some forward motion of the driven without carrying the belt with it. This is called slip of the belt and is generally expressed in percentage.

Let

S1 percentage =slip between the driven and the belt and

S2 percentage =slip between the belt and follower

$\therefore$ *velocity of the belt parring over the driver per second*

$$V = \frac{\pi d1N1}{60} - \frac{\pi d1N1}{60} \times \frac{s1}{100}$$

$$V = \frac{\pi d1N\,1}{60} - \left[1 - \frac{s1}{100}\right]$$

And velocity of the belt paring over the follower second

$$\frac{\pi d2N2}{60}=\text{v-v}\left(\frac{s2}{100}\right)$$

$$\frac{\pi d2N2}{60}=\frac{\pi d1n1}{60}\left(1-\frac{s1}{100}\right)\left(1-\frac{s2}{100}\right)$$

$$\frac{N2}{N1}=\frac{d1}{d2}\left(1-\frac{s1}{100}-\frac{s2}{100}\right)\left[\therefore\ \frac{s1xs2}{100x100}\right]$$

Neglecting

$$=\frac{d1}{d2}\left(1-\left(\frac{s1+s2}{100}\right)\right)$$

$$\frac{N2}{N1}=\frac{d1}{d2}(1-\frac{s}{100})\ (\therefore\ s1+s2=s$$

Total percentage of slip)

$$\therefore\ \frac{N2}{N1}=\frac{d1}{d2}(1-\frac{s}{100})$$

If the thickness of the belt considered

$$\frac{n2}{n1}=\frac{d1+t}{d2+t}(1-\frac{s}{100})$$

Let

r1 and r2=radii of the larger and smaller pulleys

X=distance between the centres of two pulleys (ie o1 o2)

L=total length of the belt

Length of an Open Belt Drive:

Let the belt leaves the larger pulleys at E and g and the smaller pulley at f and h as shown in figure 6.10.

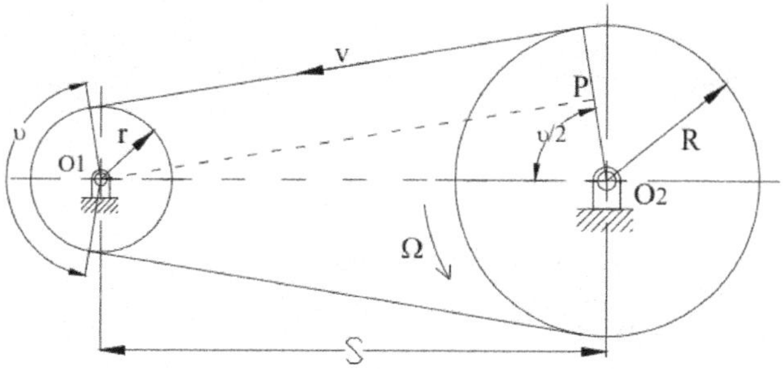

Fig. 6.10

Through o_2 draw o_2 m parallel to f

From the geometry o_2m will be l to o_1l

Let the angle mo_2 o_1 =radians

Length of the belt

$$L = Arc\ GJE + Arc + KH + HG$$

$$L = 2(Arc\ JE + EF + Arc\ FK)$$

From the geometry

$$\text{Sin} \propto = \frac{01M}{0102} = \frac{01E-EM}{0102} = \frac{r1-r2}{r}$$

Since the angle ∝ is very small therefore

$$\sin \alpha = \alpha\ in\ radians = \frac{r_1 - r_2}{x}$$

∴ Arc JE = r_1 $(\frac{\pi}{2} + \propto)$

Arc fic $= r_2$ $(\frac{\pi}{2} - \propto)$

$$EF = mo_2 = \sqrt{(O_1O_2)^2 - (O_1M)^2} =$$

$$= \sqrt{x^2 - (r_1 - r_2)^2}$$

$$EF = x\sqrt{1 - (\frac{r1-r2)}{x}}$$

Expanding this equation by trinomial theorem

$$EF = x(1-(\frac{r1-r2}{n}) + \ldots) = n - (\frac{r1-r2}{2x})^2$$

L=2 [Arc JE +EF + Arc FC]

$$= 2\left[r_1\left(\frac{\pi}{2} + \alpha\right) + x - \frac{(r_1 - r_2)^2}{2x} + r_2\left(\frac{\pi}{2} - \alpha\right)\right]$$

$$=2(r1\frac{\pi}{2} + r1\ 2 + r - \frac{r1-r2)}{2r}_2$$

$$+r2\ (\frac{\pi}{2} - \propto)$$

$$=2\left(r1\frac{\pi}{2} + R12 + r - (r1 - r2\ \right)2 + \frac{\pi}{2} - r2 \propto)$$

$$=2(\frac{\pi}{2}(r1 + r_2) + \propto (r1-r2)^2 + r2\frac{\pi}{2} - r_2 \propto)$$

$$=2(\frac{\pi}{2}(r_1+r_2) + 2(r_1-r_2) + 2n$$

L=$\pi(R1 + R2) + (R1 - r2) + 2R - (r1 - r2)^2 \rightarrow 6$

$\propto = (\frac{r1-r2)}{n}$ in 6

$$L = \pi(r_1 + r_2) + 2 \times \frac{(r_1 - r_2)}{x}(r_1 - r_2) + 2x - \frac{(r_1 - r_2)^2}{x}$$

$$= \pi\,(r_1 + r_2) + \frac{2(r_1 + r_2)^2}{x} + 2x + \frac{(r_1 + r_2)^2}{x}$$

$$L = \pi(r_1 + r_2) + 2x + 2\frac{(r_1 - r_2)^2}{x}\ (Interms\ of\ radia)$$

$$L = \frac{\pi}{2}(d_1 + d_2) + 2x + \frac{(d_1 - d_2)^2}{4x}(Interms\ of\ pulley\ dia)$$

Length of Cross Belt Drive

w.k.t length of the belt

L = Arc GJE + EF + Arc FKH + HG

$$= 2\,(Arc\,JE + EF + Arc\,FK) \qquad (1)$$

From the geometry

$$\sin\alpha = \frac{O_1M}{O_1O_2} = \frac{O_1M + EM}{O_1O_2} = \frac{r_1 + r_2}{x}$$

since α is very small

$$\sin\alpha = \alpha\ (inred\,) = \frac{r_1 + r_2}{x} \qquad (2)$$

$$\therefore Arc\,JE = r_1\left(\frac{\pi}{2} + \alpha\right) \rightarrow 3$$

$$Arc\,FK = r_2\left(\frac{\pi}{2} + \alpha\right) \rightarrow 4$$

and

$$EF = MO_2 = \sqrt{(O_1O_2)^2 - (O_1M)^2}$$

$$= \sqrt{x^2 - (r_1 + r_2)^2}$$

$$EF = x\sqrt{1 - \frac{(r_1 + r_2)^2}{x}}$$

Expanding this equation by binomial theorem.

$$EF = MO_2 = x\left[1 - \frac{1}{2}\left(\frac{r_1 + r_2}{x}\right)^2 + \cdots\right]$$

$EF = -\frac{(r_1+r_2)^2}{2x} \rightarrow 5$+++

sub 3 4 and 5 in 1 ⇒+

$$L = 2[r_1\left(\frac{\pi}{2}+\alpha\right)+x-\frac{(r_1+r_2)^2}{2x}+r_2\left(\frac{\pi}{2}+\alpha\right)]$$

$$= 2\left[r_1\times\frac{\pi}{2}+r_1\alpha+x-\frac{(r_1+r_2)^2}{2x}+r_2\alpha+r_2\frac{\pi}{2}\right]$$

$$= 2\left[\frac{\pi}{2}(r_1+r_2)+\alpha(r_1+r_2)+x-\frac{(r_1+r_2)^2}{2x}\right]$$

$$L = \pi(r_1+r_2)+2\alpha(r_1+r_2)+2x-\frac{(r_1+r_2)^2}{x} \quad \rightarrow 6$$

sub α in 6 we get

$$L = \pi\,(r_1+r_2)+2\times\frac{(r_1+r_2)}{x}(r_1+r_2)+2x-\frac{(r_1+r_2)^2}{x}$$

$$= \pi(r_1+r_2)+\frac{2(r_1+r_2)^2}{x}+2x-\frac{(r_1+r_2)^2}{x}|$$

$$L = \pi(r_1+r_2)+2x+\frac{(r_1+r_2)^2}{x} \quad - interms\ of\ radia$$

$$L = \frac{\pi}{2}(d_1+d_2)+2x+\frac{(d_1+d_2)^2}{4x} \quad interms\ of\ dia$$

Advantages

- Belt drives offer several advantages, including smooth and quiet operation, shock absorption, overload protection, and the ability to transmit power over long distances.
- They are also relatively simple to install, maintain, and replace compared to other power transmission systems.

Limitations

- Belt drives have some limitations, such as limited power transmission capacity compared to other systems like gears or chains.
- They can also experience belt slippage under high loads or when the tension is not properly maintained.
- Additionally, belt drives may require periodic belt replacement due to wear and fatigue.

Design Problems

1) A horizontal shaft running at 200 rpm is during a shaft parallel to it at 300rpm. The pulley on the driving shaft is 50 cm diameter. Find the diameter of the driven pulley under the following conditions.

a. Neglecting belt thicken

b. Taking 0.5cm for belt thickeners

c. Assuming a slip of 5% in the latter case.

Solution:

Given data

$N_1 = 200rpm$, $N_2 = 300rpm$, $S = 5\%$, $d_1 = 50cm$

To find: d_2

1. Neglect ion belt thickness

$$\frac{N_2}{N_1} = \frac{d_1}{d_2} \qquad \therefore d_2 = \frac{N_1 d_1}{N_2} = \frac{200 \times 50}{300} = 33.33\ cm$$

2. Considering the belt thickener

$$\text{we have } \frac{N_1}{N_2} = \frac{d_1 + t}{d_2 + t}$$

$$d_2 + 0.05 = (0.05 + 50) \times \frac{200}{300}$$

$$d_2 = 33.17cm$$

3. Considering slip and belt thickness

$$\frac{N_2}{N_1} = \frac{d_1 + t}{d_2 + t}\left(1 - \frac{S}{100}\right)$$

$$d_2 + t = \frac{N_1}{N_2} \times (d_2 + t)\left(1 - \frac{S}{100} S\right)$$

$$d_2 + 0.5 = \frac{200}{300}(50 + 0.5)(1 - 0.05)$$

$$\div \quad d_2 = 31.48\ cm$$

2) An engine running at 150 rpm driver a line shaft by means of a belt. The engine pulley shaft is 75cm diameter and pulley on the line shaft is 45cm. A 90cm diameter pulley on the line shaft drives a 15cm diameter pulley keyed to a dynamo shaft. Find the speed of the dynamo shaft, when

1. These is no slip
2. These is a slip of 2% at each drive.

Solution:

$N_1=150rpm$, $N_2=N_3=?$ $d_1=75cm$, $d_2=45cm$, $d_3=90cm$, $d_4=15cm$.

To find $N_4=?$

1. When these is no slip

$$\frac{N_2}{N_1} = \frac{d_1}{d_2}$$

$$N_2 = N_1 \times \frac{d_1}{d_2} = 150 \times \frac{75}{45}$$

$$N_2 = 250rpm$$

$$\therefore N_2 = N_3 \qquad Also\ \frac{N_4}{N_3} = \frac{d_3}{d_4}$$

$$N_4 = N_3 \times \frac{d_3}{d_4} = 250 \times \frac{90}{15}$$

$$N_4 = 1500rpm$$

2. When there is 2% slip

$$\frac{N_2}{N_1} = \frac{d_1}{d_2}\left(1 - \frac{S}{100}\right)$$

$$N_2 = N_1 \times \frac{d_1}{d_2}\left(1 - \frac{S}{100}\right) \rightarrow A$$

$$N_2 = 245rpm$$

$$N_3 = N_2 = 245rpm$$

Also $\frac{N_4}{N_3} = \frac{d_3}{d_4}\left(1 - \frac{S}{100}\right)$

$$N_4 = N_3 \times \frac{d_3}{d_4}\left(1 - \frac{S}{100}\right)$$

$$= 245 \times \frac{90}{15}\left(1 - \frac{2}{100}\right)$$

$$N_4 = 1440.6rpm$$

3) Two parallel shaft 6 meters apart are provided with 60cm and 80 cm diameter pulley and are connected by means of a cross belt . The direction of rotation of the follower pulley is to be reversed by changing over to an open belt drive. How much length of the belt has to be reduced?

Solution:

Given data

$d_1 = 80cm$, $r_1 = 40cm$, $d_2 = 60cm$, $r_2 = 30cm$
$x = 6m = 600cm$

To find

Change in length of belt

Length of cross belt $=\pi(r_1+r_2)+\frac{(r_1+r_2)^2}{x}+2x$

$$=\pi(40+30)+\frac{(40+30)^2}{600}+2\times600$$

$$=1428.08cm$$

Length of cross belt = $(r1+r2)+\frac{(r1+r2)}{2}+2n$

$$=(40+30)+\frac{(40+30)}{600}+2x600$$

$$=1428.08cm$$

Length of open belt = $\pi(r1+r2)+\frac{(r1-r2)2}{2}+2n$

= 1428.08cm

Length of belt to be reduced =1428.08-1420.08

Change in length =8cm

4) An engine running at 150 rpm driven a line shaft by means of a belt. The engine pulley shafts is 75cm diameter and pulley on the line shaft is 45cm.A 90cm diameter pulley on the line shafts driven a 15cm diameter pulley keyed to a dynamo shafts .find the speed of the dynamo shaft, when.

(1) There is no slip

(2)There is a slip of 2 percentage at each drive

Solution:

Given data:

N1=150rpm, N2=N3=? d1=75cm, d2=45cm, d3=90cm, d4=15cm

To find N_4=?

1) When there is no slip:

$$\frac{N2}{N1}=\frac{d1}{d2}$$

$$N2=N1x\frac{d1}{d2}=150\text{ x }\frac{75}{45}$$

N2 = 250rpm

$\therefore$ N2 = N3 also $\frac{N4}{N3}=\frac{d3}{d4}$

$$N4 = N3x\frac{d3}{d4} = 250\ x\frac{90}{15}$$

$$N4 = 1500rpm$$

2) When there is 2 percentage slip

$$\frac{N2}{N1} = \frac{d1}{d2}(1-\frac{s}{100})$$

$$N2 = N1\ x\frac{d1}{d2}(1-\frac{s}{100})$$

$$N2 = 245\text{rpm}$$

5) The initial tension in a belt drive is found to be 600 N and the ratio of frictions 1.8. The mass of the belt is 0.8 kg/m length. Determine (i) the velocity of the belt for maximum power transmission (ii) tension on the tight side of the belt when it is started (iii) tension on the tight side of the belt when running at maximum speed.

Solution:

From equation, for maximum power transmission with consideration of initial tension,

a) $v = \sqrt{\frac{T_O}{3\,m}} = \sqrt{\frac{600}{3\,x\,0.8}} = 15.8\ \text{m/s}$

b) Tension on the tight side of the belt when it is started

$T_1 = \frac{2kT_0}{k+1} = \frac{2\,x\,1.8x\,600}{1.8+1} = 771.4\ \text{N}$

c) Tension on the tight side of the bet when running at maximum speed centrifugal tension = $mv^2 = 0.8x\ 15.8^2 = 199.7$ N

d) Initial tension $T_0\ = \frac{T_1+T_2}{2} + T_C$

$600 = \frac{T_1+\left(\frac{T_1}{1.8}\right)}{2} + 199.7$

$= 514.6$ N

e) It can also be found by applying the relation

$T_1 = \frac{2k(T_0 - T_C)}{k+1} = = \frac{2\,x\,1.8\,(600 - 199.7)}{1.8+1} = 514.6\ \text{N}$

6.7 Chain Drives

Chain drives are a type of power transmission system that use a chain to transmit power between two or more sprockets as shown in figure 6.12. Here are some key aspects of chain drives:

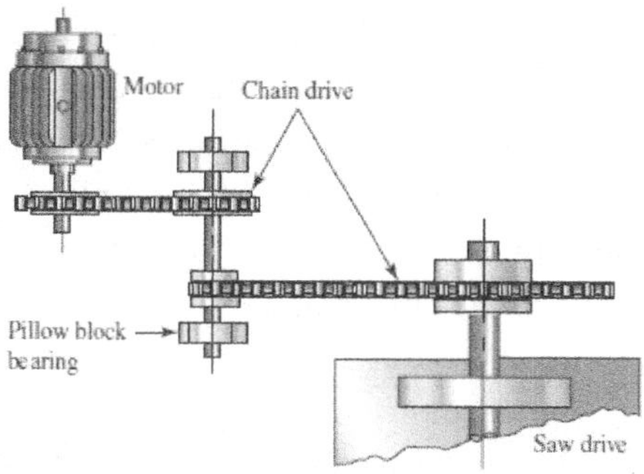

Fig. 6.12. Chain drive system

1. **Chain and sprockets:** Chain drives consist of a chain and two or more sprockets. The chain is made up of interlocking links, typically made of metal, and the sprockets are toothed wheels with grooves that engage with the chain. The chain runs over the sprockets, creating a positive engagement that allows for power transmission.

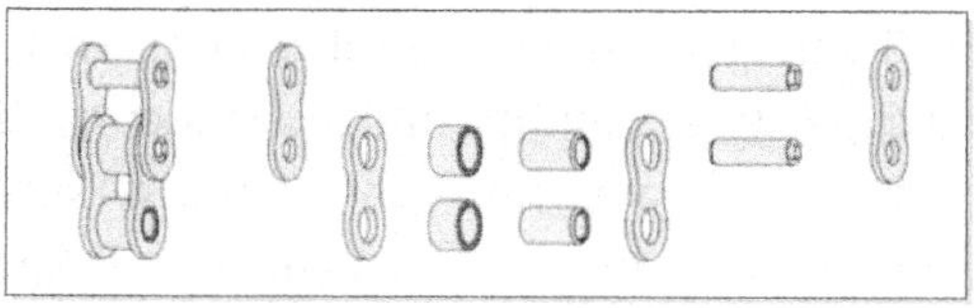

Fig. 6.13. Chain

2. **Power transmission:** The driving sprocket imparts rotational motion to the chain, which then transfers the power to the driven sprocket(s). The teeth on the sprockets mesh with the chain links, creating a positive drive that allows for high power transmission capacity. Chain drives are known for their durability and ability to handle heavy loads.

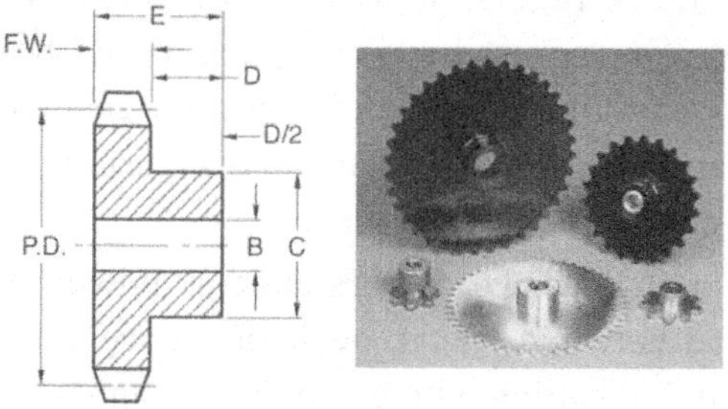

Fig. 6.14. Chain drive sprocket

3. **Types of chains:** There are different types of chains used in chain drives, including roller chains, silent chains, and leaf chains. Roller chains are the most common type and consist of cylindrical rollers that engage with the sprocket teeth. Silent chains use toothed links that engage with the sprockets without the need for rollers. Leaf chains have flat, leaf-shaped links that engage with the sprockets.

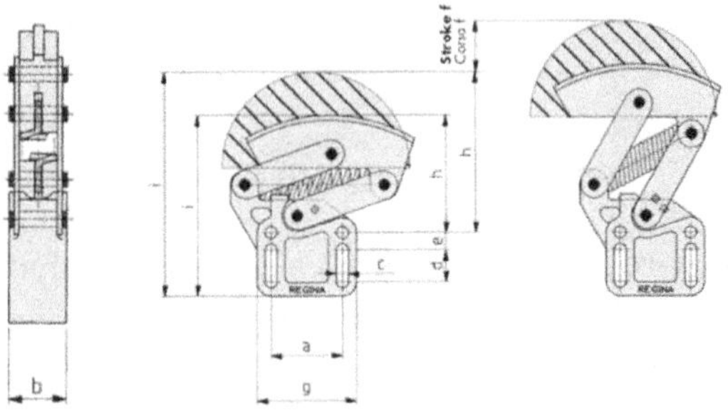

Fig. 6.15. Chain drive tensioners

4. **Advantages:** Chain drives offer several advantages, including high power transmission capacity, durability, and resistance to shock loads. They are commonly used in heavy-duty applications, such as in industrial machinery, motorcycles, bicycles, and conveyors. Chain drives also have the ability to transmit power over long distances.
5. **Maintenance:** Regular maintenance is important for chain drives to ensure optimal performance and longevity. This includes lubrication to reduce friction and wear, periodic inspection for wear or damage, and proper tensioning of the chain. Chain tension can be adjusted using tensioners or by adjusting the position of the sprockets.
6. **Limitations:** Chain drives have some limitations. They can generate noise and require regular lubrication to minimize friction and wear. Chain drives also require proper alignment and tensioning to prevent premature wear and failure. Additionally, chain drives may not be suitable for applications where cleanliness is critical, as they can generate debris and require regular cleaning.

When selecting a chain drive, factors such as power requirements, speed ratio, center distance between shafts, available space, and service conditions should be considered. Consulting with chain drive manufacturers or experts can provide valuable guidance in selecting and maintaining the appropriate chain drive for a specific application.

Fig. 6.16. Chain drive

Chain = sequence of inner link and pin link articulated to form a flexible device for power transmission

Main parameters:

- Pitch: distance between two consecutive pins
- Roller diameter: dimension of the outside diameter of the chain rollers
- Inside width: distance between the two opposite inner sides of the inner link plates

6.8 Chain Drives – Layout

While belts can be used on 3D paths, chain only works on planar paths

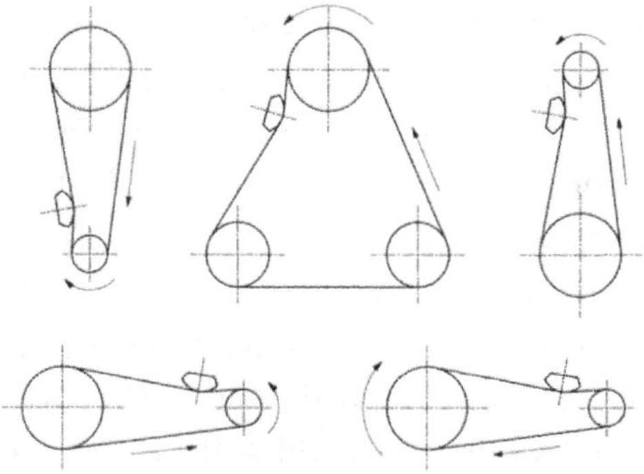

Fig. 6.17. Chain drives layout

6.9 Chain Drives – Dynamic

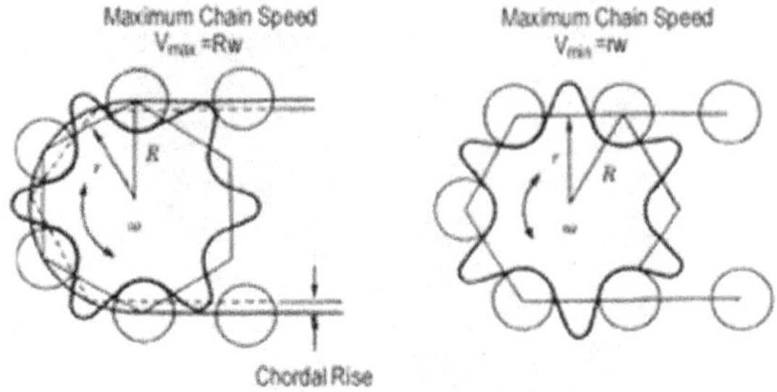

Fig. 6.18

6.10 Applications of Chain Drive

Fig. 6.19. Chain applications

6.11 Rope Drive

A rope drive, also known as a belt and rope drive or a cord drive, is a type of power transmission system that uses a flexible rope or cord to transmit power between pulleys. Here are some key aspects of rope drives:

1. **Rope or cord:** Rope drives use a flexible rope or cord made of materials such as cotton, nylon, or synthetic fibers. The rope is typically round or flat in cross-section and can be made of multiple strands twisted together for added strength.
2. **Pulleys:** Rope drives consist of two or more pulleys, also known as sheaves. The pulleys have grooves or channels that guide and grip the rope, allowing for power transmission. The driving pulley imparts rotational motion to the rope, which then transfers the power to the driven pulley(s).

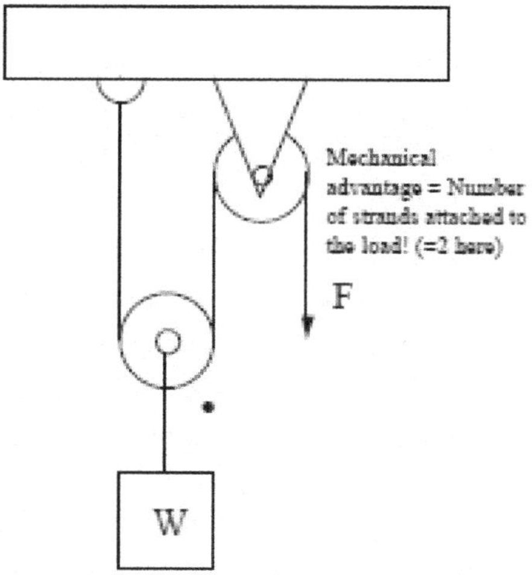

Fig. 6.20. Mechanical advantage

3. **Power transmission:** The rope wraps around the pulleys, creating frictional contact that allows for power transmission. The grip and traction between the rope and pulleys enable the transfer of torque and power. Rope drives are commonly used in applications where flexibility and shock absorption are required.

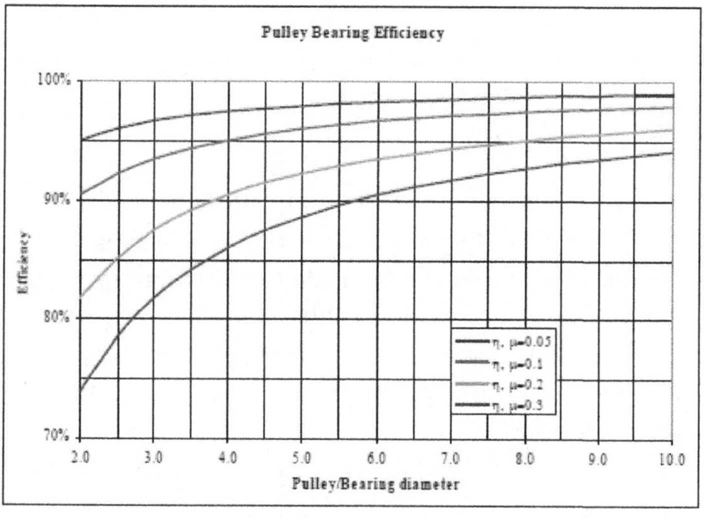

Fig. 6.21. Pulley bearing efficiency

4. **Maintenance:** Regular maintenance is important for rope drives. This includes checking and adjusting rope tension, inspecting for wear or damage, and replacing worn-out ropes as needed. Regular cleaning and lubrication may also be necessary to ensure smooth operation and prevent premature wear.

Rope drives are less commonly used today compared to other types of drives like belt or chain drives. However, they can still be found in certain applications, such as in agricultural machinery, vintage machinery, and some industrial equipment.

When considering a rope drive, factors such as power requirements, speed ratio, center distance between shafts, available space, and service conditions should be taken into account. Consulting with drive system manufacturers or experts can provide valuable guidance in selecting and maintaining the appropriate rope drive for a specific application.

6.12 Types of Ropes

The rope drives use the following two types of ropes

1. Fibre ropes
2. Wire ropes

The fibre ropes operate successfully when the pulleys are about 60 metres apart.

While the wire ropes are used when the pulleys are up to 150 metres apart.

While the wire ropes are used when the pulleys are up to 150 metres apart.

6.13 Fibres Ropes

Fiber Ropes: Fiber ropes are made from natural or synthetic fibers and are commonly used in various applications. Here are some key aspects of fiber ropes:

1. **Materials:** Fiber ropes can be made from natural fibers such as cotton, hemp, or sisal, or synthetic fibers such as nylon, polyester, or polypropylene. The choice of material depends on the specific application requirements, including strength, durability, and resistance to environmental factors.
2. **Construction:** Fiber ropes are typically constructed by twisting or braiding multiple strands of fibers together. The number of strands and the twisting or braiding pattern can vary, affecting the rope's strength, flexibility, and other properties.

3. **Applications:** Fiber ropes have a wide range of applications, including marine and boating, construction, agriculture, towing, and general-purpose use. They are often used for lifting, pulling, securing, and other tasks that require strength and flexibility.
4. **Advantages:** Fiber ropes offer several advantages, including good strength-to-weight ratio, flexibility, and ease of handling. They are generally less expensive than wire ropes and are resistant to corrosion. Fiber ropes also provide good shock absorption and are less likely to cause damage to the objects they come into contact with.
5. **Limitations:** Fiber ropes have some limitations. They may have lower tensile strength compared to wire ropes, making them less suitable for heavy-duty applications. Fiber ropes can also be susceptible to degradation from UV exposure, moisture, and chemicals, which can affect their strength and lifespan. Regular inspection and maintenance are necessary to ensure their safe and reliable use.

6.14 Wire Ropes

Wire ropes are made from multiple strands of metal wires twisted together to form a strong and flexible structure. Here are some key aspects of wire ropes:

1. **Construction:** Wire ropes are typically constructed by twisting multiple strands of steel wires together. The individual wires are helically laid around a central core, forming a rope-like structure. The number of strands and wires per strand can vary, depending on the desired strength and flexibility.
2. **Applications:** Wire ropes are commonly used in heavy-duty applications that require high strength and durability. They are widely used in industries such as construction, mining, oil and gas, cranes and hoists, elevators, and marine applications. Wire ropes are suitable for lifting, pulling, towing, and other tasks that involve heavy loads.
3. **Advantages:** Wire ropes offer several advantages, including high tensile strength, durability, and resistance to abrasion and crushing. They can withstand heavy loads and provide reliable performance in demanding environments. Wire ropes also have good resistance to UV exposure and can handle high temperatures.
4. **Limitations:** Wire ropes have some limitations. They can be more expensive than fiber ropes and require specialized tools and techniques

for installation and maintenance. Wire ropes are also susceptible to corrosion, especially in marine or corrosive environments. Regular inspection, lubrication, and replacement of worn-out wires are necessary to ensure their safe and reliable use.

When selecting between fiber ropes and wire ropes, factors such as the specific application requirements, load capacity, environmental conditions, and budget should be considered. Consulting with rope manufacturers or experts can provide valuable guidance in selecting the most suitable rope for a specific application.

Advantages:

Rope drives offer several advantages, including flexibility, shock absorption, and the ability to transmit power over long distances. They can accommodate misalignment between pulleys and are suitable for applications where vibration or shock loads are present. Rope drives also provide a smooth and quiet operation.

- They give smooth steady and quiet service
- The power maybe taken off in any direction
- They give high mechanical efficiency
- They are little affected by the outdoor condition.
- These are lighter in weight

6.15 Classification of Wire Ropes

According to the direction of twist of the individual wires and that of strands relative to each other the wire ropes may classified as follows

1. Cross (or) regular lay ropes
2. Parallel (0r) Long lay ropes
3. Composite (or) reverse laid ropes

1) Cross (or) regular lay ropes:

In these types of ropes the direction of twist of wires in the strands is opposite to the direction of twists of the strands.

2) Parallel (or) Lang lay ropes:

In these types of ropes the direction of twist of the wires in the strands is same as that of strands in the rope as shown in figure. These ropes have better because surface but is harder to splice and twists more easily when loaded. These ropes are more flexible and resists wear more effectively. Since such ropes have the tendency to spin therefore these are used in lifts and hoists with guide ways.

3) Composite (or) reverse laid ropes:

In these types of ropes the wires in the two adjacent strands are twisted in the opposite direction as shown in figure.

Transmissions – Summary

Characteristic	Friction wheel	Spur gears	Flat belts	Trapezoidal belts	Toothed belts	Chains
Max power [kW]	80	80e3	200	350	120	400
Max torque [kNm]	5	7000	3	5	1	40
Max linear speed [m/s]	20	20	100	30	60	10
Efficiency	0.95	0.97	0.97	0.97	0.96	0.95
Power function os speed	y	n	y	y	y	y
Max ratio (1 stage)	6-18	6-10	6-8	6-10	6-10	6-10
Tensioning required	y	n	y	y	n	n
Load on bearing	high	low	high	high	low	low
Build precision	average	high	low	low	low	average
Presence of sliding	y	n	y	y	n	n
Noise	low	average	low	low	low	high
Overload limiter	y	n	y	y	n	n
Cost	low	high	low	average	average	average

Fig. 6.22

7

Introduction to Brake

The design of a brake system involves various components and considerations to ensure effective and reliable braking. A disc brake is a type of brake that uses the calipers to squeeze pairs of pads against a disc or a "rotor" to create friction. This action slows the rotation of a shaft, such as a vehicle axle, either to reduce its rotational speed or to hold it stationary. The energy of motion is converted into waste heat which must be dispersed.

The most fundamental difference between traditional rim brakes and disc brakes is where the braking forces are applied. Rim brakes clamp directly on to the sides of the wheel rim itself. In this way, the rim serves as a main structural component of the wheel, the mounting base for the tyre and the braking surface all in one. In contrast, disc brakes move all braking duties to a separate rotor that is much smaller in diameter and mounted directly to the hub - much like everyday automobiles or motorcycles, and pretty much all other wheeled vehicles. The brake caliper is still mounted to the frame and fork but is situated much closer to each wheel axle.

Another key difference is how each type of brake is usually operated. With a few rare exceptions, rim brakes are 'cable-actuated', meaning the levers are connected to the caliper with braided steel cables that slide through some sort of housing. Disc brakes are more often than not of the fully hydraulic variety, where the cable and housing are replaced by a non-compressible fluid and a hose in a fully sealed system. When you pull the lever on a hydraulic brake, it pushes a plunger in a 'master cylinder', which then pushes that fluid through a hose to the caliper at the other end. That hydraulic pressure is what pushes the caliper pistons out and clamps the pads onto the rotor.

The disc is usually made of cast iron, but may in some cases be made of composites such as reinforced carbon–carbon or ceramic matrix composites. This is connected to the wheel and/or the axle. To slow down the wheel, friction material in the form of brake pads, mounted on the brake caliper, is forced mechanically, hydraulically, pneumatically, or electromagnetically against both sides of the disc. Friction causes the disc and attached wheel to slow or stop.

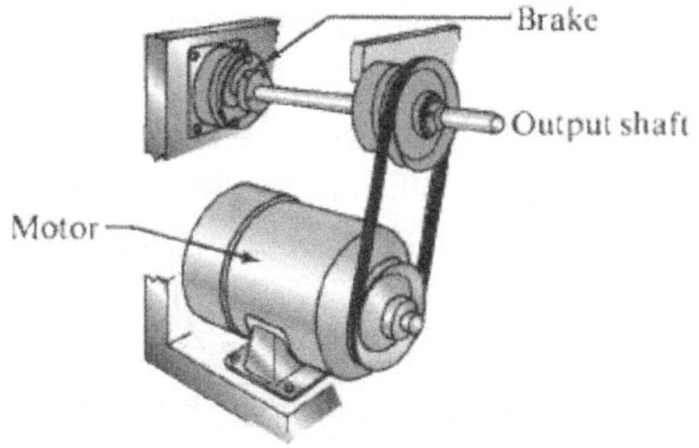

Fig. 7.1. Brake applications

While there are different types of brakes used in different applications, here are some key aspects of brake design:

1. **Brake Mechanism:** The brake mechanism converts the kinetic energy of a moving object into heat energy through friction. Common brake mechanisms include disc brakes, drum brakes, and calliper brakes. The choice of mechanism depends on factors such as the application, load requirements, and space constraints.
2. **Friction Material:** The friction material, often referred to as brake pads or brake shoes, is a critical component that provides the necessary friction to stop or slow down the moving object. The friction material is typically made of a composite material that can withstand high temperatures, provide consistent friction performance, and have good wear resistance.
3. **Actuation System:** The actuation system applies force to the friction material to engage the brake. It can be hydraulic, mechanical, or pneumatic, depending on the specific application. Hydraulic systems are commonly used in automotive brakes, while mechanical systems are used in applications where hydraulic or pneumatic systems are not feasible.
4. **Cooling and Heat Dissipation:** Braking generates heat, and effective cooling and heat dissipation are essential to prevent brake fade and maintain braking performance. Brake systems may incorporate cooling

fins, ventilation channels, or even active cooling mechanisms such as air ducts or cooling fans to dissipate heat efficiently.

5. **Control and Modulation:** Brake systems often include mechanisms for control and modulation of braking force. This allows for precise and gradual application of the brakes, preventing sudden stops or skidding. Anti-lock braking systems (ABS) and electronic brake force distribution (EBD) are examples of advanced control systems used in modern vehicles.
6. **Safety Features:** Brake systems may incorporate safety features such as parking brakes, emergency brakes, or fail-safe mechanisms to ensure that the brakes can be engaged even in the event of a failure in the primary braking system.
7. **Maintenance and Serviceability:** Brake systems should be designed for ease of maintenance and serviceability. This includes features such as accessible brake components, easy replacement of brake pads or shoes, and clear indicators for wear or damage.

When designing a brake system, factors such as the required braking force, operating conditions, temperature range, and expected lifespan should be considered. Compliance with relevant safety standards and regulations is also crucial. Consulting with brake system manufacturers or experts can provide valuable guidance in designing an effective and reliable brake system for a specific application.

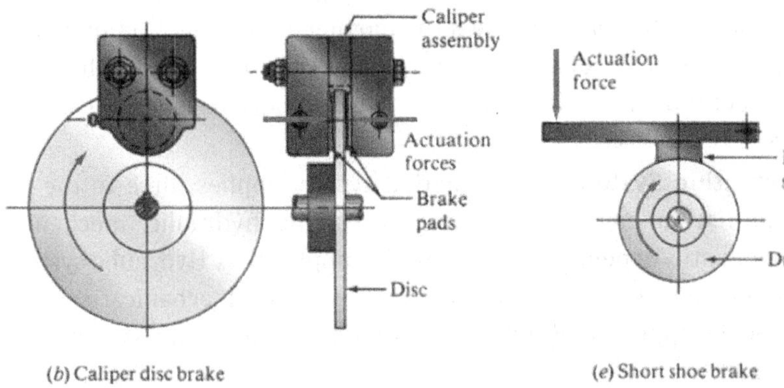

Fig. 7.2. Disc and shoe brake

7.1 Types of Brakes

There are several types of brakes used in various applications, each with its own advantages and characteristics. Here are some common types of brakes:

1. **Disc Brakes:** Disc brakes use a rotating disc (rotor) and callipers to apply friction and stop the rotation of a wheel or shaft. The callipers contain brake pads that clamp onto the disc when the brakes are applied. Disc brakes are commonly used in automotive applications due to their excellent heat dissipation and consistent braking performance.
2. **Drum Brakes:** Drum brakes consist of a rotating drum and brake shoes that press against the inner surface of the drum to create friction and slow down or stop the rotation. Drum brakes are often used in applications where cost, simplicity, and space constraints are important factors, such as in some rear wheels of automobiles and in industrial machinery.
3. **Calliper Brakes:** Calliper brakes are a type of disc brake where the calliper contains one or more pistons that push the brake pads against the disc. They are commonly used in bicycles, motorcycles, and some automotive applications. Calliper brakes can be either mechanical (cable actuated) or hydraulic (fluid actuated).
4. **Drum-in-Hat Brakes:** Drum-in-hat brakes, also known as internal expanding brakes, are a combination of drum and disc brakes. They have a small drum brake integrated into the center of a disc brake rotor. This design is often used in some automotive applications, particularly for parking brakes.
5. **Electromagnetic Brakes:** Electromagnetic brakes use the principle of electromagnetism to generate braking force. When the electromagnetic field is activated, it creates a magnetic force that attracts or holds the brake disc or rotor, causing it to slow down or stop. Electromagnetic brakes are commonly used in industrial machinery, elevators, and some automotive applications.
6. **Hydraulic Brakes:** Hydraulic brakes use hydraulic fluid to transmit force from the brake pedal to the brake mechanism. They are commonly used in automotive applications due to their ability to provide high braking force and consistent performance. Hydraulic brakes can be found in disc brakes, drum brakes, and other brake types.

7. **Regenerative Brakes:** Regenerative brakes are a type of braking system commonly used in electric and hybrid vehicles. They convert the kinetic energy of the vehicle into electrical energy, which is then stored in a battery for later use. This helps to improve energy efficiency and extend the range of electric vehicles.

These are just a few examples of brake types, and there are many other specialized brakes used in specific applications. The selection of the appropriate brake type depends on factors such as the application requirements, load conditions, space constraints, and desired performance characteristics.

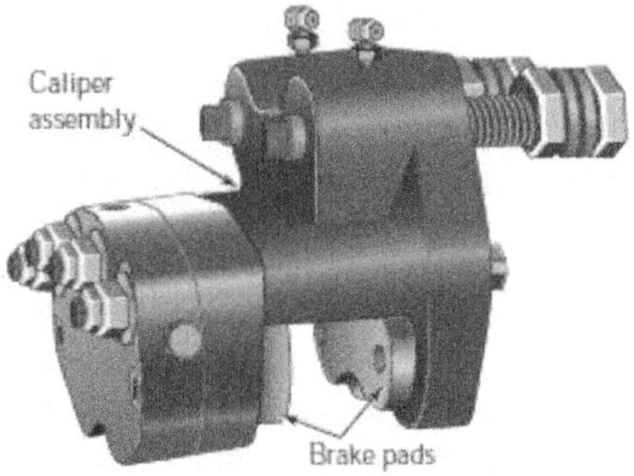

Fig. 7.3. Schematic diagram of Disc brake

7.2 Hydraulic Brakes

Modern cars use hydraulic brakes. In a hydraulically actuated system, the cables or rods of the mechanical system are replaced by fluid-filled lines and hoses. The brake: pedal linkage operates a piston in a ***master cylinder*** to pressurize the fluid inside the lines and hoses. Fluid pressure in each wheel cylinder forces the friction material against the drum or rotor.

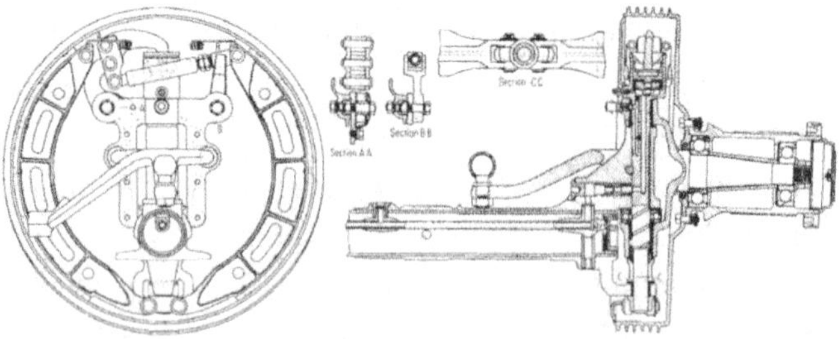

Fig. 7.4. Hydraulic brake

7.3 Single Block (or) Shoe Brake

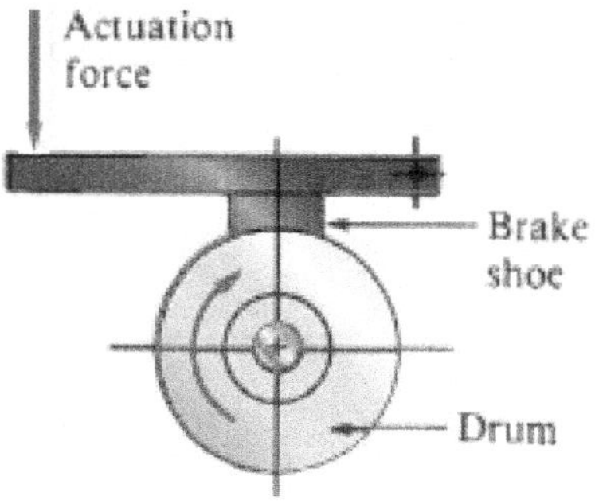

Fig.7.5. Single block brake

The friction between the block and the brake down causes the retarding of the drum.

Applications

Railway trains and tram cars.

The block is pressed against the drum by a force (F) applied on one end of a lever. The other end of the lever is pivoted on a fixed fulcrum O.

Let as assume that

r = Radius of drum

RN= Normal reaction of the block.

F = Force applied at lever end.

μ = Coefficient of friction.

μR_N= Frictional Force.

T_B =Braking Torque.

$F_b = \mu R_N$

$T_b = F_b . r = \mu . R_N . r$

Case (i)

Assume the line of action of tangential braking force (F_b) passes through the fulcrum of the lever as shown in figure.

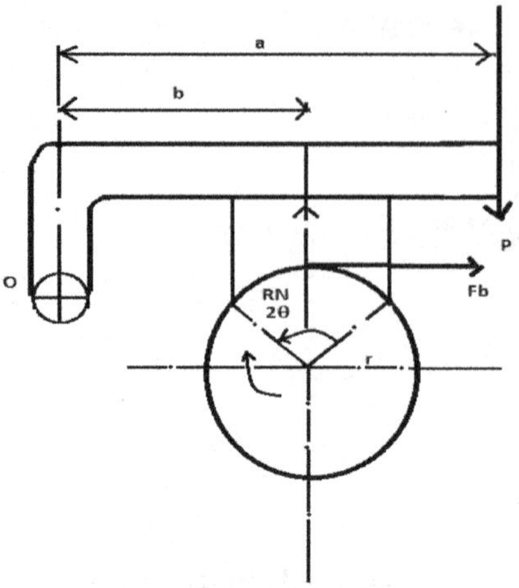

Fig. 7.6. Single shoe brake

a) Clockwise rotation of braking wheel

Taking moment about 'O'

$$P \times a = R_n \times b \ (moment\ by\ F_b\ is\ zero)$$

$$\therefore R_n = \frac{P.a}{b}$$

Then braking torque $T_b = \mu . R_N . r$

$$= \frac{\mu.P.a.r}{b}$$

Now anticlockwise rotation

$$P \times a = R_n \times b$$

$$R_n = \frac{P.a}{b}$$

$$\therefore T_b = \mu . R_N . r = \frac{\mu . P . a . r}{b}$$

Design Problem

1) A differential band brake has a drum radius 400mm. The two ends of the band are fixed to the pins on both sides of fulcrum lever at 40 mm and 200 mm from fulcrum. The angle of contact is 270 degrees. Taking coefficient of friction as 0.2 determine the braking torque developed when a force of 600 N is applied to the lever at a distance of 800 mm from the fulcrum.

Solution:

Given data:

$\theta = 225^0 = 270\times\frac{\pi}{180} = 4.71^0$

$\mu = 0.20$

$r = 400\ mm = 400 \times 10^{-3}m$

$P = 600\ N$

$L = 800 \times 10^{-3}$

$a = 200 \times 10^{-3}m$, $b = 40\ mm = 40 \times 10^{-3}m$

Tension in tight side and slack side of the belt,

$\frac{T_1}{T_2} = e^{\mu} \times \theta$

$T_1 = e^{\mu} \times \theta \times T_2$

$T_1 = 2.565 \times T_2$

1) For clockwise rotation of drum

$$P = \frac{T_2 \times a - T_1 \times b}{l}$$

$$600 = \frac{T_2 \times 200 \times 10^{-3} - 2.565T_2 \times 40 \times 10^{-3}}{800 \times 10^{-3}}$$

$600 \times 800 \times 10^{-3} = 0.0974 \times T_2$

$T_1 = 12640.65\ N$

Braking torque

$T_B = (T_1 - T_2) \times r = (12640.65 - 4928.13)400 \times 10^{-3} = 3085.00\ N\text{-}m$

2) A 400 mm radius brake drum contacts a single shoe as shown in figure 6.2, and sustains 200 N-m torque at 500 rpm. For a coefficient of friction 0.25, determine:

a. Normal force on the shoe.

b. Required force F to apply the brake for clockwise rotation.

c. The dimension c required to make the brake self-locking, assuming the other dimensions remains the same.

d. Heat generated.

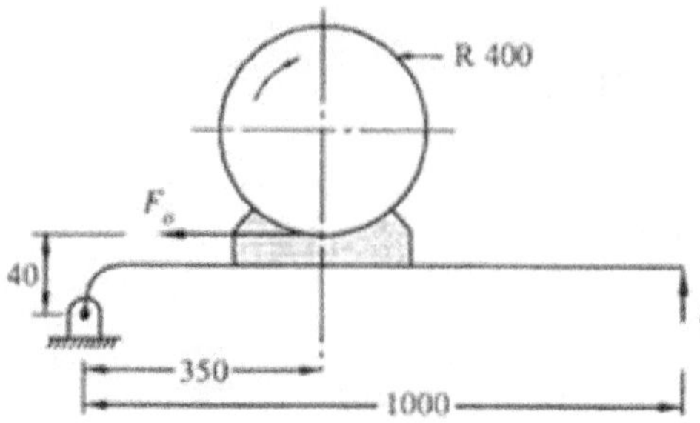

Fig. 6.2

Given data:

R = 400 mm, M_1= 200 N-m, n=500 rpm, μ = 0.25, a = 350 mm, i = 1000 mm,

b= l-a = 1000 -350 =650 mm, c = 40 mm

Tangential friction force $F_\theta = \frac{M_1}{r} = \frac{200\times10^3}{400} = 500$ N

Normal force $F_\theta = \frac{F_\theta}{\mu} = \frac{500}{0.25} = 2000$ N

When the force F_θ acts towards the fulcrum (Clockwise rotation)

Actuating force $F_\theta = \frac{F_\theta a}{a+b}\left[\frac{1}{\mu} - \frac{c}{a}\right]$

$= \frac{500\ x\ 350}{350+650}\left[\frac{1}{0.25} - \frac{40}{350}\right] = 680$ N

Heat generated $H_g = \mu\, p\, A_c\, \text{v} = F_n \text{v}$

$= 0.25 \times 2000 \times \frac{\pi \times800\times500}{600\times1000} = 1071.98$ W

$= 10.472$ kW

Heat generated $H_g = 10.472$ kJ/s

8

Introduction to Clutch

Clutches are mechanical devices used to engage and disengage power transmission between two rotating shafts. They are commonly used in automotive vehicles, industrial machinery, and various other applications.

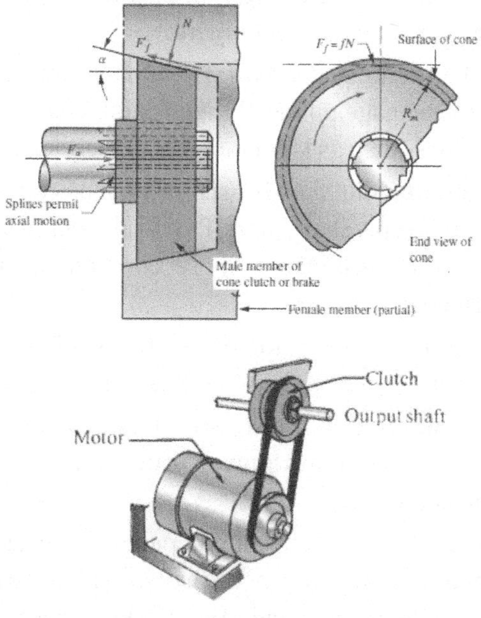

Fig. 8.1. Clutch applications

Here are some key aspects of clutches:

1. **Function:** The primary function of a clutch is to connect and disconnect the engine or power source from the transmission or driven shaft. When the clutch is engaged, power is transmitted from the engine to the transmission, allowing the vehicle or machinery to move. When the clutch is disengaged, power transmission is interrupted, enabling gear changes or stopping the motion.

2. **Types of Clutches:** There are several types of clutches, including:
    - **Friction Clutches:** Friction clutches use friction surfaces, such as clutch plates or discs, to transmit power. They are commonly used in automotive vehicles and consist of a pressure plate, clutch disc, and release mechanism.
    - **Electromagnetic Clutches:** Electromagnetic clutches use an electromagnetic field to engage and disengage power transmission. They are often used in applications where rapid engagement and disengagement are required, such as in industrial machinery.
    - **Hydraulic Clutches:** Hydraulic clutches use hydraulic fluid to transmit force and engage or disengage power transmission. They are commonly used in heavy-duty applications, such as commercial vehicles and construction equipment.
    - **Centrifugal Clutches:** Centrifugal clutches use centrifugal force to engage and disengage power transmission. They are commonly used in small engines, such as lawn mowers and go-karts.
3. **Clutch Components:** Clutches consist of various components, including a clutch disc or plate, pressure plate, flywheel, release bearing, and clutch pedal or actuation mechanism. These components work together to engage and disengage the clutch.
4. **Clutch Operation:** The operation of a clutch involves three main stages:
    - **Engaging:** When the clutch pedal is released, the pressure plate applies force to the clutch disc, pressing it against the flywheel. This creates friction and allows power transmission between the engine and transmission.
    - **Disengaging:** When the clutch pedal is pressed, the release mechanism or bearing moves the pressure plate away from the clutch disc, releasing the friction and interrupting power transmission.
    - **Slipping:** In some cases, clutches can be partially engaged, allowing for gradual power transfer and smooth engagement. This is known as clutch slipping and is often used during gear changes or in situations where a gradual transfer of power is required.
5. **Clutch Wear and Maintenance:** Clutches are subject to wear and may require periodic maintenance or replacement. Factors such as clutch material, usage conditions, and proper adjustment can affect the lifespan

and performance of a clutch. Regular inspection, lubrication, and adjustment are important to ensure optimal clutch operation.

The selection of the appropriate clutch type depends on factors such as the application requirements, torque capacity, engagement speed, and space constraints.

Friction Disc

Friction disc, also known as a friction plate or clutch disc, is a component used in various mechanical systems, particularly in automotive clutches. It plays a crucial role in transmitting power and controlling the engagement and disengagement of the clutch.

Key aspects of friction discs:

1. **Construction:** A friction disc is typically made of a flat, circular plate with friction material attached to both sides. The friction material is usually made of a composite material that includes a mixture of organic fibres, resins, and friction modifiers. The disc may also have a hub or splines for connection to the clutch assembly.
2. **Function:** The primary function of a friction disc is to transfer torque from the engine to the transmission by engaging and disengaging the clutch. When the clutch pedal is pressed, the pressure plate releases the friction disc, allowing for smooth gear changes. When the clutch pedal is released, the pressure plate applies pressure to the friction disc, causing it to engage with the flywheel and transmit power.
3. **Friction Material:** The friction material on the disc is designed to provide high friction and wear resistance. It allows for efficient power transfer while minimizing slippage and heat generation. The composition and design of the friction material can vary depending on the specific application requirements, such as the torque capacity, operating temperature, and durability.
4. **Design Considerations:** The design of a friction disc takes into account factors such as the size, shape, and number of friction surfaces, as well as the type and thickness of the friction material. These factors influence the friction characteristics, torque capacity, and overall performance of the clutch system.
5. **Maintenance and Replacement:** Friction discs are subject to wear and may need to be periodically inspected and replaced. Excessive wear or

damage to the friction material can lead to reduced clutch performance, slippage, or complete failure. Regular maintenance, including proper lubrication and adjustment of the clutch system, is important to ensure the longevity and reliable operation of the friction disc.

Friction discs are widely used in automotive clutches, industrial machinery, and other applications where controlled power transmission and engagement are required. The specific design and characteristics of friction discs can vary depending on the intended application and the requirements of the system.

8.1 Types of Clutches

- Positive clutches.
- Friction clutches.

1) Positive clutches

The simplest type of a positive clutch is a jaw or claw clutch. The jaw clutch permits one shaft to drive another through a direct contact of interlocking jaws.

2) Friction clutches:

Types of friction clutches.

- Disc (or) plate clutches (single disc or multiple disc clutch)
- Cone clutches
- Centrifugal clutches.

8.2 Design of a Disc or Plate Clutch

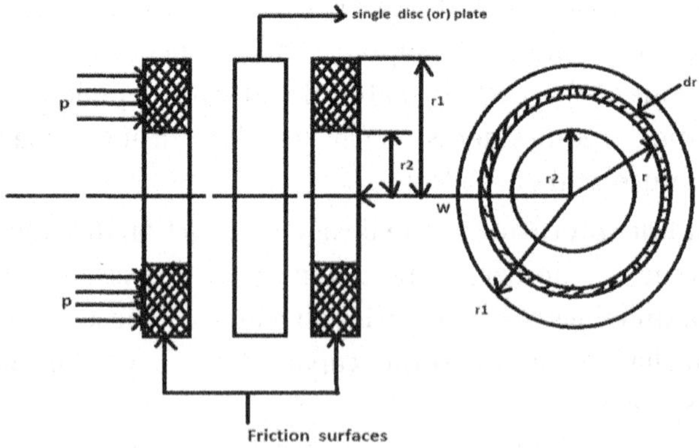

Fig. 8.2. Plate Clutch

T= Torque transmitted by the clutch

P = Intensity of axial pressure with which the contact surfaces are held together.

r_1 and r_2 = External and internal radii of frictional forces.

r = mean radius of the friction force and

μ = coefficient of friction.

Consider an elementary ring of radius rand thickness 'dr' as shown in figure.

W.k.t Area of the contact surface or friction surfaces = = $2\pi r.dr$

∴ Normal or axial force on the ring

$$\delta w = Pressure \times Area$$

$$\delta w = P \times 2\pi r \times dr.$$

and the frictional force on the ring acting tangentially at radius r.

$$F_r = \mu \times \delta w = \mu \times P \times 2\pi r \times dr.$$

∴Frictional force acting on the ring.

$$T_r = F_r \times r = \mu.p \times 2\pi.dr \times r$$

$$T_r = 2\pi\mu.p.r^2 dr$$

We shall now consider the following two cases.

1) When there is a uniform pressure.

2) When there is a uniform axial wear.

1) Considering uniform pressure:

w.k.t

$$\delta w = P \times 2\pi r \times dr.$$

∫ing

$$w = 2\pi p \int_{r2}^{r1} (r1^2 - r2^2)$$

$$P = \frac{w}{\pi(r1^2 - r2^2)} \rightarrow 1$$

Total friction torque.

$$T_r = 2\pi\mu p. \int_{r2}^{r1} r2.dr$$

$$T = 2\pi\mu . p[\frac{r^3}{3}]_{r2}^{r1} \ = 2\pi\mu P\left[\frac{r1^3 - r2^3}{3}\right]$$

sub 1

$$= 2\pi\mu\frac{w}{(T(r1^2 - r2^2)}\left[\frac{r1^3 - r2^3}{3}\right]$$

$$= \frac{2}{3}\mu . w\left[\frac{r1^3 - r2^3}{r1^2 - r2^2}\right]$$

$$T = \mu . w . R$$

Mean radius of the friction surface $R = \frac{2}{3}\left[\frac{r1^3 - r2^3}{r1^2 - r2^2}\right]$

Considering uniform axial wear:

Assume:

The work of friction is proportional product of normal pressure (P) and the sliding velocity (v).

∴Normal wear α work of fiction αPV

PV = K (a constant)

or $P = \frac{K}{V}$

Let P be the normal intensity of pressure at a distance 'r' from the arms of the clutch

$$p . r = c \quad p = \frac{c}{v}$$

$$\delta w = p . 2\pi r . dr$$

sub p

$$= \frac{c}{r}\ 2\pi r dr$$

$$dw = 2\pi c dr$$

$$c = \frac{w}{2\pi(r1 - r2)}$$

W.k.t the frictional torque acting on the ring

$$T_r = 2\pi\mu . pr^2\ dr = 2\pi\mu \times \frac{c}{r} \times r^2 \mathrm{dr}$$

$$Tr = 2\pi\mu c . r . dr$$

∴Total frictional torque acting on the frictional surface.

$$T = \int_{r2}^{r1} 2\pi\mu crdr$$

$$= 2\pi\mu c[\frac{r^2}{2}]_{r2}^{r1}$$

$$= 2\pi\mu c\left[\frac{r1^2 - r2^2}{2}\right]$$

$$= \pi\mu c[(r1^2) - (r2^2)]$$

$$= \pi\mu \times \frac{w}{2\pi(r1 - r2)}[r1^2 - r2^2]$$

$$= \frac{1}{2}\mu.w(r1 + r2) = \mu.w.R$$

$$R = \frac{r1 + r2}{2}$$

Design Problems

1) Determine the maximum, minimum and average pressure in a plate clutch when the axial force is 4KN. The inside radium of the contact surface and the outside radius is 100mm.

Solution:

Assume uniform wear.

Given data:

W=4KN,

r_2=50mm, r_1=100mm

Maximum pressure

$P_{max} \times r2 = C$

$C = 50P_{max.}$

Total force on the contact surface.

$W = 2\pi C(r_1 - r_2)$

4000=2π50 P_{Max} (100-50)

4000=15710 P_{Max} $C = P_{max} * r_2$

$P_{Max} = 0.2546N/mm^2$

Minimum pressure

$P_{min} \times r_1 = c$

$4000 = 2\pi c(r_1 - r_2) = 2\pi \times 100 P_{min}\ (100 - 50)$

$= 31420\ P_{min.} \qquad C = P_{min} \times r_1$

$\therefore P_{min} = 0.1273 N/mm^2$

Average Pressure

$$P_{av} = \frac{W}{\pi[(r1^2 - r2^2]} = \frac{4000}{\pi[(100)^2 - (50)^2]} = 0.17 N/mm^2$$

2) A Plate clutch having a single driving plate with contact surfaces on each side is required to transmit 110KW at 1250rpm .The outside diameter of the contact surfaces is to be 300 mm. The co efficient of friction is 0.4

a) Assume a uniform pressure of 0.17N determine the inner diameter of the friction surfaces.

b) Assuming the same dimensions and the same total axial thrust determine the maximum torque that can be transmitted and the maximum intensity of pressure when uniform wear conditions have been reached.

Given data:

P =110KW r_1=150mm $\mu = 0.4$ P=0.17N/mm^2

To find r_2, T, Pmaxz

(i) Inner diameter of the friction surface (d_2) (or) r_2

w.k.t

$$T = \frac{p \times 60}{2\pi N} = \frac{110 \times 10^3 \times 60}{2\pi \times 1250}$$

$$T = 840 \times 10^3 Nm.$$

Axial thrust with which the contact surfaces are held together

$W = pressure \times area = P \times \pi[(r1)^2 - (r2)^2 = 0.17 \times \pi[(150)^2 - (r2)^2]$

$W = 0.534[(150)^2 - (r2)^2] \rightarrow 1$

Mean radius of the contact surface for uniform pressure conditions.

$$R = \frac{2}{3}\left[\frac{(r1)^3 - (r2)^3}{(r1)^2 - (r2)^2}\right]$$

$$R = \frac{2}{3}\left[\frac{(150)^3 - (r2)^3}{(150)^2 - (r2)^2}\right]$$

∴ Torque transmitted by the clutch (T)

$$T = n\mu.w.R$$

$$840 * 10^3 = 2\times 0.4\times 0.534[(150)^2 - (r2)^2]\times \frac{2}{3}\left[\frac{(150)^3 - (r2)^3}{(150)^2 - (r2)^2}\right]$$

$$= 0.285[(150)^3 - (r2)^3]$$

$$(r2)^3 = 150)^3 - 2.95\times 10^6$$

$$r2 = 75mm$$

$$d2 = 150mm.$$

(2) Maximum torque transmitted:

W.K.T axial thrust

$$w = 0.534[(150)^2 - (r2)^2]$$

$$= 0.534[(150)^2 - (75)^2]$$

$$w = 9011N.$$

Mean radius of the contact surfaces for uniform wear condition.

$$R = \frac{r1 + r2}{2} = \frac{150 + 75}{2} = 112.5mm$$

∴ Maximum torque transmitted

$$T = n.\mu.w.R = 2 \times 0.4 \times 9011\times 112.5$$

$$T = 811\times 10^3 Nmm.$$

Maximum intensity of pressure:

For uniform area condition

$$P.v = C$$

$$P_{max}\times r2 = C \quad C = P_{max}\times 75$$

W.k.T axial thrust (W)

$$9011 = 2\pi c(r1 - r2)$$

$9011 = 2\pi P_{max} \times 75(150 - 75)$

$P_{Max} = 0.255\ N/mm^2$.

3) A car engine has its rated output of 12KW. The maximum torque developed is 100 N-m. The clutch used is of single plate type having two active surfaces. The axial pressure is not to exceed $85KN/m^2$. The external diameter of the friction plate is 1.25 times the internal diameter. Determine the dimensions of the friction plate and the axial force exerted by the springs coefficient of friction=0.3.

Solution

Given data:

P =12KW=$12^{*} \times 10^3 W$.

T=100 N-m n=2. $P_{max} = 85\ KN/m^2 = 85 \times 10^3 N/m^2$

$$d1 = 1.25d2\ or\ \frac{d1}{d2} = 1.25\ (or) \frac{r1}{r2} = 1.25$$

μ =0.3

(i) Dimensions of the Friction plate:

Assume uniform wear:

T=100 N-m.

Design torque [T]=T.KS

Service factor KS=k1+k2+k3+k4.

Refer pageno.790.

K1=0.33 (for machines with low starting torque characteristics ,turbines and line transmission).

K2=1.25 (Metal cutting m/c tool, wood working machine).

K3=0.32(for 1000 rpm)

K4=0.9(assume 48 engagement)

$\therefore ks = k1 + k2 + k3 + k4 = 0.33 + 1.25 + 0.32 + 0.90$

ks = 2.8

Design torque (T) =100×2.8=(∴T.KS)

=280Nm.

since the intensity of pressure is maximum r2

$P_{Max} \times r2 = C \quad C = P_{Max} x r2$

axial force exerted by the springs $=85 \times 10^3 \times r2 N/m$

$W = 2\pi c(r1 - r2) = 2\pi 85 \times 10^3 x r2(r1 - r2) \qquad (\therefore r1 = 1.25r2)$

$W = 2\pi c(r1 - r2) = 2\pi 85 \times 10^3 \times r2(1.25r2 - r2)$

$W = 1.335 \times 10^5 \, r2^2 \, N.$

W.k.t Torque transmitted [T]=$n.\mu.w\left(\frac{r1+r2}{2}\right)$

$$280 = 2 \times 0.3 \times 1.335 \times 10^5 r2^2 \left(\frac{1.25r2 + r2}{2}\right)$$

r2=0.1459nm =145.9mm

r1=1.25r2 =1.25×0.1459

r1=182.3mm

(ii) Axial force exerted on the springs

$W = 2\pi c(r1 - r2) = 2\pi 85 \times 10^3 x r2(r1 - r2)$

$W = 2841.79N$

9

Introduction to Gear Trains

A gear train is one or more pairs of gears operating together to transmit power. Figure 9.1 shows examples of a simple gear train, a reverted gear train and a non-reverted gear train. Gear trains are mechanical systems that consist of multiple gears meshed together to transmit power and motion between rotating shafts. They are used to change the speed, torque, and direction of rotation in various applications.

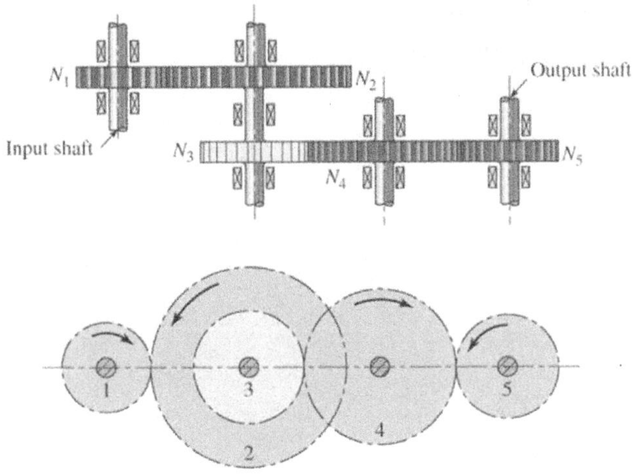

Fig. 9.1. Gear train

Key aspects of gear trains:

1. **Types of Gears:** Gear trains can include different types of gears, such as spur gears, helical gears, bevel gears, worm gears, and planetary gears. Each type has its own unique tooth profile and configuration, which determines its specific characteristics and applications.
2. **Gear Arrangements:** Gear trains can be arranged in different configurations to achieve specific speed and torque relationships.

Common gear arrangements include parallel shaft, intersecting shaft, and planetary gear trains.

3. **Speed and Torque Relationships:** The gear ratio determines the speed and torque relationship between the input and output shafts in a gear train. The gear ratio is determined by the number of teeth on the gears involved. A higher gear ratio results in a lower output speed and higher output torque, while a lower gear ratio results in a higher output speed and lower output torque.
4. **Efficiency and Power Loss:** Gear trains introduce some power loss due to friction and mechanical inefficiencies. The efficiency of a gear train depends on factors such as gear quality, lubrication, alignment, and load conditions. Proper maintenance and lubrication are important to minimize power loss and ensure smooth operation.
5. **Applications:** Gear trains are used in a wide range of applications, including automotive transmissions, industrial machinery, clocks, watches, and robotics. They are essential for transmitting power and motion in a controlled and efficient manner.
6. **Gear Train Analysis:** The analysis of gear trains involves calculating the gear ratios, determining the direction of rotation, and evaluating the overall performance of the system. This analysis helps in designing gear trains for specific applications and optimizing their performance.

When designing or selecting a gear train, factors such as the required speed and torque ratios, space limitations, load conditions, and desired efficiency should be considered.

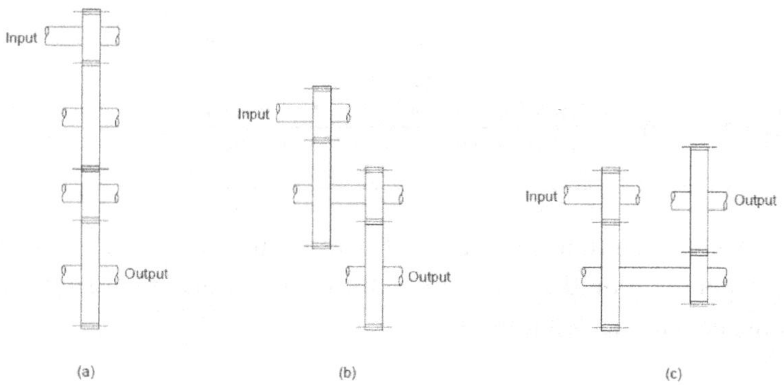

Fig. 9.2. Gear train analysis

9.1 Simple Gear Train

When there is only one gear on each shaft it known as simple gear train as shown in figure a.

Speed ratio:

It is the ratio of the speed of the driver to the speed of the driven or follower and ratio of speeds of any pair of gears in mesh is the inverse of their nu8mber of teeth.

$$Speed\ ratio = \frac{n_1}{n_2} = \frac{T_1}{T_2}$$

Train value:

The ratio of the speed of the driven or follower to the speed of the driver is known as train value of the gear train.

$$\text{Train value} = \frac{\mathrm{N_1}}{\mathrm{N_2}} = \frac{\mathrm{T_1}}{\mathrm{T_2}}$$

Since the driving gear 1 is in mesh with the intermediate gear 2 therefore speed ratio for these two gears is

$$\frac{N_2}{N_1} = \frac{T_2}{T_1}$$

The inter emolliate gear 2 is in mesh with the driven gear 3 therefore speed ratio for these two gears is

$$\frac{N_2}{N_3} = \frac{T_3}{T_2}$$

The speed ration of the gear train B is

$$\frac{\mathrm{N_1}}{\mathrm{N_2}} \times \frac{\mathrm{N_2}}{\mathrm{N_3}} = \frac{\mathrm{T_2}}{\mathrm{T_1}} \times \frac{\mathrm{T_3}}{\mathrm{T_2}}$$

(or)

$$\therefore \frac{N_1}{N_3} = \frac{T_3}{T_1}$$

ie speed ratio $= \dfrac{speed\ of\ driver}{speed\ of\ driver} = \dfrac{no.of\ teeth\ on\ driven}{no.of\ teethon\ driver}$

Train value $= \dfrac{speed\ of\ driven}{speed\ of\ driver} = \dfrac{no.of\ teeth\ on\ driver}{no.of\ teeth\ on\ driven}$

From above we see that the speed ratio and train value in a simple train of gears is independent of the size and number of intermediate gears .These intermediate gears are called idle gears.

9.2 Compound Gear Train

When there are more than one gear on a shaft it pound train of gear. These gears are useful in bridging over the sp the driver and the driven as shown in figure 8.

Since gear 1 is in mesh with gear 2 therefore its s

$$\frac{N_1}{N_2} = \frac{T_2}{T_1}$$

For 3 and 4

$$\frac{N_3}{N_4} = \frac{T_4}{T_3}$$

And for gears 5 and 6

$$\frac{N_5}{N_6} = \frac{T_6}{T_5}$$

The speed ratio of compound gear train is obtaiiplying eqn 1 2 and 3

$$\frac{N_1}{N_2} \times \frac{N_3}{N_4} \times \frac{N_5}{N_6} = \frac{T_2}{T_1} \times \frac{T_4}{T_3} \times \frac{T_6}{T_5}$$

$$\text{ie speed ratio} = \frac{\text{Speed of the first driver}}{\text{Speed of the last driven or follower}}$$

$$\text{Train value} = \frac{\text{Speed of the last driven or follower}}{\text{Speed of the first driver}}$$

$$= \frac{\text{Product of the no.of teeth on the driver}}{\text{Product of the no.of teeth ont he driver}}$$

9.3 Reverted Gear Train

When the axis of the first gear (ie first driver) ane last driven or follower) are coaxial then the gear train is known as r train

Since the distance between the centres of the shaand 2 as well as gears 3 and 4 is same

$$r_1 + r_2 = r_3 + r_4$$

Also the circular pitch or module of all the geed to be same therefore number of teeth on each gear is directortional to its circumference or radius

$$T_1 + T_2 = T_3 + T_4$$

$$\text{Speed ratio} = \frac{\text{Product of no.of teeth on drivens}}{\text{Product of no.teeth on drivens}}$$

$$\frac{N_1}{N_4} = \frac{T_2 \times T_4}{T_1 \times T_3}$$

9.4 Epicyclic Gear Train

A simple epicyclic gear train is shown in figure w and the arm C have a common axis at o_1 about which they can rotate.

The gear B meshes with gear A and has its axis on the arm at o_2 about which the gear B can rotate. If the arm is fixed the gear train is simple and gear a can drive gear b or vice versa but if gear a is fixed and the arm is rotated about the axis of gear a then the gear b is forced to rotate upon and around gear a. such a motion is called epicyclic and the gear train arranged in such a manner that one or more of their members move upon and around another member move upon and around another member are known as epicyclic gear trains (epi means upon and cyclic means around). The epicyclic gear trains may be simple or compounds.

Epicyclic gear train with bevel gears

Epicyclic or planetary gear train is one in which the axis of rotation of at least one of the gear rotate about the fixed axis of rotation of another gear. A sample epicyclic gear train is shown in . The gear 1 and arm have a common axis at O_1, about which the arm can rotate. The gear 2 meshes with gear 1 and has its axis on the arm at O_2 about which the gear 2 rotates. If the arm is fixed and gears 1 and 2 are free to rotate about O_1 and O_2, then the gear train is simple gear train. If the gear 1 is fixed and the arm is free to rotate about the axis O_1, then the gear train is called epicyclic gear train. The advantage of gear train is that a very high velocity ratio can be obtained with moderate diameter gears. The differential mechanism used in automobile is a common example of the application of epicyclic gear train.

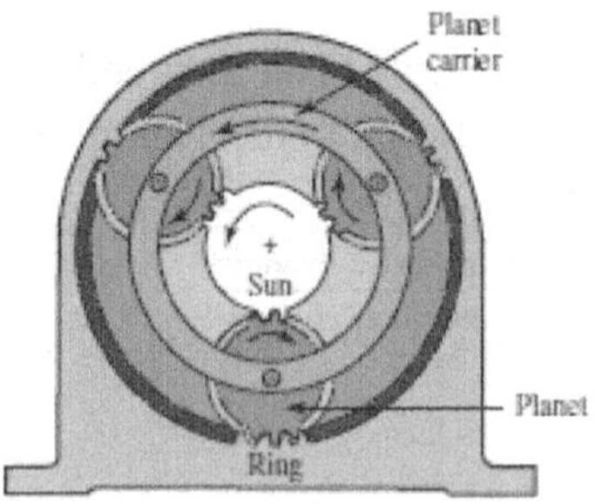

Fig. 9.3. Planetary gear

Example: differential gear of the automobile

Gear Train Problems:

1. Consider the gear train shown in Figure. 9.4. Calculate the speed of gear five.

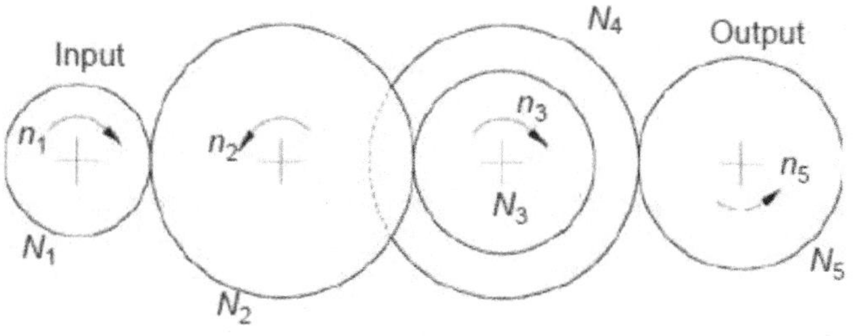

Fig. 9.4

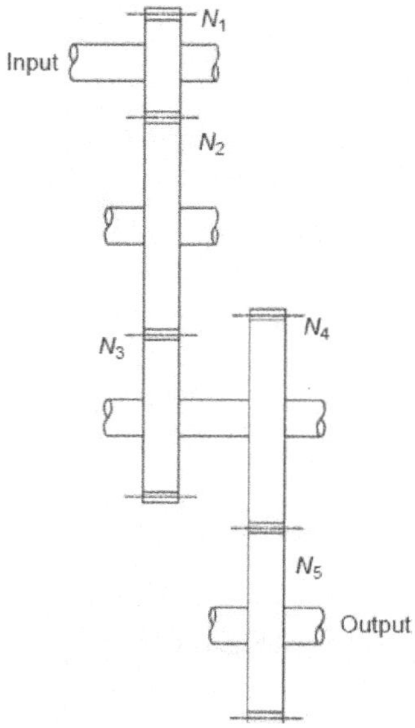

Fig. 9.5. Gear train output

Solution:

$$n_2 = -\frac{N1}{N2} n_1$$

$$n_3 = -\frac{N2}{N3} n_2$$

$n_4 = N_3$ (On the same shaft)

$$n_5 = -\frac{N4}{N5} n_4$$

$$n_5 = -\frac{N4\,N2\,N1}{N5\,N3\,N2} n_1$$

For the double reduction gear train with an idler shown in Figure 8.4, if the input speed is 1750 rpm in a clockwise direction what is the output speed?

Solution:

$$n_5 = -\frac{N4}{N5} n_4$$

$$n_4 = -\frac{N3}{N4} n_3$$

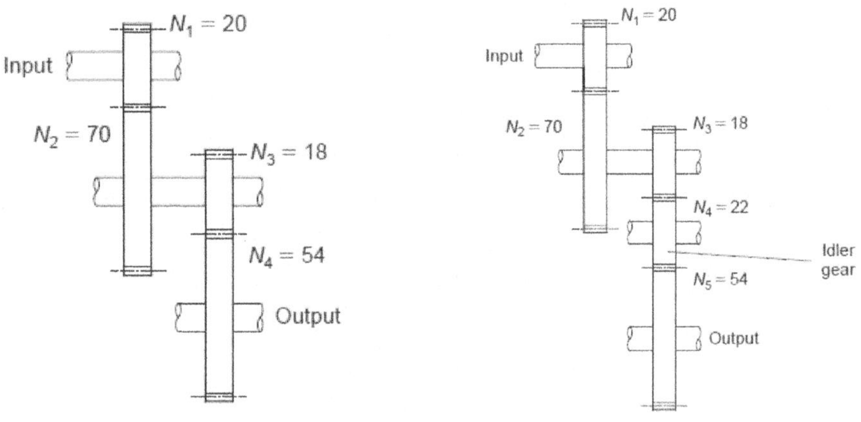

Fig. 9.6

$n_3 = N_2$

$$n_2 = -\frac{N1}{N2} n_1$$

$$n_5 = -\frac{N4\,N3\,N1}{N5\,N4\,N2} n_1$$

$$= -\frac{22}{54}\frac{-18}{22}\frac{-20}{70}(-1750)$$

10

Introduction to Gear Drives

Gears are toothed cylindrical wheels used for transmitting mechanical power from one rotating shaft to another. Several types of gears are in common use. This chapter introduces various types of gears and details the design, specification and selection of spur gears in particular. Many power producing machines, or prime movers, such as internal combustion (IC) engines, industrial gas turbine engines and electric motors produce power in the form of rotary motion. The operating characteristics of prime movers vary according to their type and size, and a change of speed is often necessary to transform the torque speed characteristic of a prime mover to a useful output characteristic. When transmitting power from a source to the required point of application, a series of devices is available including gears, belts, pulleys, and chains, hydraulic and electrical systems. Generally if the distances of power transmission are large, gears are not suitable and chains and belts can be considered.

Fig. 10.1. Gear drives

Fig. 10.2. Types of Gears

10.1 Classification of Gears

Gears can be divided into several broad classifications.

1. Parallel axis gears:
   - (a) Spur gears
   - (b) Helical gears
   - (c) Internal gears.
2. Non-parallel, coplanar gears:
   - (a) Bevel gears
   - (b) Face gears,
   - (c) Conical involute gearing.
3. Non-parallel, no coplanar gears (nonintersecting axes):
   - (a) Crossed axis helical
   - (b) Cylindrical worm gearing
   - (c) Single enveloping worm gearing,
   - (d) Double enveloping worm gearing,
   - (e) Hypoid gears,
   - (f) Spiroid and helicon gearing,
   - (g) Face gears (off centre).
4. Special gear types:
   - (a) Square and rectangular gears,
   - (b) Elliptical gears,

10.2 Selection of Gears

- American Gear Manufacturers Association (AGMA)

- AGMA 2000-A88, Gear Classification and Inspection Handbook - Tolerances and Measuring Methods for Unassembled Spur and Helical Gears, including Metric Equivalents
- American Society of Mechanical Engineers (ASME)
  - ASME Y14.7.1 Gear Drawing Standards - Part 1: For Spur, Helical, Double Helical and Rack
  - ASME Y14.7.2 Gear and Spline Drawing Standards - Part 2: Bevel and Hypoid Gears

10.3 Useful Range of Gear Ratios

The range of gear ratios in a gear drive depends on the specific configuration and types of gears used. Here are some examples of gear ratios for different types of gear drives:

1. **Spur Gears:** Spur gears have straight teeth and are the simplest type of gears. The gear ratio is determined by the number of teeth on the driving gear (pinion) and the driven gear. For example, if the pinion has 10 teeth and the driven gear has 40 teeth, the gear ratio would be 4:1.

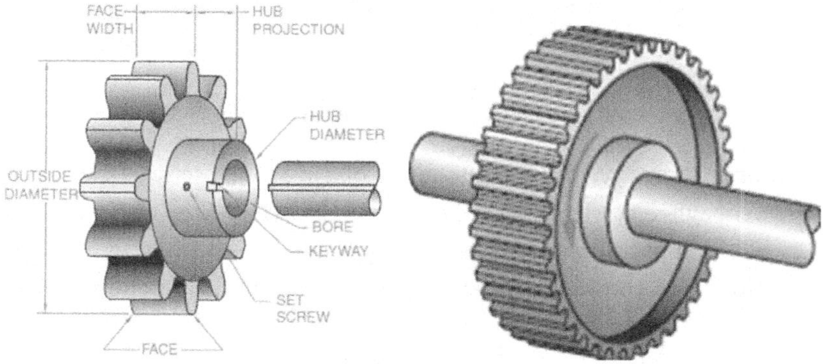

Fig. 10.3. Spur gear

2. **Helical Gears:** Helical gears have angled teeth that are helically cut around the gear. They offer smoother and quieter operation compared to spur gears. The gear ratio is determined in the same way as spur gears, based on the number of teeth on the pinion and driven gear.

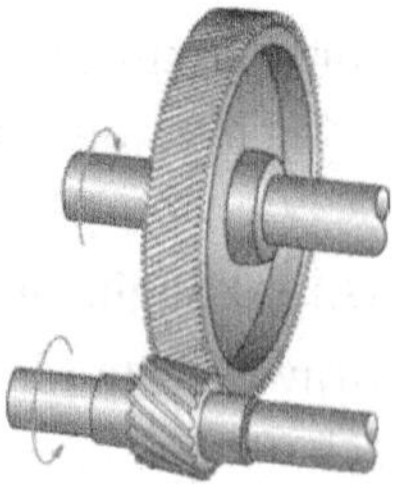

Fig. 10.4. Helical gear

3. **Bevel Gears:** Bevel gears have teeth that are cut on a conical surface. They are used to transmit power between intersecting shafts. The gear ratio is determined by the number of teeth on the bevel gears. For example, if the pinion has 20 teeth and the driven gear has 40 teeth, the gear ratio would be 2:1.

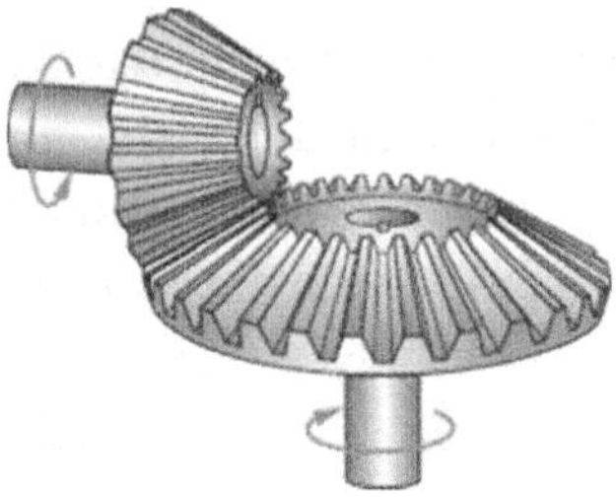

Fig. 10.5. bevel gear

4. **Worm Gears:** Worm gears consist of a worm (a screw-like gear) and a worm wheel (a gear with helical teeth). They are used for high gear reduction ratios and are known for their self-locking ability. The gear ratio is determined by the number of teeth on the worm wheel and the number of threads on the worm.

Fig. 10.6. Worm gear

5. **Planetary Gears:** Planetary gears, also known as epicyclic gears, consist of a central sun gear, planet gears, and a ring gear. They offer a wide range of gear ratios and are commonly used in automotive transmissions. The gear ratio in a planetary gear system is determined by the number of teeth on the sun gear, planet gears, and ring gear.

The actual range of gear ratios will vary depending on the specific gear drive design and the number of gear stages used. Gear drives can provide a wide range of gear ratios, from low ratios for high torque applications to high ratios for speed reduction. The gear ratio determines the relationship between the rotational speeds and torques of the driving and driven shafts.

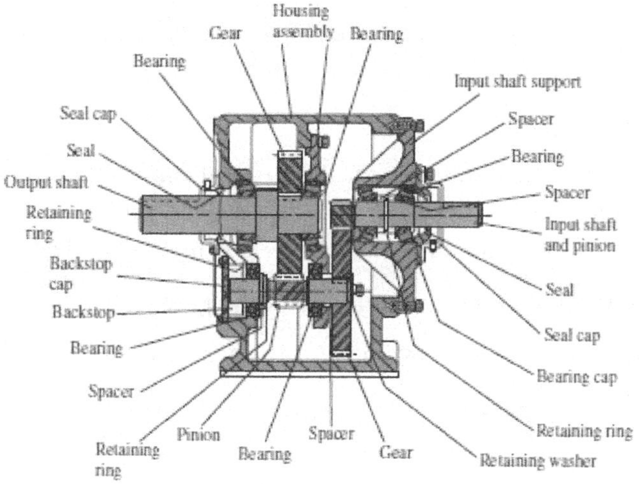

Fig. 10.7 Gear Box

When selecting a gear drive, it is important to consider the desired gear ratio range to ensure that it meets the requirements of the application. Consulting with gear drive manufacturers or experts can provide valuable guidance in selecting the appropriate gear drive with the desired range of gear ratios.

Classification of Gear Drives

The gears or toothed wheels may be classified as follows.

1) According to the position of areas of the shaft:

The areas of the shafts between which the motion is to be transmitted may be

a) Parallel
b) Intersecting
c) Non intersecting and non-parallel

a) Parallel:

These gears have teeth parallel to the axis of the wheel. These gears called spur gears and the arrangement is known as spur gearing. He local gearing in which the teeth are inclined to the axis helical gearing in which teeth are inclined to the arms.

b) Intersecting

The two non-parallel or intersecting but coplanar shafts connection by gears are called bevel gears and the arrangement is known as bevel gearing.

c) Non intersecting and non-parallel:

The non-intersecting and non-parallel i.e. non coplanar shafts connected by gears is shown in figure. These gears are called skew bevel gears or spiral gears and the arrangement is known as skew bevel gearing or spiral gearing.

2) According to the peripheral velocity of the gears:

According to the peripheral velocity of the gears may be classified as
a) Low velocity
b) Medium velocity
c) High velocity
  a) Low velocity: less than 3m/s
  b) Medium velocity: between 3 and 15 m/s
  c) High velocity: more than 15 m/s

3) According to the type of gearing

a) External gearing
b) Internal gearing
c) Rack and Pinion

External gearing: Two wheels is called spur wheel or gear and the smaller wheels is called pinion. In an external gearing the motion of the two wheels is always unlike.

Internal gearing: In internal gearing the gears of the two shafts mesh internally with each other as shown in figure the larger of these two wheels is called annular wheels and the smaller wheels is called pinion.

4) According to the position of teeth on the gear surface:

a) Straight

b) Inclined

c) Curved

10.4 Terms Used in Gears

The following terms which will be mostly used in this chapter should be clearly understood at this stage.

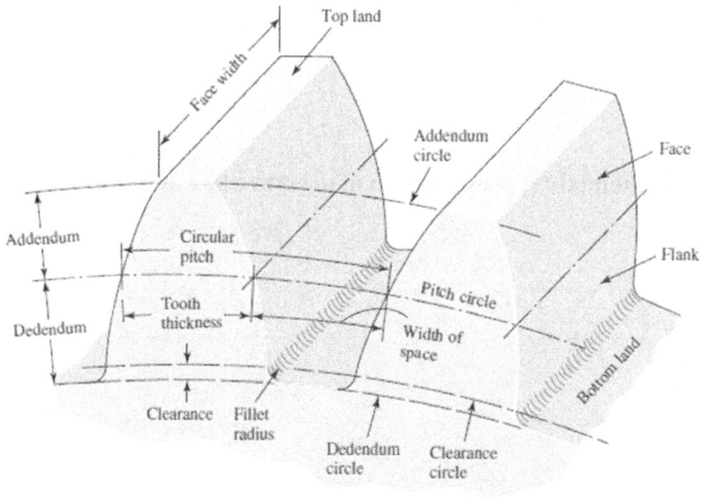

Fig. 10.8. Spur gear terminology

1) Pitch circle:

It is an imaginary circle which by pure rolling action would give the same motion as the actual gear.

2) Pitch circle diameter:

It is the diameter of the pitch circle the size of the usually specified by the pitch circle diameter it is also called as pitch diameter.

3) Pitch point:

It is common point of contact between two pitch circles.

4) Pressure angle or angle of obliquity:

It is the angle between the common normal to two gear teeth at the point of contact and the common tangent at the pitch point. It is usually denoted.

The standard pressure angles are 14 half and 20 degree.

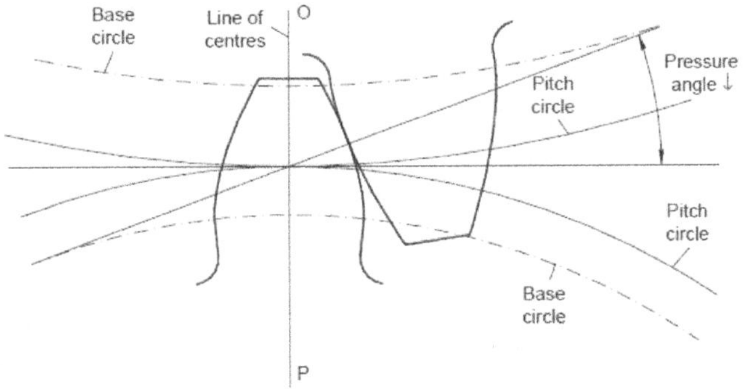

Fig. 10.9. (a) Schematic representation of pressure line and pressure angle

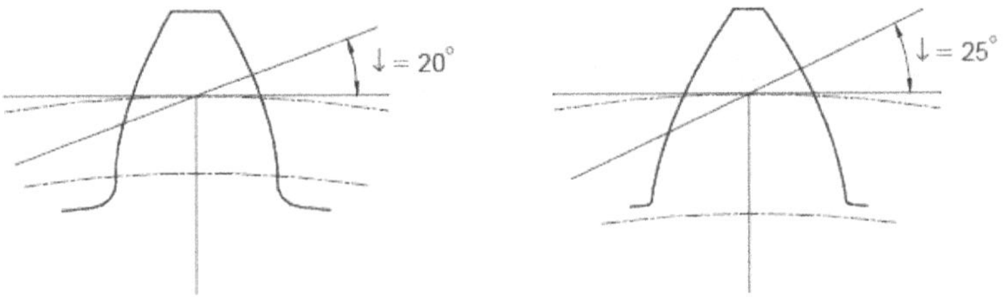

Fig. 10.9. (b) Full depth involute form

5) Addendum:

It is the radial distance of a tooth from the pitch circle to the top of the tooth.

6) Dedendum:

It is the radial distance of the tooth from the pitch circle to the bottom of the tooth.

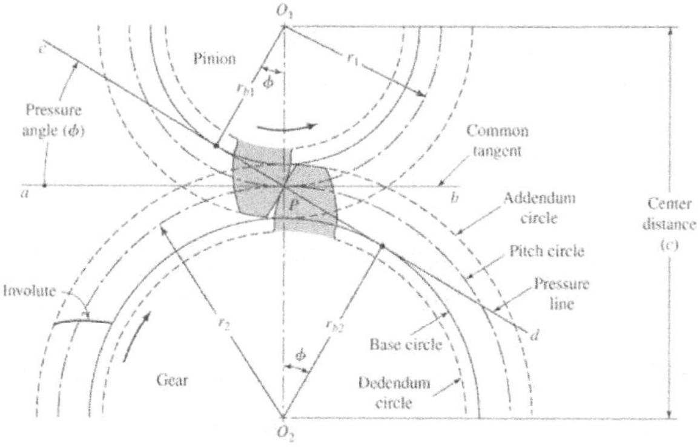

Fig. 10.10. Gear terminologies

7) Addendum circle:

It is the circle drawn through the top of teeth and is concentric with the pitch circle.

8) Dedendum circle:

It is the circle drawn through the bottom of the teeth it is also called root circle.

Root circle diameter = Pitch circle diameter

9) Circular pitch:

It is the distance measured on the circumference of the pitch circle from a point of one tooth to the corresponding point on the next tooth. It is usually denoted by pc circular pitch pc $\pi D/T$.

D = diameter of the pitch circle

T = number of teeth on the wheel

10) Diametric pitch:

It is the ratio of number of teeth to the pitch circle diameter in millimetre it is denoted by m

Module, m = $\frac{D}{T}$.

11) Module:

It is the ratio of the pickle diameter in millimetre to the number of teeth. It is denoted by m.

Module, M = $\frac{D}{T}$.

12) Clearance:

It is the radial distance from the top of the tooth to the bottom of the tooth in a meshing gear.

13) Total depth:

It is the radial distance between the addendum and Dedendum circle of the gear. It is equal to the sum addendum and Dedendum.

14) Working depth:

It is the radial distance from the addendum circle to the clearance circle it is equal to the sum of the addendum of the two meshing gears.

15) Tooth thickness:

It is the width of the space between the two adjacent teeth measured along the pitch circle.

16) Tooth space:

It is the width of space between the two adjacent teeth measured along the pitch circle.

17) Back lash:

It is the difference between the tooth space and the tooth thickness as measured on the pitch circle.

18) Face of the teeth:

It is the surface of the tooth above the pitch surface.

19) Top land:

It is surface of the top of the tooth.

20) Flank of the tooth:

It is the surface of the tooth below the pitch surface.

21) Face width:

It is the width of the gear tooth measured parallel to its axis.

22) Profile:

It is the curve formed by the face and flake of the tooth.

24) Path of contact:

It is the path traced by the point of control of two teeth from the beginning to the end of engagement of a given pair of teeth.

10.5 Velocity Ratio of Gear Drive

The velocity ratio of a gear drive is a measure of the speed relationship between the driving and driven gears in the gear system. It is defined as the ratio of the angular velocity (rotational speed) of the driving gear to the angular velocity of the driven gear.

The velocity ratio can be calculated using the formula:

Velocity Ratio = (Number of Teeth on Driven Gear) / (Number of Teeth on Driving Gear)

For example, if the driving gear has 20 teeth and the driven gear has 40 teeth, the velocity ratio would be:

Velocity Ratio = 40 / 20 = 2

This means that for every revolution of the driving gear, the driven gear will make two revolutions in the opposite direction. The velocity ratio determines the speed reduction or speed increase between the driving and driven gears.

It's important to note that the velocity ratio only considers the speed relationship and does not take into account other factors such as torque, power, or efficiency. These factors can vary depending on the specific gear drive design and the load conditions.

When selecting a gear drive, the desired velocity ratio should be considered to ensure that it meets the speed requirements of the application. Consulting with gear drive manufacturers or experts can provide valuable guidance in selecting the appropriate gear drive with the desired velocity ratio.

10.6 Gear Ratio

The gear ratio in a gear drive is a measure of the speed and torque relationship between the driving and driven gears. It is defined as the ratio of the number of teeth on the driven gear to the number of teeth on the driving gear.

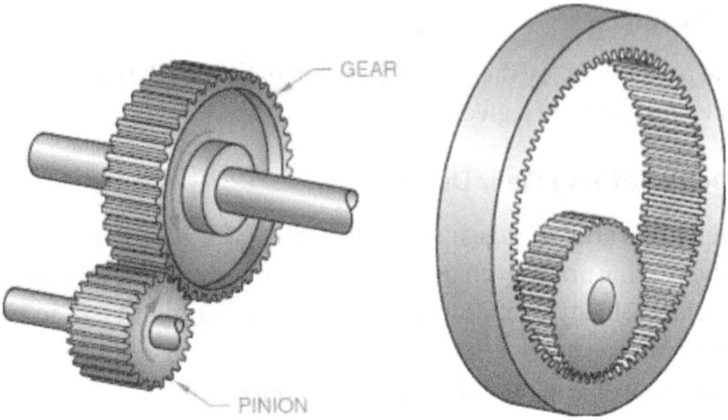

Fig. 10.11 Gear ratio

The gear ratio can be calculated using the formula:

Gear Ratio = (Number of Teeth on Driven Gear) / (Number of Teeth on Driving Gear)

For example, if the driving gear has 20 teeth and the driven gear has 40 teeth, the gear ratio would be:

Gear Ratio = 40 / 20 = 2

This means that for every revolution of the driving gear, the driven gear will make two revolutions in the opposite direction. The gear ratio determines the speed reduction or speed increase between the driving and driven gears.

The gear ratio also affects the torque relationship between the gears. In a gear drive, the torque is inversely proportional to the gear ratio. A higher gear ratio (larger driven gear compared to the driving gear) will result in a lower output torque, while a lower gear ratio (smaller driven gear compared to the driving gear) will result in a higher output torque.

It's important to note that the gear ratio is specific to each gear stage in a gear drive system. In multi-stage gear drives, the gear ratios of each stage are multiplied together to determine the overall gear ratio of the system.

When selecting a gear drive, the desired gear ratio should be considered to ensure that it meets the speed and torque requirements of the application. Consulting with gear drive manufacturers or experts can provide valuable guidance in selecting the appropriate gear drive with the desired gear ratio.

Fig. 10.12 Gear applications

$$V=\frac{N2}{N1}$$

Let the pitch circle diameters of a and b be d_1 and d_2 respectively

In case the driving gear a rotates with N_1 rpm (ω_1 rad/sec) in clockwise direction

Then the driven gear B rotates with N_2 rpm (ω_2 rad/sec) in anti-clockwise direction

The peripheral velocity of driven gear b is equal to $\frac{\omega_1 d_1}{2}$

The peripheral velocity of driven gear b is equal to $\frac{\omega_2 d_2}{2}$

The gear drive is positive the peripheral velocity of driven gear will be equal to peripheral velocity of driven gear.

$$\therefore \omega_2 \frac{d_2}{2} = \omega_1 \frac{d_1}{2}$$

$$\frac{\omega_2}{\omega_1} = \frac{d_1}{d_2}$$

(or)

$$\frac{N_2}{N_1} = \frac{d_1}{d_2}$$

We Know That

Circular pitch Pc1 (gear b)

$$P_{C1} = \pi \frac{d_1}{T_1}$$

Where T_2 is the no. of teeth on driven gear b

Two gears will mesh together correctly only if the gears have the circular pitch

$$\therefore \ P_{C1} = P_{C2}$$

$$\pi \frac{d_1}{T_1} = \pi \frac{d_2}{T_2}$$

$$\frac{d_1}{t_1} = \frac{d_2}{t_2} \ or \ \frac{d_1}{d_2} = \frac{T_1}{T_2}$$

From 1 and 2

$$\frac{N_2}{N_1} = \frac{T_1}{T_2}$$

i.e. velocity ratio or gear ratio $L = \frac{N_2}{N_1} = \frac{T_1}{T_2} = \frac{d_1}{d_2}$

10.7 Steps for Gear Drive Design

1. From design requirements, identify speed of pinion, n_P, desired output speed of gear, n_G, and power to be transmitted, P.
2. Choose type of material for the gears (steel, cast iron, bronze, etc.)
3. Determine overload factor, Ko, using table 9-5
4. Calculated $P_{des} = K_oP$ and calculate a trial value for the diametral pitch, P_d. Note diametral pitch must be a standard size (Table 8-2).
5. Specify N_p and N_G to meet VR requirement. Calculate center distance, D, OD to make sure there aren't any interference issues.
6. Specify face width using recommended range: $8/Pd < F < 16/Pd$.
   - Remember, increasing face width reduces St and Sc but consider alignment factor. Face width is normally less than 2X Dp.
7. Compute transmitted load, Wt, pitch line speed, vt, quality number, Qv, and other factors required for calculating bending stress and contact stress.
8. Summarize design

Forces Acting on Gear

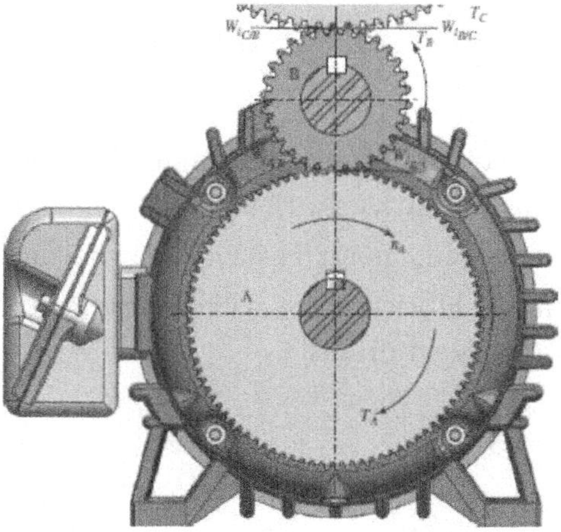

Fig. 10.13. Forces acting on gear

10.8 Gear Applications

- Factory automation
- Packaging machine
- Industrial robots
- Food processing machine
- Car production machine
- Machine tool industry
- Material handling
- Printing machine
- Automatic cutting / welding machine
- Machine for medical/cosmetic field
- Construction machine
- Wood / Glass processing machine
- Agricultural machinery

Advantages:

- It transmits exact velocity ratio
- It may be used to transmit large power
- It may be used for small centre distances of shafts

- It has high efficiency
- It has reliable service
- It has compact layout

Disadvantages:

- Since the manufacture of require special tools and equipment's therefore it is costlier than other drives.
- The error in cutting teeth may cause vibration and noise during operation.
- It requires suitable lubricant and reliable method of applying it for the proper operation of gear drives.

Design Problems

1) A toothed wheel has 120 teeth, its module is 1.5mm. Find the circular pitch, pitch diameter and the diametral pitch:

Solution:

Given Data:

T = 120 m = 1.5mm

(i) Pitch diameter:

Module m = D/T

D = m x T = 1.5 x 120 = 180 mm.

D = 180mm.

(ii) Circular pitch (P_C):

$$P_C = \frac{\pi \, x \, D}{T} = \frac{\pi \, x \, 180}{120} = 4.712\text{mm}.$$

(iii) Diametral pitch (P_d) $= \frac{T}{D} = \frac{120}{180} = 0.667$ tooth/mm.

2) Two spur wheels a and b on parallel shafts are in mesh. A has 40 teeth and rotates at 250 rpm. B is rotate at 100 rpm. Find the no. of teeth on B.

Solution:

Given data: $T_A = 40$, $N_A = 250$ rpm, $N_B = 100$rpm

To find: T_B

We have, $\frac{N_B}{N_A} = \frac{T_A}{T_B}$

$$T_B = T_A \times \frac{N_A}{N_B}$$

$$= 40 \times \frac{250}{100} = 100$$

$$T_B = 100$$

Two matting spur gears have 60 and 40 teeth. Their common module is 5mm determine the centre to centre distance between the gear axes.

Solution:

Given data:

$$\mathrm{T_1 = 60,\ m = 5mm,\ T_2 = 40}$$

To find: l

$$\text{Module } \mathrm{m} = \frac{\mathrm{d}}{\mathrm{T}}$$

$$\mathrm{d_1 = mT_1 = 5 \times 60 = 300mm}$$

$$\mathrm{d_2 = mT_2 = 5 \times 40 = 200mm}$$

We Know that

$$L = r_1 + r_2 = \frac{d_1}{2} + \frac{d_2}{2} = \frac{300}{2} + \frac{200}{2}$$

$$= 150 + 100 = 250$$

$$L = 250\ mm$$

3) A pair of 4 diametral pitch/20^0 full depth involve, spur gears with a face width of 60 mm is made of steel having 400 HB. The pinion has 28 teeth and runs at 1200 rpm. The gear ratio is 4. What power can be transmitted an indicated by the Lewis equation? Check for dynamic and wear loads Assume σ_0 = 210 Mpa and$\sigma_{\sigma s}$ 70 Mpa.

Given data:

b = 60mm

T_P = 28 teeth

N_p = 1200 rpm

G =4

$\sigma_{ep} = 210$

σ_{es} =70Mpa

Solution:

w.k.t

$$G = \frac{T_g}{T_p} = T_g - GT_p = 4 \times 28 = 112 teeth.$$

Assuming a module of 6mm

$$V = \frac{\pi D_P N_P}{60}$$

[D_P = 6 X28 =168]

=10.55 m/s

since V is less than 12.5 m/s

$$C_V = \frac{3}{3+V} = \frac{3}{3+10.55} = 0.22$$

Exercises

1) A shaft running at 250 rpm is driven by a15 KW motor running at 876 rpm through a pairs of 20^0 full depth spur gears . If the central distance is to be approximately 400 mm (±3mm) allowed design the spur gear drive. Use C30 and C45 steels for pinion and gear respectively.

2) 7.5 KW is to be transmitted from 4.7 to 4.9 a motor shaft rotating at 1440rpm to another shaft with a speed reduction of 3:1. The starting torque may be taken as 50% higher than the mean torque. The gears should be made of heat treated steel and the shaft of mild steel. The pinion should have a minimum of 20 teeth. Design the gear drive.

3) Determine the module, face and 4.9 to 4.10 teeth for a pair of gears if they are to transmit 3.75KWat 1800 rev/min of the pinion for intermittent service. The material is to be good grade cast iron and the pinion is to have 18 teeth 20^0 full depth VR=2.5.

4) A pair of gears connecting parallel shafts is to transmit 415 Nm torsional moment at 2800 rev/min of the pinion. The teeth are to be 200 stub of heat

treated alloy steel. The width of the face is limited to 38 mm. The driven gear rotates at 1800 rev/min. Select the necessary module and check for wear.

5) Design the full depth 20 deg teeth of a pair of cast iron spur gears to transmit intermittently 7.5 kW at 625 rev/min of the pinion. The velocity ratio should be above 3.5.The pinion is to have not less than 22teeth. Find the module, face width and diameters of the gears strength alone considered check for dynamic load.

6) A 10 KW, 750 rpm induction motor is to drive a pump set running at 300 rpm through a pair of spur gears. The starting torque of the motor may be taken as 2.5 times the rated torque design the gear pairs and check for dynamic load.

7) Design a pair of 20^0 full depth spur gears to transmit 15 KW at 1400 rpm to another shaft a rotating at 720 rpm. Design the gear device and check for dynamic load.

8) A pair of spur gears with 20°, full-depth, involute teeth transmits 50 hp. The pinion is mounted on the shaft of an electric motor operating at 1150 rpm. The pinion has 18 teeth and a diametral pitch of 5. The gear has 68 teeth.

Compute the following

1. The rotational speed of the gear
2. The velocity ratio and the gear ratio for the gear pair
3. The pitch diameter of the pinion and the gear
4. The center distance between the shafts carrying the pinion and the gear
5. The pitch line speed for both the pinion and the gear
6. The torque on the pinion shaft and on the gear shaft
7. The tangential force acting on the teeth of each gear
8. The radial force acting on the teeth of each gear
9. The normal force acting on the teeth of each gear

9) A pair of spur gears with 20°, full-depth, involute teeth transmits 0.75 hp. The pinion is mounted on the shaft of an electric motor operating at 3450 rpm. The pinion has 24 teeth and a diametral pitch of 24. The gear has 110 teeth.

Compute the following:

1. The rotational speed of the gear
2. The velocity ratio and the gear ratio for the gear pair
3. The pitch diameter of the pinion and the gear
4. The center distance between the shafts carrying the pinion and the gear

5. The pitch line speed for both the pinion and the gear
6. The torque on the pinion shaft and on the gear shaft
7. The tangential force acting on the teeth of each gear
8. The radial force acting on the teeth of each gear
9. The normal force acting on the teeth of each gear

10. A pair of spur gears with 20°, full-depth, involute teeth transmits 7.5 hp. The pinion is mounted on the shaft of an electric motor operating at 1750 rpm. The pinion has 20 teeth and a diametral pitch of 12. The gear has 72 teeth.

Compute the following:

1. The rotational speed of the gear
2. The velocity ratio and the gear ratio for the gear pair
3. The pitch diameter of the pinion and the gear
4. The center distance between the shafts carrying the pinion and the gear
5. The pitch line speed for both the pinion and the gear
6. The torque on the pinion shaft and on the gear shaft
7. The tangential force acting on the teeth of each gear
8. The radial force acting on the teeth of each gear
9. The normal force acting on the teeth of each gear

10.9 Helical Gears

Helical gears are a type of gear system that consists of cylindrical gears with helical teeth. Unlike spur gears, which have straight teeth, helical gears have teeth that are cut at an angle to the gear axis. This angled tooth design allows for smoother and quieter operation compared to spur gears.

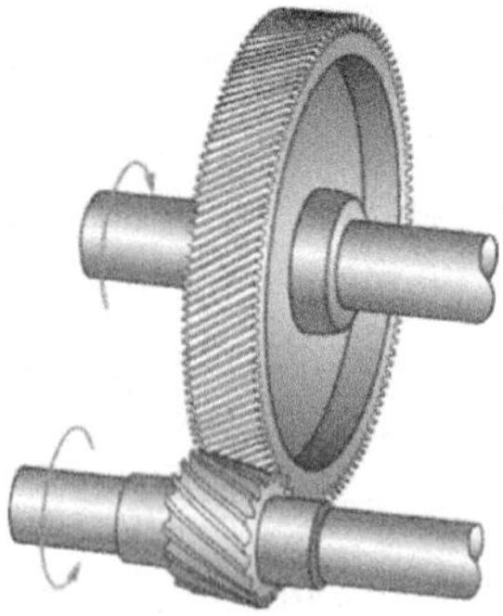

Fig. 10.20. Helical gear

Here are some key aspects of helical gears:

1. **Tooth Profile:** The teeth of helical gears are cut in a helical shape, forming a helix angle with respect to the gear axis. This helical tooth profile allows for gradual engagement and disengagement of the gear teeth, resulting in reduced noise and vibration during operation.
2. **Contact Pattern:** The helical tooth design creates a larger contact area between the gear teeth compared to spur gears. This increased contact area distributes the load more evenly, resulting in higher load-carrying capacity and improved efficiency.
3. **Axial Thrust:** Helical gears generate an axial thrust force due to the helix angle of the teeth. This axial thrust needs to be properly managed and balanced to prevent excessive axial movement of the gears. Various methods, such as thrust bearings or double helical gears (herringbone gears), can be used to counteract the axial thrust.
4. **Efficiency:** Helical gears offer higher efficiency compared to spur gears, especially at higher speeds and under heavy loads. The gradual engagement of the teeth reduces impact and sliding friction, resulting in less power loss and improved overall efficiency.
5. **Noise and Vibration:** The helical tooth design helps to reduce noise and vibration in gear systems. The angled teeth allow for smoother meshing, minimizing gear noise and providing quieter operation. However, helical gears can still produce some axial thrust-related noise, which can be mitigated through proper design and lubrication.
6. **Applications:** Helical gears are widely used in various applications, including automotive transmissions, industrial machinery, power generation equipment, and many other gear-driven systems. They are particularly suitable for applications that require high torque transmission, smooth operation, and low noise levels.
7. **Manufacturing and Assembly:** The manufacturing process for helical gears involves specialized gear-cutting techniques, such as hobbing or shaping, to create the helical tooth profile. The assembly of helical gears requires precise alignment to ensure proper meshing and minimize noise and wear.

When designing or selecting helical gears, factors such as the desired gear ratio, torque requirements, speed range, noise considerations, and space constraints should be taken into account.

Helical Angle:

It is a constant angle made by the helices with the axis of rotation.

Axial Pitch:

It is the distance parallel to the axis between similar faces of adjacent teeth. It is the same as circular pitch and is therefore denoted by Pc.

Formative or Equivalent no. of teeth for helical gears:

$$T_E = \frac{T}{Cos^3 \propto}$$

where

T = Actual no. of teeth on a helical gear.

α = Helix angle.

10.10 Proportions for Helical Gear (AGMA)

Pressure angle = 15^0 to 25^0

Helix angle =20^0 to 45^0

Addendum = 0.8 m (Maximum)

Dedendum = 1m (Maximum)

Minimum total depth = 1.8 m

Minimum Clearance = 0.2m

Thickness of tooth =1.5708 m

10.11 Strength of Helical Gear

Modified levis equation is given by

$W_T = (\sigma_o \text{ x } C_v) b \text{ x } \pi \text{ x } m \text{ x } 4$

W_T = Tangential tooth load

σ_o = Allowable static stress

C_v = Velocity Factor

b = Face width

M = Module

y = Tooth form factor (or) Lewis factor.

$C_V = \frac{6}{6+v}$ for peripheral velocities from 5 to 10$\frac{m}{s}$.

$C_V = \frac{15}{15+v}$ for peripheral velocities from 10 to 20$\frac{m}{s}$.

$C_V = \frac{0.75}{0.75+\sqrt{v}}$ for peripheral velocities greater than 20$\frac{m}{s}$.

$C_V = \frac{0.75}{1+v} + 0.25$ for non metallic gears.

2) Dynamic tooth Load is given by

$$W_d = W_T + \frac{21V(bc\,COS^2\alpha + WT)COS\alpha}{21V + \sqrt{bc\,COS^2\alpha + WT}}$$

3) Static tooth Load (or) endurance strength of the tooth is given by

$$W_S = \sigma_e b\pi m y'$$

4) The maximum or limiting wear tooth load for helical gear is given by

$$W_W = \frac{D_p bQK}{cos^2\alpha}$$

$$K = \frac{(\sigma es)^2 sin\phi N}{1.4}\left[\frac{1}{E_p} + \frac{1}{E_q}\right]$$

ϕ_N = Normal Pressure angle.

1) A pair of helical gears are to transmit 15 KW. The teeth are 20^0 stub in diametral. The pinion runs at 10000 rpm and has 80 mm pitch diameter. The gear has 320 mm pitch diameter. If the gears are made of cast steel having allowable static strength of 100 Mpa , determine a suitable module and face width from static strength considerations and check the gears for wear given σ_{es} = 618MPa.

Solution:

Given Data:

p = 15 KW

$\phi = 20^0$

$\alpha = 45^0$

N_p =10000 rpm

D_P = 80mm

D_Q = 320mm

σ_{op} = 100MPa

σ_{es} = 618 MPa

$$T = \frac{P \times 60}{2\pi N_P} = \frac{15 \times 10^3 \times 60}{2\pi \times 10000}$$

T =14.32 Nm

Tangential Tooth Load on the pinion

$$W_T = \frac{T}{\frac{D_P}{2}} = \frac{14.32}{\frac{0.08}{2}} = 358N.$$

W.K.T

$$\mathrm{T_p} = \frac{\mathrm{D_p}}{\mathrm{m}} = \frac{80}{\mathrm{m}}$$

Equivalent no. of teeth is given by

$$T_E = \frac{T_P}{cos^3 \propto} = \frac{\frac{80}{m}}{cos^3 45^0} = \frac{226.4}{m}$$

Tooth form factor for 20^0 stub teeth

$$Y_p = \frac{0.175 - 0.95}{T_E}$$

$$Y_p = \frac{0.175 - 0.95 \times m}{226.4}$$

$$Y_p = 0.175 - 0.00419m.$$

W.k.t

$$V = \frac{\pi D_P N_P}{60} = \frac{\pi \times 0.08 \times 10000}{60} = 42m$$

∴ Velocity Factor Cv

$$C_V = \frac{0.75}{0.75} = \frac{5.55}{5.55 + \sqrt{V}} = \frac{5.55}{5.55 + \sqrt{42}} = 0.4614$$

$$C_V = 0.4614$$

b = 12.5 m (max . face width 12.5 m to 20 m)

$\therefore\ W_T = \left(\sigma_{op} \times C_V\right) b\pi m y' p$

= (100 x 0.4614) x12.5 m x π m(0.175-0.00419m)

= 409 m^2 (0.175-0.00419m)

=72m^2-1.5m^3

m =2.3 say 2.5 mm.

∴b= 12.5 m

=12.5 x2.5 =31.25 = 32.

check the gears for wear

$$V.R = \frac{D_q}{D_P} = \frac{320}{80} = 4$$

Ratio factor

$$Q = \frac{2 \times VR}{VR + 1} = \frac{2 \times 4}{4 + 1} = 1.6$$

W.K.T

$\tan\phi_N = \tan\phi\cos\alpha = \tan 20^0 \cos 45^0$

$\tan\phi_N = 0.2573$

$\phi_N = 14.4^0$

$$E_P = E_q = 193.2\frac{KN}{m^2}\,(page\ no. 186\ Table\ 12.7)$$

Load Stress factor

$$K = \frac{(\sigma_{es})^2 Sin\emptyset N}{1.4}\left[\frac{1}{E_P} + \frac{1}{E_q}\right]$$

$$= \frac{(618)^2 \times \sin 14.4^\circ}{1.4}\left[\frac{1}{193.2\times10^3} + \frac{1}{193.2\times10^3}\right]$$

$$= \frac{94980.6\times0.01035}{1.4}\ [5.175]$$

$= 67843.31\ X\ 1.035\ X10^{-5}$

K = 0.7023 N/mm^2

w.k.t max or limiting load for wear

$$W_W = \frac{D_p b Q K}{\cos^2 \alpha}$$

$$=\frac{80\times32\times1.6\times0.7023}{cos^2 45} = 5753.24N$$

$$W_W = 5753.24N$$

∴ W_W is much greater than W_T

∴ Design is satisfactory.

10.12 Worm Gear

A worm gear is a type of gear system that consists of a worm (a screw-like gear) and a worm wheel (a gear with helical teeth). It is a compact and efficient gear arrangement used in various applications, particularly where high gear reduction ratios and self-locking capabilities are required.

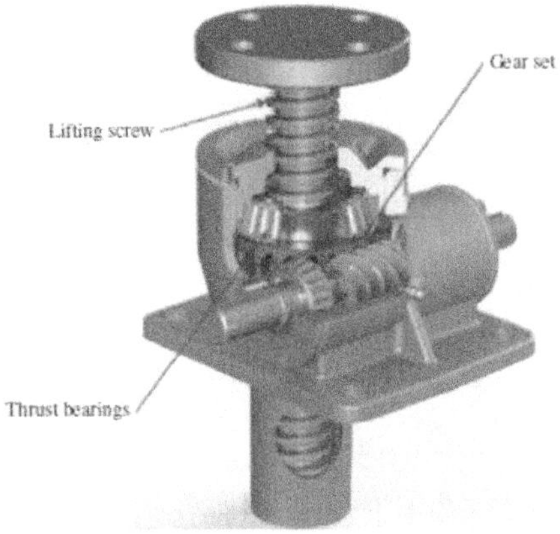

Fig. 10.21. Worm gear applications

Key aspects of worm gears:

1. **Function:** The primary function of a worm gear is to transmit rotational motion and torque between non-parallel shafts. The worm, which is a cylindrical screw-like gear, meshes with the teeth of the worm wheel, resulting in a gear reduction ratio between the input and output shafts.
2. **Gear Ratio:** Worm gears provide high gear reduction ratios, typically ranging from 5:1 to 100:1 or even higher. The gear ratio is determined by the number of teeth on the worm wheel and the pitch of the worm. The gear reduction ratio is calculated by dividing the number of teeth on the worm wheel by the number of starts on the worm.
3. **Self-Locking:** One of the unique characteristics of worm gears is their self-locking capability. Due to the angle of the helical teeth on the worm